Praise for Robert Hofler

"Theater critic Hofler (*Mon*... *Dunne*) delivers a spellbinding ... seminal 1973 film *The Way*... sparkles, and he successfully blends histrionics with on-screen magic. The captivating result makes clear that the drama happening behind the camera can be just as gripping as what's in front of it."
—Publishers Weekly (starred review)

"*The Way They Were* has it all: huge egos on collision courses, great showbiz gossip, and insight into how Hollywood movies once got made. But at its center is the love story between Arthur Laurents, a Broadway legend with the sharpest of tongues; and Tom Hatcher, who put up with it all. It's a complicated love story to be sure, but that's what makes Robert Hofler's book so compelling."
—Michael Riedel, author of *Razzle Dazzle: The Battle for Broadway*

"No one captures the magic of moviemaking, from Fade In to Fade Out, better than Robert Hofler. In *The Way They Were*, he delivers a riveting account of a cinematic epic full of colorful details and characters who leap off the page. Filled with prodigious research, shrewd insight, and driven by a powerful narrative, the book provides a luminous chronicle of personalities ready for their close-ups and the business that enables them."
—Bob Spitz, author of *The Beatles* and *Dearie: The Remarkable Life of Julia Child*

Please turn the page for more outstanding praise!

"You know the movie: Barbra Streisand and Robert Redford fall in love, but history gets in the way. To mark the fiftieth anniversary of *The Way We Were*, Hofler, a theater critic and author of a handful of books about Hollywood-related subjects, has produced a thoroughly entertaining account of how the film got made. This was one of those movies that could easily have been a disaster. Nearly everything went wrong: the casting process was a nightmare; the script needed a lot of work (at least according to one of the film's stars); and the first cut of the movie, the one shown to audiences in previews, stunk up the place. And yet, somehow, what emerged from the ordeal was a movie that was a hit when it came out and quickly slipped into the "beloved" category, where it has remained for half a century. Hofler knows the trick of writing a "making of" book: to give the behind-the-scenes story a measure of the excitement, even the suspense, of an actual movie. He nails it."
—*Booklist*

"And you thought Katie and Hubbell's relationship was complicated? Wait until you delve into the making of *The Way We Were*. In scrupulous journalistic detail, Robert Hofler relates the behind-the-scenes internecine conflicts and intricacies of one the screen's great romances. What surfaces is a backstory as captivating—and, at times, as heartbreaking—as *The Way We Were* itself."
—Stephen M. Silverman, author of *David Lean* and *The Catskills: Its History and How It Changed America*

"Just in time for the film's 50th anniversary, theater critic Hofler digs deep to find the drama that went on behind the scenes . . . This is a detailed and well-researched biography of a popular film that avid fans and film students will likely find fascinating."
—*Library Journal*

**ROBERT
HOFLER**

The
WAY they
WERE

**How EPIC BATTLES
and BRUISED EGOS
Brought a Classic
HOLLYWOOD
LOVE STORY
to the SCREEN**

CITADEL PRESS
Kensington Publishing Corp.
www.kensingtonbooks.com

CITADEL PRESS BOOKS are published by

Kensington Publishing Corp.
900 Third Avenue
New York, NY 10022

All Kensington titles, imprints, and distributed lines are available at special quantity discounts for bulk purchases for sales promotion, premiums, fund-raising, educational, or institutional use. Special book excerpts or customized printings can also be created to fit specific needs. For details, write or phone the office of the Kensington Special Sales Manager: Attn. Special Sales Department. Kensington Publishing Corp, 900 Third Avenue, New York, NY 10022. Phone: 1-800-221-2647.

CITADEL PRESS and the Citadel logo Reg. U.S. Pat. & TM Off.

First Kensington Hardcover Edition: February 2023
First Paperback Edition: February 2025

ISBN: 978-0-8065-4233-1

ISBN: 978-0-8065-4234-8 (ebook)

10 9 8 7 6 5 4 3 2 1

Printed in the United States of America

To the memory of Ernest Lloyd Wright

The
WAY they
WERE

Chapter 1

Barbra Streisand and Katie Morosky

"**A**rthur remembers it being a hundred twenty-five pages. I remember reading a fifty-page treatment," said Barbra Streisand. Regardless of how many pages Arthur Laurents had written of a synopsis, or an outline or a so-called "treatment," Streisand wanted those pages, titled *The Way We Were*, and she wanted them now. "I fell in love with it!" she gushed.

More important, Streisand put her enthusiasm into the only words that count in Hollywood. "I want this to be my next movie," she told the producer Ray Stark.

Stark had produced *Funny Girl* on Broadway and also brought it to the screen, with Streisand reprising the role of Fanny Brice, who happened to be the producer's mother-in-law. The New York theater had long been home to Jewish artists who refused to hide their heritage. The movies, not so much. Streisand in the movie *Funny Girl* was historic, a Jewish actress playing a proudly Jewish character. *The Way We Were* would build on that breakthrough, providing Streisand with her first dramatic role in which being Jewish was again central to the story. With

The Way We Were, she was going back to the well of *Funny Girl*, only she was delving deeper. Much deeper.

Again, it was the fairy tale of Cinderella, who, falling in love with the handsome Prince Charming, sheds her sooty persona and is made to feel beautiful. The fact that Omar Sharif in the movie version of *Funny Girl* wasn't Jewish, despite playing a character named Nicky Arnstein, diluted the romance's Semitism to make it more palatable to general audiences. What Laurents delivered with *The Way We Were* would be radically different due to the male lead character. What he wrote puts on display the various tropes of what it meant to be Jewish in America and how different it was to be Gentile in America. He then let his two protagonists, Katie Morosky and Hubbell Gardiner, meet in the most intimate of contexts: love and marriage. Katie represents discrimination, morality, and a fraught past; Hubbell represents privilege, aestheticism, and a wide-open future. The political split embodied by the two characters is obvious. More subtle is the aesthetics divide, which has Katie telling Hubbell, "I'm not attractive in the right way, am I? I don't have the right style for you, do I?"

What could go wrong when such a couple fell in love and got married and had a baby?

Jews have a name for Gentiles, especially those with whom they are involved in a romantic relationship. The Gentile woman is called a shiksa; the Gentile man is called a shegetz. Laurents often used another name that encapsulated both the shiksa and the shegetz. He called them a "fantasy WASP."

He didn't use the term to describe only Katie's Hubbell. He used it to describe a Gentile character named Alex in the play *My Good Name*, which he wrote two decades later and which was first produced in 1997. Alex is married to a woman named Rachel (the name of Katie and

Hubbell's baby in *The Way We Were*), who is essentially a middle-aged Katie. She loves the "sound of crystal" in the Palm Court at the Plaza Hotel (where Katie and Hubbell last see each other). For Rachel, the music of that expensive cutlery represents the seductive aestheticism of her wealthy Anglo-Saxon and Protestant businessman husband. It means the same thing to Katie when she dines there with Hubbell in Laurents's novel, *The Way We Were*, which was published a year before the film's release. The sound of crystal as both Rachel and Katie hear it also means that they do not really belong at the Palm Court. They are both outsiders. Not so subtly on Laurents's part, the Rachel of *My Good Name* has written a book of poems titled *Crystal Nights*, which has nothing to do with eating and drinking at the Plaza's Palm Court and everything to do with Kristallnacht, or the Night of Broken Glass, the November 1938 pogrom in Nazi Germany, during which thousands of synagogues and businesses were destroyed and hundreds of Jews murdered. Rachel, like Katie, is a very moral woman and a political activist. What is either of these female characters doing in the company of a fantasy WASP, or shegetz, much less falling in love with and marrying one?

It's a question Ray Stark did not ask himself upon reading the treatment for *The Way We Were* on a cross-country flight home to Los Angeles in the spring of 1970. He did not see a debate on morality and aestheticism in the 123 pages (not fifty or 125 pages) that Laurents had given him in New York City. The producer was smarter than that. Raymond Otto Stark, in 1931, at age fifteen, was the youngest student ever admitted to Rutgers University, in New Brunswick, New Jersey. When he read the treatment for *The Way We Were*, he saw money, and he saw another massive hit starring Streisand, whom he just happened to have under contract at the time. She owed him not one but two more movies after their screen collaborations of *Funny Girl* and *The Owl and the Pussycat.*

Stark rushed to a telephone at LAX the moment his airplane landed. He didn't wait for his chauffeur to limousine him to his Holmby Hills mansion, home to a menagerie of statues, their rock-hard buttocks a favorite topic of conversation when the producer escorted female guests he wanted to bed across the grounds. Who didn't want their backside compared to an Alberto Giacometti or a Henry Moore? At the airport, Stark phoned Laurents to say, "It's wonderful. I want to do it."

Stark commissioned him on the spot, and Laurents delivered a first draft of *The Way We Were* screenplay in a matter of weeks. According to documents, it became the property of Rastar Productions at Columbia Pictures Corporation in Hollywood on August 14, 1970.

The fifty-four-year-old writer had provided the books for the classic Broadway musicals *West Side Story* and *Gypsy*, but nothing with the name Arthur Laurents on it had found much approval from either the critics or the public since the late 1950s. Suddenly, with *The Way We Were*, Laurents again stood on the receiving end of telephone calls overflowing with effusive approval.

"You know what you're proposing here? This is dynamite!" film director Sydney Pollack told Laurents as soon as he read the treatment. "This will be the first-ever blacklist movie, the first one to show how it was."

Laurents knew the subject firsthand. He had lived that right-wing political nightmare in the late 1940s, after writing the screenplay for Alfred Hitchcock's *Rope,* among other movies. Over the years, Laurents never gave an interview without failing to mention how his movie career got upended when the House Un-American Activities Committee (HUAC) swung into action in 1947 and declared not only the State Department, but also the motion picture industry a hotbed of communism. Hollywood had one major asset over Capitol Hill, and HUAC stood ready to exploit it. "It started there because the [House] Un-American Activities Committee knew it could get publicity if it investigated celebrities," Laurents recalled.

American voters barely knew the names of their representatives in the US Congress, much less anyone working in the State Department, but in those "soon to disappear" days before every citizen owned a TV set, they went to the movies by the tens of millions on a weekly basis. John Wayne and James Stewart weren't commies. But maybe Charlie Chaplin and John Garfield were. And who knew how many others working there in Tinseltown were Reds, especially in an industry founded and run by Jews?

For HUAC, it all came down to publicity, and even a lowly screenwriter like Laurents got caught in the committee's mischief-making sweep through the Hollywood Hills when, in 1950, *Red Channels,* a right-wing pamphlet subtitled *The Report of Communist Influence in Radio and Television* and published by three ex-FBI agents, listed him as a subversive. For a few months in 1952, he even lost his US passport, and all because the *Daily Worker*, the official publication of the Communist Party USA, had once reviewed *Home of the Brave*, his 1946 Broadway play about anti-Semitism in the army. It was a horrible time to be an American, and Laurents eventually escaped back to Broadway. Who knew that one day he would get a screenplay out of those evil, dark days in La-La Land? If nothing else, *The Way We Were* would be his sweet revenge.

Streisand, unlike Laurents and Pollack, was less interested in the film's politics—at least in the beginning, before she found herself on President Richard Nixon's so-called "enemies list" a few months before the 1973 release of *The Way We Were*. Among the film's principals, only Stark could have cared even less about politics. In the beginning, Streisand's real interest lied elsewhere: She had heard somewhere that the esteemed film director David Lean once decreed that if a script contained five great scenes, it would be a success. She counted five such scenes in *The Way We Were*, all of them featuring her—that is, there were five great scenes, each of them featuring *her* playing Katie Morosky, the 1930s Jewish campus communist, who falls in love with the college's Gentile golden-boy athlete, Hubbell Gardiner. She especially liked a scene that envisions Katie at home in her tiny Manhattan apartment, crying on the phone—even in his treatment, Laurents had completely fleshed it out with dialogue—and begging Hubbell to take her back after they've just broken up in the wake of World War II. "I can't sleep, Hubbell," she says. "It would help if I could talk to someone . . ."

What also impressed Streisand was a small detail that Laurents stuck in his treatment: Katie never uses a four-letter word *until* she moves to Hollywood. "That's me! You've got it!" exclaimed Streisand. The foul word spoken isn't the f-bomb. Stark would remove all those from the script. In the scene, Katie calls a Hollywood agent who has named names to HUAC "a shit." Streisand got to say it for the cameras, but along with about another sixty minutes focusing on the Hollywood blacklist in the movie, the entire scene hit the cutting-room floor even before preview audiences got a first look at *The Way We Were*.

Streisand and Stark and Laurents and Pollack. It was a bizarre, lopsided rectangle of big talent and even bigger egos, with Robert Redford soon to be the reluctant odd man looking for a way out to escape this box of movie popcorn or, as he put it, that "Ray Stark ego trip." It's why making the movie turned into such a nightmare and why, ultimately, the movie became a Hollywood classic. Since the American Film Institute started keeping track of such monumental stuff, *The Way We Were* has always found itself ensconced on the list of the Top Ten Movie Romances of all time, in the august company of *Casablanca* and *Gone with the Wind*.

Pollack bore the day-to-day horrors of shepherding *The Way We Were* to the screen, and he claimed that Stark, because of his four-picture contract with Streisand, had "an ownership thing" with the star.

"Ray and Barbra, it was a very, very complicated relationship," said Judith Rascoe, a Stark employee who worked as a script consultant on *The Way We Were*. While Stark expected the star to pay obeisance, Streisand never forgot—or, more likely, never forgave—Fran Arnstein Stark for putting her through the indignity of a pre–*Funny Girl* casting contest. The producer's wife didn't want just any singer to play her famous mother onstage. Fanny Brice's daughter insisted on an endless decathlon of meetings and auditions, only to prefer an actress who was not Jewish. She wanted an actress who was an even bigger star on Broadway than her mother ever had been. Her first choice for the role was the theater's singing sweetheart. Fran wanted Mary Martin to play her mother.

Funny Girl composer Jule Styne remembered one of those go-see auditions and how the young Streisand "looked awful . . . All her clothes were out of thrift shops. I saw Fran Stark staring at her, obvious distaste on her face." Taking cues from his wife, Ray Stark said of the young Streisand, "She's terrible . . . [S]he'll never play my mother-in-law."

At the time, the popular comedienne Kaye Ballard was campaigning hard for the role, and even added the Brice standard "My Man" to her nightclub repertoire. No surprise, she also ran into a roadblock thrown up by the Brice/Arnstein offspring. "Fran Stark had this fantasy that her mother was this beautiful, delicate creature," said Ballard. "Fanny was beautiful after you got to know her, but not beautiful in the way [Fran] wanted to portray her."

With Streisand, it wasn't just the old, funky clothes that this Jewish girl from Brooklyn would make fashionable and chic in record time. With Streisand, there was the Nose. In a review of her cabaret act in 1961, *Variety* cracked that "perhaps a little corrective schnoz bob might be an element to be considered." A critic at the *New York Journal-American* delivered an even crueler attack, calling her "an amiable ant-eater."

Brice herself eventually "tired of being a sight gag," as she put it, and submitted her nose to a surgeon's knife and hammer. On that sensitive subject of nasal reconstruction, which she assiduously eschewed, Streisand might have agreed with the sardonic Dorothy Parker, who once wrote that Baby Snooks had "cut off her nose to spite her race." Radio fans of Brice didn't know the word *schnoz* from *schnook* from *schmuck*, but twenty years later, in the early 1960s, TV watchers couldn't mistake Streisand's calling herself a "nice Jewish girl" in repeated appearances on Mike Wallace's *PM East*, *The Jack Paar Show*, and *The Tonight Show*. These appearances took place before Styne composed "People" and "Don't Rain on My Parade," songs that he wrote specifically for her voice, with its multi-octave range, songs that went from E below middle C to a high F.

And even earlier, Streisand had made being Jewish and being from Brooklyn (in that order) part of her schtick in cabaret appearances at the basement venue Bon Soir in Greenwich Village. It was where Styne first heard her and became an early avid fan.

Laurents heard the young singer a few months later. Hot off writing the books for *West Side Story* and *Gypsy*, he momentarily put aside his typewriter to direct his first Broadway musical. His assistant on *I Can Get It for You*

Wholesale remembered Streisand's audition for Laurents. "When she came to *Wholesale*, what a wreck she was," said Ashley Feinstein. "Barbra wore strange clothes and black-dyed hair. Impossible to think she would ever be on the screen. She was also this Jewish girl from Brooklyn, and she had no compunction about letting people know she was Jewish."

Her audition for *Wholesale*, set in New York's Garment District during the Great Depression, inspired the young Streisand to indulge her penchant for antique clothes. "Since the action took place in the 1930s, I showed up in a 1930s fur coat that I'd bought in a thrift shop for ten dollars," she remembered. For that audition, Streisand requested a chair, a most unusual request, because she wanted to sing sitting, not standing.

Laurents, like Styne, fell in love at that first hearing, if not at first sight. The director-writer recalled, "She walked in and knocked me out. In those days what Barbra looked like was not considered attractive." Always the contrarian, Streisand's Broadway mentor didn't leave it there. "All this talk about her nose is nonsense," Laurents would quickly add. "She actually has a lovely nose. It's the eyes that are a problem."

Laurents cast the nineteen-year-old novice actress in *Wholesale* to play the musical's daffy secretary. As originally conceived by book writer Jerome Weidman, Miss Marmelstein is a fifty-year-old spinster. Laurents ignored that little character trait and kept the teenager in the show, despite the constant complaints leveled against her by the show's tyrannical producer. "David Merrick was after me every night to fire her because she wasn't attractive," said Laurents. The producer, already known on Broadway as "the Abominable Showman," wanted nothing but pretty girls in his musicals, even if they were playing dumpy middle-aged secretaries.

Laurents, however, saw something in rehearsals that also stunned Streisand's largely gay following at the Bon Soir. "She was incredibly sexual onstage," he said. Merrick was one of those straight men who didn't see it. Perhaps he never saw it, but there was no not noticing the audience's reaction when, out of town in Philadelphia, Streisand sang "Miss Marmelstein" as she coasted across the stage in an office chair on rollers. Laurents gave the show's choreographer, Herbert Ross, credit for the chair. The performer who played the singing secretary on wheels remembered it differently.

"We disagreed about the 'Miss Marmelstein' number," said Streisand. "She was the overworked secretary, and I envisioned her singing that song in a secretarial chair that rolls. That's why I asked for a chair during the audition. Arthur and Herb Ross had a different concept, with lots of the cast walking behind me while I was at my desk. But it never seemed to work until opening night in Philadelphia when they finally gave in and said, 'Do it in your goddamn chair!' It stopped the show that night . . . and they weren't very happy with me afterwards."

The new musical was supposed to revive the moribund careers of singer-actress Lillian Roth and Ballet Theatre's Harold Lang, a former Laurents boyfriend, whose last Broadway success had been a decade earlier in the first major revival of *Pal Joey*. Roth and Lang were the two names known to Broadway ticket buyers, and comeback stories were always good box office. The introduction of a new star was even better box office, and Laurents saw something immediately in the young Streisand that straight men like Merrick could not, because he and others like him could not get beyond her nose. Streisand had *it*, and it wasn't only her incredible voice and her great comic timing but that she also exuded sex.

Here was a woman who enjoyed sex, just like her gay

following did, and she was getting it, just like they were, despite all the odds of her unconventional appearance and their unconventional sexual orientation. And she was getting it with straight men whom gay men could only fantasize about sleeping with. It's what linked Streisand to such other icons of the gay world as Bette Davis and Judy Garland, who, not being conventionally pretty, weren't afraid to flaunt their sexual aggression. Having lots of sex wasn't only for the glamorous idols adored by homosexuals, women like Joan Crawford and Marlene Dietrich. Years later, it would be Laurents who recognized that it was Streisand and not Redford, the conventionally pretty one, who brought sex to the pairing in *The Way We Were*. "She gives him sex and he gives her class," he said, parroting what Katharine Hepburn once said about Ginger Rogers and Fred Astaire. (Truth be told, Redford always had more sex appeal than Astaire, and Streisand always had more class than Rogers.)

Despite Streisand's *Wholesale* success, Stark and his wife, Fran—especially his wife, Fran—did not envision Fanny Brice being played by this young Jewish upstart from Brooklyn with that nose. They didn't take Stephen Sondheim's advice before Bob Merrill replaced him as the *Funny Girl* lyricist. "You've gotta have a Jewish girl!" Sondheim insisted. "And if she's not Jewish, she at least has to have a nose."

Streisand never forgot the way that Starks and Merrick treated her. She flaunted being the star that didn't get a nose job, and she defused the issue with humor. In a *Life* magazine interview, she revealed, "There is a joke about a girl who went to the hairdresser and said, 'Give me a Barbra Streisand look.' So he took the hairbrush and broke her nose." Her sense of humor, however, never completely washed away the resentment. It fueled Streisand. Even her first *Playbill* bio announced that Miss Streisand "is not a

member of [the] Actors Studio." The flip side of resentment is a lack of gratitude, but that grudge complex was
to come a little later. Yes, the producer's "ownership thing"
with the star was "very, very complicated."

No doubt Laurents's relationship with Streisand would
have been even more "complicated" if the writer had accepted Stark's original offer that he, Laurents, write the
book for the stage musical *Funny Girl*. Laurents expressed
no interest in the subject; among other things, he'd recently written another backstage story, *Gypsy*, and it was
doubtful he would improve on what most critics considered the best book ever written for a musical.

Although their working relationship ended with *I Can
Get It for You Wholesale*, which ran for three hundred
performances, Streisand stayed in touch with Laurents,
most notably right after the release of her LP debut, *The
Barbra Streisand Album*, in 1963. By then Streisand had
already graduated from her kooky antique-clothing-store
getups to her very exotic Nefertiti look, with the flamboy-
antly contoured eyes and hair. Beyond fashion advice, she
wanted performance tips from her stage mentor. A couple
of years before, Laurents had told her not to lower her
face when performing at the Bon Soir. She thought it had
something to do with her nose. No, the shadows emphasized her double chin, he replied.

Now, she expected praise from Laurents for a first album
that had garnered raves from the critics. Having just ended
her January engagement at the Blue Angel and looking to
open for Liberace at the Riviera in Las Vegas, she felt inse-
cure about performing solo at such a big venue. Could
Laurents offer any advice?

Yes, but not the kind she wanted. Laurents gave her a
lambasting, and that included an accusation that she had
imitated his good friend Lena Horne, among other crimes,
on her album. The comment provoked Streisand to write

Laurents a six-page handwritten letter in pencil to let him know that she'd never even heard Lena Horne sing, so how could she "copy" her?

Streisand also wrote that she appreciated Laurents's critique but thought he really wanted to "hurt" and not to advise. She went on to reveal something that would soon become an interview staple for her. As she put it to a *New York Times* reporter the following year, and in only slightly different words to Laurents in her letter, "People will no longer come to see a new talent they've heard about. I now have to live up to their concept of a great success. I'm not the underdog, the homely kid from Brooklyn they can root for anymore. I'm fair game."

The man who threw a grenade at *The Barbra Streisand Album* was not the same man who'd directed Streisand in *Wholesale*. The man who attacked her for copying Lena Horne was not the same man who'd made chicken noodle soup in his apartment on Fifty-Ninth Street and brought it to rehearsals every day in order for the cast to get their needed nourishment. Laurents could be a real mensch. Laurents could also be a real schmuck. For instance, after *Wholesale* opened, he quickly became critical of Streisand's mutable performances, telling her, "You're never gonna make it in showbiz. You're too undisciplined. You never do it exactly the same way."

Laurents, the "schmuck," was the one who answered the plea for a little stage help before her Las Vegas debut. Streisand concluded the letter to Laurents on a gracious note, thanking him for his "honesty." She could always count on him for the stark, brutal, and often hurtful truth, and she went on to ask her erstwhile director to write something for her. She knew how to stroke him. She called him "a great writer."

Streisand and Laurents were both Jewish. They had both grown up in Brooklyn and had even graduated from the same high school, Erasmus Hall. When Streisand read his *The Way We Were* treatment—it had taken him only eight years to write something for her—she said of Katie Morosky, "That's me! You've got it!" Laurents would unequivocally admit the same thing about Katie, although it would take him until 2011, at the age of ninety-three, to write in his posthumously published memoir, *The Rest of the Story*, "Katie Morosky, the campus political progressive played by Barbra Streisand, is mainly me."

To get to that admission, the writer had done a dance of three or four veils, at times obfuscating his own complete ownership of the role. In the wake of the film's immediate box office success, Laurents often mentioned a number of real-life women who were supposedly his real inspiration for Katie Morosky. In a Turner Classic Movies special Valentine's Day presentation on February 14, 2022, host Dave Karger told viewers that Laurents based Streisand's "fiery" character in *The Way We Were* on "a woman he knew during his college days." Writers as smart as Neal Gabler also fell for the ruse. In his 2016 Streisand biography, the author of the celebrated study *An Empire of Their Own: How the Jews Invented Hollywood* claimed that a Jewish communist coed named Fannie Price—yes, it rhymes with Fanny Brice—was the real Katie Morosky. Upon the film's release, reporters even tracked down the erstwhile radical, who at the time had been teaching high school in upstate New York. Ms. Price didn't believe Barbra Streisand was playing her any more than Laurents ever believed it.

Homosexual playwrights in the early 1970s remembered with vivid dread an infamous essay by the esteemed critic Stanley Kauffmann, and for years, those same writers often had to lie about their source material to protect what they had written. The title of the piece, which was published in 1966 in the *New York Times*, said it all: "Homosexual Drama and Its Disguises." Without naming names, Kauffmann lambasted Tennessee Williams, William Inge, and Edward Albee—or, as he put it, "three of the most successful American playwrights"—for writing works that presented "a badly distorted picture of American women, marriage, and society in general." The essay's clear subtext was that Williams was really Blanche DuBois in *A Streetcar Named Desire*, Albee was really Martha in *Who's Afraid of Virginia Woolf?*, and Inge was really Lola Delaney in *Come Back, Little Sheba*; and therefore those three female characters embodied a distortion of womanhood.

Years before "Homosexual Drama and Its Disguises" became a blot on Kauffmann's otherwise illustrious résumé, Laurents had gone around telling friends and associates in the theater that he was really Leona Samish in *The Time of the Cuckoo*, his one and only success as a playwright on Broadway. He could be gutsy that way. "[T]he central character, a woman, is based on me," Laurents boasted. (Much later in life, he also admitted basing the tyrannical stage mother Rose in *Gypsy* on himself when David Saint, his executor and the person he called "my closest friend," challenged him, saying, "I know where Rose came from. She's you.") In the immediate homophobic turbulence created by Kauffmann's essay in the almighty *New York Times*, Laurents stopped mentioning his close connection to Leona Samish. He also played it safe with *The Way We Were*. When asked about Katie, he didn't mention himself. For years after the release of the movie, he mentioned Fannie Price.

"In the beginning, I only knew that Ray Stark hired Arthur Laurents to write a script for me, which I thought was a great idea," Streisand recalled. "It was only later that I learned how personal it was for him. But it was also personal to me, because Arthur has said he used my own personality, as well as my own political activism, for Katie."

In the beginning, Laurents also mentioned Fannie Price to Streisand. To paraphrase the movie's now-legendary theme song, it wasn't the only case of "mem'ries" obstructing the corners of someone's mind, much less the facts. In the middle of Stark's ferocious fights with Pollack to control the final cut of *The Way We Were*, the producer falsely reminded his director in a memo dated only three weeks into shooting on the picture (October 10, 1972) that when he had arm-twisted David Begelman, then head of production at Columbia Pictures, to green-light the project, he had always imagined it as a movie "starring Barbra Streisand and Robert Redford and directed by Sydney Pollack."

Chapter 2

Robert Redford and Hubbell Gardiner

Perhaps Ray Stark briefly imagined Robert Redford in the role of Hubbell Gardiner, but he never fought for him the way Sydney Pollack did or, to a lesser extent, Barbra Streisand did or, to an even lesser extent, Arthur Laurents did. In fact, three months before shooting started, it was Stark who decreed, "We've got Streisand. What do we need Redford for?" The producer thought Ryan O'Neal, Streisand's erstwhile boyfriend and costar in the just-released comedy *What's Up, Doc?*, would do just fine playing Katie's fantasy WASP.

Not since Clark Gable owned Rhett Butler had an actor been more identified with a yet-to-be-filmed role than Redford was with Hubbell. At least that's the way Pollack, Streisand, and Laurents argued the situation with Stark, who proved far more malleable on the casting of the blond star despite his memo of October 10, 1972. After writing that praiseworthy missive, he was more prone to say, "We've got Streisand!" whenever the subject of who should play Hubbell came up.

"Ray Stark seemed to think that any blond actor would do, but I wouldn't give up on Redford," said Streisand.

O'Neal would be ready to go. Indeed, he was ready to go even as late as June 1972—eight months after Redford had first been offered the role—as Redford still hadn't committed to the film, despite the August start date for *The Way We Were*. O'Neal may even have accepted the role as Laurents originally envisioned it, that is, with Hubbell's story being subsidiary to Katie's and his character being "unheroic."

Pollack, for his part, wouldn't direct the film with O'Neal. "Barbra had never worked with a really strong leading man," he contended. "She has a tendency to take over a picture, just by the size of her talent and larger-than-life presence. It's hard for a costar to stay in the same ring with her." According to the director, only Redford could compete. "In acting, you have to sense that there's a reserve somewhere, that you're seeing the top of the iceberg. Redford makes you come to him as a performer," Pollack went on to explain. "He holds his ground, and you either enter his turf or you don't get it. Period. He will not court you."

As Laurents conceived the character, Hubbell does not court Katie. Only later, thanks to adjustments made by other writers, does Hubbell show any interest in Katie during their college time together. Laurents wrote a character who is barely aware of Katie in the year 1937, and more important, he wrote Hubbell as a featured role. The problem was, Redford didn't play featured roles. Not in 1972.

Redford and Pollack had already made two films together, *This Property Is Condemned* and *Jeremiah Johnson*, and were close friends by the time Stark first proposed *The Way We Were* to them. Pollack harbored his own ideas for beefing up the male lead, to make Hubbell more attractive, to give the character more to do, to make Redford want to play him. And so began the incessant wooing of the star, much to Stark's immediate ire and much to Laurents's later fury. Stark and Redford had never gotten along, and that falling-out went back to a movie they made together five years earlier, when the actor among them was not yet a star.

Redford put it succinctly, saying, "Stark had no affection for *This Property Is Condemned*, which he sold to Warners as part of his portfolio, and really dumped." It was the actor's first leading role, having appeared opposite Jane Fonda and Marlon Brando in *The Chase* the year before. Stark found Redford to be something of an ungrateful upstart, while Redford found Stark to be everything he hated about Hollywood. He also feared the producer epitomized what the movie business might turn him into: a vulgarian, or worse. For a brief moment, around the time of *This Property Is Condemned*, Redford believed he "was starting to go Hollywood without noticing." Those horrors included his buying a "flashy" Lincoln Continental, which, when the new movie star came to his senses, he took back to the dealer two weeks later. (That one Lincoln Continental aside, Redford went on to purchase at least twenty different Porsches.) Redford even used his least favorite movie producer as a metaphor for what he hated about Hollywood. "Everything was as phony as the statues in Ray Stark's garden," he opined, unaware at the time that many of those same statues would one day be bequeathed to the permanent collection at the Getty Museum in Los Angeles.

Equally phony, Redford thought, was something called *The Way We Were*. Or as Redford put it to Pollack when the director first told him this terrific story about a young Jewish communist who falls in love with a young, gor-

geous Gentile college jock. "It sounds to me like another
Ray Stark ego trip," Redford replied. "I don't even want
to read it."

Even before he became a movie star, Redford knew exactly what kinds of roles he wanted to play and what
kinds he didn't. One of those latter roles was Nick in the
film version of Edward Albee's *Who's Afraid of Virginia
Woolf?* Unquestionably the most anticipated film of 1966,
it starred Elizabeth Taylor and Richard Burton at the height
of their post-*Cleopatra* fame, and as if that weren't entic-
ing enough, the project provided Mike Nichols with his
screen directorial debut. A few years before, Nichols had
directed Redford on Broadway in Neil Simon's *Barefoot in
the Park*, and the theater wunderkind couldn't believe
how a young actor would even consider turning down the
extraordinary opportunity to be part of such a starry en-
semble in such an important screen adaptation as *Virginia
Woolf.*

"Nick just died in the text," Redford explained without
remorse. "I felt he started powerfully, but the author didn't
know what to do with the character, and so he trailed off
after the first half. I didn't want that part." Redford thought
even less of the character of Hubbell, who he didn't think
"started powerfully" but did trail off from there.

Something else also bothered the actor about the Nick
character, and it was a concern that resurfaced in a major
way with Hubbell, much to Stark's and Laurents's dismay.
Late in *Who's Afraid of Virginia Woolf?*, it is revealed that
the macho Nick, who was a prizewinning boxer in college,
isn't everything he promises to be at first glance. When it
comes to having extramarital sex with his colleague's wife,
the rapacious Martha, Nick is labeled a big "flop."

In his original *The Way We Were* screenplay, Laurents
wrote a second love scene between Katie and Hubbell, in
which he tells her, "It'll be better this time." It was a line

lifted from Laurents's novel. It was also a line that Robert Redford would never utter.

The actor had assiduously avoided playing any role that capitalized on his awesome chiseled face and his dazzling golden hair, which had been more strawberry blond in his youth. He had learned to play against type, because in his earlier Broadway career, Redford seemingly coasted along on his male beauty in the back-to-back hits *Sunday in New York* and *Barefoot in the Park*. Essentially those 1960s plays were glorified sitcoms before more adventurous TV fare, like *All in the Family* and *M*A*S*H*, made such fluff obsolete on the stage. Those two comedic roles didn't require much more of him as an actor than great looks and, to be honest, equally great comic timing and charm. It's as if Redford didn't want to capitalize on what had made him a Broadway star when it came to the movies, because, in fact, it was his incredible physical beauty that got in the way of live audiences and theater critics (and later movie critics) recognizing his real talent as a subtle and gifted actor.

Pollack, a former acting coach, was never one of those people. "Redford is one of the great screen actors," he proclaimed. "Almost all of Redford's performances are underrated . . . [W]e tend to be suspicious of romantic actors." The film director used the word *romantic*, but he said it in 1995. Before *The Way We Were* came along, Redford hadn't played a straight-up romantic role in a drama. Hubbell would be his first. Until then, he'd learned to downplay his rare good looks by rarely playing a lover. Streisand handled her rare, unusual looks by almost always playing one. Streisand and Redford together? How different could two stars be?

"Redford and I were very different on the surface," said Streisand. "I was raised in a Jewish family in Brooklyn, playing skelly with bottle caps in the street. He was the blond, suntanned California guy, surfing and riding horses—while I was afraid of them. But inside, we were alike: shy, sensitive, and both of us appreciated the mystery of relationships."

Regarding her costar, Streisand tended to make the mistake casting directors did early in Redford's career. His very humble upbringing in Van Nuys and Sawtelle, two Los Angeles neighborhoods, wasn't all that much different from Streisand's in Brooklyn.

The young Redford especially objected when casting directors categorically rejected him for blue-collar roles. They told him he looked too Ivy League. He recalled being told more than once, "If you didn't look as if you had graduated from Harvard, we could believe you as a garbage collector." Or a factory worker. Or a cop. Or a thug.

"Well, I've got news for those people. I did collect garbage," he claimed. "I don't know what the inside of Harvard looks like." He made it clear: "This business of being over-privileged really makes me burn."

Hubbell in *The Way We Were* is nothing if not privileged. It defines the character. Blond, Gentile, Ivy League, and with wealthy friends who entertain friends on posh Beekman Place. And it doesn't get any more privileged than Beekman Place, on the far East Side of Midtown Manhattan. What Redford didn't want to exploit was what Pollack needed from him to make the romance in *The Way We Were* work on-screen—that look of privilege.

Early in their collaboration, during a moment of pique, Laurents asked Pollack what he thought *The Way We Were* was all about. Pollack told him, "I think this is the story of a girl who thinks she isn't pretty, and a guy who is afraid that he is only pretty." Pollack never used that line on Redford. He'd deeply admired the actor's talent ever since they performed together in Redford's first film, *War Hunt*, in 1961. Acting talent was one thing, but pretty was something else entirely, although for male actors of an earlier era, the latter sometimes made it difficult for anyone to see the former. The inherent narcissism of actors was commonly thought to attract homosexuals to the profession. Pollack's father wanted his son to become a dentist, and when the kid instead expressed interest in the theater, Dad warned him it was "a place for fags." The young Pollack chose working with homosexuals in New York over working with people's teeth in Lafayette, Indiana. It wasn't such a difficult jump, since the future movie director had always "felt like a fish out of water."

Redford would remark that his director friend's innate ambivalence was what drew Pollack to the role of Hubbell. "He identified with the character of an uncommitted man," said Redford, who, being committed and certain of himself, as many handsome, heterosexual, and Gentile men tend to be, found nothing of interest in the role.

Laurents would say it was Pollack's "envy" of men like Redford—and, by extension, the character of Hubbell—that drew him to *The Way We Were*. Homosexuality permeated the movie project, if for no other reason than an openly gay man had conceived and written it. That was a fact. The fiction of *The Way We Were* had everything to do with how much Laurents borrowed from his own life to write the characters Katie and Hubbell.

Early in his film career, Redford felt he got brutally burnt playing a closeted movie star in *Inside Daisy Clover*, opposite Natalie Wood. The 1965 movie was released decades before playing a homosexual on-screen translated into an Academy Award for William Hurt (*Kiss of the Spider Woman*, 1985), Tom Hanks (*Philadelphia*, 1993), and Philip Seymour Hoffman (*Capote*, 2005), among others. Worse than playing a homosexual in 1965 was playing a homosexual movie star. Complicating Redford's frustration was his misguided assumption that the character Wade

Lewis was merely "narcissistic" and not full-blown gay. Gavin Lambert, a homosexual, made Lewis's sexual orientation clear in his 1963 novel, *Inside Daisy Clover*, as well as in his original screenplay. Rewrites were made at Redford's insistence to blur the character's same-sex attractions. Not rewritten were scenes in which Lewis is talked about by other characters in a way that makes it clear, or as clear as it could be made in 1965, in the dying days of the Production Code, that Daisy Clover's new husband prefers sex with men.

Feeling he had been tricked regarding *Inside Daisy Clover*, Redford turned down the film adaptation of Albee's *Who's Afraid of Virginia Woolf?*, and he followed that decision by also repeatedly turning down Laurents's *The Way We Were*. His director friend didn't care what Redford thought. "I spent literally eight months beating him to death in order to get him to do it," said Pollack. "I would not let him off the hook."

The director had been in the reverse position on the two men's previous film, then in postproduction. With the American Western *Jeremiah Johnson*, it was Redford who had to convince Pollack. "He did it with me on *Jeremiah*," said Pollack. "It was payback time." Little did Pollack know at the time how much easier Redford's task was regarding *Jeremiah Johnson* than his would be regarding *The Way We Were*.

After Redford called *The Way We Were* "another Ray Stark ego trip," Pollack resorted to putting his pitch in writing on December 4, 1971. That three-page, single-spaced typewritten memo, addressed to Bob Redford, began with the strong admonition not to read "this now." At the time, Redford was doing double duty as actor and producer on *The Candidate*, in which he played a political idealist who's running to be governor of the state of California. Pollack knew firsthand the difficulties of having to deal with the brass at Warner Bros., since those hard-nosed executives were the same men responsible for bringing *Jeremiah Johnson* to the screen. Pollack begged his friend not to read anything regarding *The Way We Were* unless he was in "a great mood." Regardless, Pollack made his pitch in writing, and it was a strong pitch, because he firmly believed that the Laurents story could be turned into a movie that was both "GOOD and commercial." The word *good* was the only one that the director put all in caps in the thousand-plus-word memo.

Pollack knew he could easily handle one of Redford's major problems. The actor had voiced his concerns about Streisand and, as he told the director, "the whole concept of basing a movie on Barbra as a serious actress." He went on to assert, "She ha[s] never been tested." Redford also questioned working with Streisand. Period. As he put it, "Her reputation is as a very controlling person. She will direct herself. It'll never work." And not the least of his qualms, he mused, Would *The Way We Were* somehow be turned into a musical? "She's not going to sing, is she?" Redford asked. "I [don't] want her to sing in the middle of the movie."

Pollack told him not to worry. He'd sold himself to Streisand by emphasizing his early career as an acting teacher at the Neighborhood Playhouse, run by the thespian guru Sanford Meisner. "That really got me," said Streisand, who'd admired that iconic theater ever since her early days as a struggling actor in Greenwich Village. "In those days, I wanted to be an actress, not a singer," she added.

Meisner, together with Lee Strasberg and Stella Adler, had introduced American actors to the Method, a training approach based on acting techniques created by director-actor Konstantin Stanislavski in early twentieth-century Russia. Streisand's *Playbill* bio for *I Can Get It for You*

Wholesale, in which the young Broadway debutante touted not being "a member of [the] Actors Studio," that mecca of the Method, exposed an itch that she was never really able to scratch away, not even when she won an Oscar for best actress in 1969 for *Funny Girl*.

"Barbra was smart," said Pollack. "She liked my Sandy Meisner connection, because she was ambitious as an actress, to learn." The same had been true of Jane Fonda, whom Pollack directed in *They Shoot Horses, Don't They?* The 1969 film about a brutal Depression-era dance contest gave the actress, most famous at the time for comedic fluff like *Barbarella* and potboilers like *The Chapman Report*, her first of seven Oscar nominations. Fonda went so far as to thank the director. "Because no one ever treats me as an artist. I am never requested to act. Just to star in," she told Pollack.

According to the director, Streisand also saw *The Way We Were* as a departure. "Barbra wanted to 'go straight' with this movie, not to rely on what we normally expect of her—the timing, the gestures, the facial expressions. She wanted to use fewer tricks," said Pollack.

Redford's greatest concern, however, was not his controlling, challenging, or even challenged costar. It was Hubbell. As the film's director, Pollack could not control what Laurents wrote or would go on to write and rewrite and rewrite. Pollack could only promise that he'd work with Laurents, and if that arrangement didn't achieve the desired changes and needed improvements, he would hire other writers to turn the character into something Redford not only could play but also wanted to play. Whatever Pollack may have told Laurents—"This is dynamite!"—it is evident in his correspondence with Redford that he didn't have an especially high regard for Laurents's overall skills as a writer. He especially disparaged his handling of the Hollywood characters in *The Way We Were*, calling the approach "camp," a word that at the time was code for "gay."

The Hollywood milieu, coupled with what could possibly be homosexual-tinged material, was especially sensitive. Beyond the controversy of homosexual writers and their dramas, not to mention their disguises, Redford stood with many Hollywood executives and pundits who believed that audiences didn't want to see movies about Hollywood. He went so far as to call it a "taboo." The critical and box office debacle of *Inside Daisy Clover*, a double blow that led Natalie Wood to attempt suicide, was followed by even more embarrassing Hollywood-themed failures, like *The Oscar* and *The Legend of Lylah Clare*, 1960s flops that brought down stars as big and varied as Kim Novak, Peter Finch, and Stephen Boyd.

Pollack scoffed at Redford's movies-about-movies phobia and mentioned films like *Sunset Boulevard* and *All About Eve*. Pollack called those screenplays by Billy Wilder and Joseph Mankiewicz "exciting" but forgot to mention that the two film classics, both from 1950, were made over two decades ago and that *All About Eve* is set on Broadway, not in Hollywood. Nonetheless, he promised Redford that the scenes set in the movie world could be handled in a similar way that was also "very real and even understated." He believed film directors and writers too often made a common mistake regarding Hollywood: it was an inherently theatrical place, and they tended to go off the rails by making it even "more theatrical." And again, he used that word *camp*.

To help convince Redford, Pollack did extensive research on the Hollywood blacklist, and in the process, he turned Laurents's original story into a kind of roman à clef, in which every character—whether it be a movie agent, screenwriter, producer, or director—is a stand-in for a historic figure from the late 1940s. By deconstructing

The Way We Were, he urged his actor friend to think of "the real people." It was a trick Laurents also used often to give the veneer, if not the weight, of truth to his fiction.

As Pollack described it to Redford, the legendary film director John Huston, who brought *The Maltese Falcon* and *The African Queen* to the screen, is the George Bissinger character in *The Way We Were*. Similar to what Bissinger does in the screenplay, Huston had traveled to Washington, D.C., in 1947 to plead for the rights of Dalton Trumbo, Ring Lardner, Edward Dmytryk, and other blacklisted writers and directors, men who quickly came to be known as the Hollywood Nineteen and then, when the committee later narrowed its focus, the Hollywood Ten. Joining Huston in that effort were Humphrey Bogart, Lauren Bacall, Gene Kelly, Danny Kaye, and other movie stars, who organized and attended meetings called a Conference on the Subject of Thought Control in the US in July 1947 at the posh Beverly Hills Hotel. (Movie stars who would testify before HUAC to condemn purported communist activity in Hollywood included Gary Cooper, Adolphe Menjou, Robert Montgomery, Ronald Reagan, and Robert Taylor.)

Later that year, Huston led the effort to form the Committee for the First Amendment. Bogart, being the far more famous face, quickly became the unofficial head of the group when many of them flew to the nation's capital on an airplane, supplied by billionaire mogul Howard Hughes, to protest the right-wing House Un-American Activities Committee. Prior to that ill-fated trip, Bogart released a statement, which read:

"This has nothing to do with communism. It's none of my business who's a communist and who isn't. The reason I am flying to Washington is because I am an outraged and angry citizen who feels that my civil liberties are being taken away from me and that the Bill of Rights is being abused and who feels that nobody in this country has any right to kick around the Constitution of the United States, not even the Un-American Activities Committee."

Bogart's participation was especially gutsy: in 1939 HUAC had called him to the Capitol to confirm that he had never belonged to the Communist Party.

Laurents didn't put a Bogart movie-star figure in *The Way We Were*. Instead, he let his character Katie Morosky be that political idealist leading the Hollywood pack, despite the fact that in his novel and screenplay, she is a mere reader at the motion picture company Zenith International Pictures. With his Bissinger character, he wrote the part of the disillusioned activist, which had been Huston. The *Maltese Falcon* director was the first among the starry members of the Committee for the First Amendment to undergo a complete change of heart. After witnessing one accused screenwriter after another get into an on-the-floor brawl with members of the House Un-American Activities Committee, Huston announced publicly, "It was a sorry performance. You felt your skin crawl and your stomach turn. I disapproved of what was being done to the Ten, but I also disapproved of their response. They had lost a chance to defend a most important principle."

Pollack emphasized to Redford that the Bissinger character does a similar about-face, much to Katie's horror in *The Way We Were*. The next character on Pollack's list to be dissected was Hubbell's agent, Rhea Edwards. He saw her as a stand-in for the real-life Hollywood agent and producer Meta Rosenberg, a former communist, who went on to testify before HUAC as a friendly witness in 1951. Employing a little dramatic license, Laurents moved Edwards's testimony to 1947 in his story, giving Katie a chance to rebuke the agent character in bruising style: "I think you're a shit."

Pollack saw the famous MGM executive and producer Dore Schary as the producer character J.J., who, like

Schary, is supportive of the liberal cause and then, like Schary, abandons it to salvage his career. There were also the real-life blacklisted screenwriters Dalton Trumbo and Salka Viertel. In his critique to Redford, Pollack outed Viertel as "Greta Garbo's lover!" Trumbo, for his part, had committed the mortal sin of writing a silly comedy titled *Tender Comrade*, in which Ginger Rogers spouts such leftist propaganda as "Share and share alike—that's democracy." In her 1947 testimony before HUAC, Rogers's mother, Lela, cited the line as prime evidence that communists had infiltrated and seized control of the motion-picture industry.

Viertel, beyond being Garbo's confidante, was renowned for her Santa Monica Canyon soirees, which attracted such European émigrés as Christopher Isherwood and Bertolt Brecht. The author of *The Threepenny Opera* and other classics of the German theater would go on to be one of the Hollywood Nineteen before his purposefully incoherent testimony to HUAC in 1947 absolved Brecht of any suspicion. In Pollack's opinion, the foreign-born Viertel was the Paula Reisner character, a screenwriter and a world-weary intellectual from Eastern Europe who bonds with Katie and whom Hubbell calls a "dyke." In the Laurents story, Trumbo became the blacklisted screenwriter character Brooks Carpenter, punished for speaking out against HUAC and forced to beg Hubbell to be a "front" to sell his screenplays.

In a way, Redford didn't need a who's who sales pitch with regard to the Hollywood blacklist. While he grew up in Sawtelle, a blue-collar community in Los Angeles, Charles Robert Redford enjoyed an early education at the tony Brentwood Grammar and at Emerson Junior High School in Westwood. It was there that he met and dated such socially connected girls as Jill Schary, daughter of Dore Schary, and Carol Rossen, daughter of Robert Rossen, a blacklisted screenwriter turned director. Rossen won an Oscar for his *All the King's Men* screenplay in 1949, then suddenly found himself out of work only two years later, when he invoked the Fifth Amendment while testifying before HUAC in 1951. Redford and Carol Rossen would have been teenagers when that calamity devastated her family. The young Redford may not have been privy to all the political implications of his girlfriend's father being thrown out of work, but he saw firsthand how the blacklist nearly destroyed one family.

He also heard other HUAC horror stories. Redford had recently worked with three movie colleagues whose lives had been adversely affected by that right-wing committee. In 1969 he starred in the film *Tell Them Willie Boy Is Here*, directed by blacklisted screenwriter-director Abraham Polonsky. Redford's film *The Candidate*, to be released in 1972, costarred actor Melvyn Douglas, who had found himself "graylisted" in the 1950s, when his wife, Congresswoman Helen Gahagan Douglas, ran for the US Senate on the Democratic ticket and immediately became targeted as "the Pink Lady" by her Republican opponent. Congresswoman Douglas lost that race but achieved considerable revenge by coining the nickname "Tricky Dick" for Richard M. Nixon. And finally, and perhaps most prominently, there was Redford's former but longtime agent. She was none other than Meta Rosenberg herself, the woman on whom the Rhea Edwards character is based in Pollack's analysis of *The Way We Were*.

Pollack's biggest sales job to Redford came when he tried to create a historical counterpart for Hubbell. In fact, he came up with several, and they included Salka Viertel's son, Peter, a screenwriter whose ex-communist wife, Jigee, according to dubious reports by Laurents, divorced him so he could keep his career in Hollywood. Pollack also threw into the Hubbell mix another name: the *On the Water-*

front author Budd Schulberg, Jigee's former ex-communist husband, who went on to name names before HUAC in 1951. Like Hubbell, Schulberg was a novelist turned screenwriter, and he ran into trouble with the Communist Party when he penned his first book. Before the 1941 publication of *What Makes Sammy Run?*, officials in the party demanded that Schulberg make extensive changes to the text to reflect the party's principles. Schulberg refused and immediately left the Community Party. He used that experience as his justification for later naming names to HUAC.

Pollack mentioned another possible Hubbell prototype. He was the Oscar-winning editor-turned-director Robert Parrish, who, being blond, looked a little like Hubbell if Hubbell were played by Redford. Left out of Pollack's matchups for the male lead of *The Way We Were* was any mention either of Laurents, who'd been a screenwriter in Hollywood during the blacklist era, or of his longtime partner, Tom Hatcher, who was blond, handsome, and Gentile. Mention of either man might have been considered "camp."

Beyond all the historical figures that Pollack could squeeze on to the head of Hubbell, the director found something to admire in the character. He found Hubbell to take "the more existential view of things." The character knew that the Hollywood Ten and their liberal supporters would one day work again for the Hollywood executives who had enforced the blacklist. Which was, in fact, what happened to political liberals like Marlon Brando and Arthur Laurents, who went on to work with HUAC informers, like directors Elia Kazan and Jerome Robbins, respectively, in the years to come. Regarding Hubbell, Pollack called his "a long view of life. Katie sees as far as her nose."

Pollack reminded Redford that they had been looking for a love story to do together, and while he readily admitted *The Way We Were* wasn't "exactly" what they had in mind, he saw that as a positive. "It's off," he claimed. Also, Streisand and Redford together would create "sparks." The two of them on screen together for the first time would be unconventional. "Off." *The Way We Were* would not end up being her picture, Pollack promised, and he even went so far as to downplay Katie as a "self-explanatory" character.

When Redford complained that Hubbell was "one-dimensional," Pollack countered that the character was not a weak "cop-out." He even paraphrased something written by F. Scott Fitzgerald, and the director used that famous quote to call Hubbell "a man who sees and feels too much." Katie sees life in black and white; Hubbell sees the nuances, the shades of gray, and therefore cannot be politically committed like his activist wife. Finally, Pollack turned downright contrite, apologizing for being "so hard" in his pitch.

To come up with his roman à clef matchup, Pollack had gone to a source with even more intimate knowledge of the blacklist than Laurents. He went to Dalton Trumbo. To help Pollack in his research of the era, the blacklisted screenwriter mentioned a book, *Wanderer*, the 1963 autobiography by Sterling Hayden. The actor had enjoyed a recent screen comeback playing the corrupt policeman Captain McCluskey in Francis Ford Coppola's *The Godfather*. Despite the years, Hayden had never stopped agonizing over his disgraceful 1951 testimony before HUAC, writing, "I don't think you have the foggiest notion of the contempt I have had for myself since the day I did that thing."

Hayden had joined the Committee for the First Amendment in 1947 and was one of the reasons members of that group, like Bogart and Bacall, felt they'd been duped in their efforts to help the blacklisted screenwriters. Hayden, like Trumbo, failed to reveal his communist past to the group. Upset, Bogart went so far as to write an article titled "I'm No Communist" for *Photoplay* magazine. It was a magazine assignment he could not refuse after a newspaper columnist and TV host threatened him. Ed Sullivan told Bogie, "The public is beginning to think you're a Red!" Jack Warner at Warner Bros. also lobbied hard for the actor's conversion, eager to protect the studio's upcoming picture *The Treasure of the Sierra Madre*, starring Bogart and directed by Huston. Even Bacall joined the fray, commenting, "We didn't realize until much later that we were being used to some degree by the Unfriendly Ten," as she ruefully dubbed the unemployed screenwriters. *Variety*, the entertainment industry's bible, reported on Bogart and Bacall's political about-face and put its sentiments into a memorable headline: COMMIE CARNIVAL CLOSES: AN EGG IS LAID. The starry Committee for the First Amendment returned to Los Angeles from the capitol with fur coats hanging between their legs.

Pollack's communications with Trumbo in 1971 produced some questionable results. The screenwriter detected similarities between Hayden and the Hubbell character, calling them both "a good guy who is trapped by the committee into becoming an informer and thereby destroyed." He also thought they were both morally ambivalent men who looked back at their heroic World War II experience as a high point.

After reading *Wanderer*, Pollack wrote to Trumbo, telling him the book gave him "clues" to understanding Hubbell. "I think the blacklist should be dead center to the drama rather than keeping it to one side . . . Secondly, it fulfills the metaphor of Hubbell as America. And thirdly, it gives him something to do." Those "clues" took Pollack down a path that he'd eventually abandon, because in the end, those "clues" did nothing to impress Redford. After reading Pollack's memo, the actor remained adamantly unimpressed. "I don't want to go through a picture where all I say is, 'Okay, stop doing that,' and I have no point of view of my own," he said. As if that weren't bad enough, he added, "And all I am supposed to be is this blond, blue-eyed hunk of romance that all the girls go crazy over, and I have absolutely nothing else to do in the picture."

If nothing else, Redford knew his effect on women. His comment also spoke to a larger truth: actresses in Hollywood weren't the only ones who had to fight to show they were more than a pretty face. One of Redford's most famous costars explained it well. "If blue eyes are what it's all about, and not the accumulation of my work as a professional actor, I may as well turn in my union card right now and go into gardening," said Paul Newman.

Pollack could openly tell Laurents that Hubbell was "a guy who is afraid that he is only pretty." He could not tell it to Redford. He knew better than anyone that the last thing his blond friend wanted was to play a pretty man.

Pollack soon found himself in a bind. He needed to make *The Way We Were* more political and less romantic to interest Redford. He also needed to make *The Way We Were* less political and more romantic to please Stark and Columbia Pictures. "There was resistance from the studio, resistance from everybody to making a real commitment to deal head-on with this McCarthy issue," said Pollack.

The director never stopped making the error that put Senator Joe McCarthy into the 1947 mix of Laurents's original story. McCarthy claimed that there were fifty-seven communists in the US State Department; other days he said there were 250. But those false accusations did not surface until 1950, by which time the Republican senator from Wisconsin chaired the powerful Government Operations Committee in the Senate. While McCarthy's political influence essentially ended in 1954, when the US Senate censured him, the blacklist supported by McCarthy and film industry leaders like Jack Warner, Harry Cohn, and Walt Disney continued to be enforced in Hollywood for another six years. Pollack's frequent references to McCarthy to describe the Hollywood section of *The Way We Were* only fueled Laurents in his accusations that the director was "uninformed" on the subject.

Chapter 3

Sydney Pollack and Arthur Laurents

Before he lost complete control of his screenplay, Arthur Laurents continued to dream big about the praise that Ray Stark and Barbra Streisand and Sydney Pollack lavished on his Hollywood blacklist, star-crossed love story. In addition to completing in record time a first draft of the screenplay, he turned his story into a novel, also titled *The Way We Were*, which Harper & Row would publish in March 1972. Regarding the movie, it took a big leap toward reality on January 19 of that year, when Laurents received a letter of "confirmation" from Stark. The producer had booked rooms at the Beverly Hills Hotel for the end of that month to provide the writer and Pollack three whole days to do a page-by-page analysis of the screenplay. Stark wanted the Beverly Hills confab to be followed immediately by a much longer get-together, either in Sun Valley or Aspen, where the two men would do a line-by-line "rewrite" of the screenplay. Stark stressed that Stephen Grimes, the movie's production designer, needed a "next to final draft" no later than March to begin his work on the sets.

Stark cautioned that he wanted the two men to be working on the screenplay and not hashing over "again" who would be playing Hubbell. Robert Redford continued to reject *The Way We Were*. At this moment in the creative process, the producer wasn't very hands-on regarding script changes, and the only alteration he had suggested ended up being completely disregarded by Laurents. Stark wrote to Laurents that the Hubbell character should be a philosophy student who just happens to take a creative writing class in college. Stark called it a "cliché" that Hubbell would be a novelist who sells out to the Hollywood establishment.

Whether the role meant playing a writer or a philosopher, Redford definitely didn't want to play Hubbell. And just as definitely, Pollack didn't give up. He thought he could get the script into shape so it would change the actor's mind.

During his meetings with Laurents at the Beverly Hills Hotel, Pollack casually mentioned the name of a young writer he had used on his previous films, starting with *They Shoot Horses, Don't They?* Maybe David Rayfiel could be brought on to improve the *Way We Were* script, he suggested. Laurents observed a rare moment of control and did not reply. If he had, he would have blown the palm leaves off the wallpaper in the corridors of the Beverly Hills Hotel. Nearly three decades later, Laurents still hadn't gotten over the slight that Pollack wanted him to take writing lessons from someone without any screenwriting credits. "Very talented, David was, a talent Sydney was sure would be recognized as soon as one of David's own screenplays was produced," he wrote in his 2000 memoir. Left out of *Original Story By* was how prescient Pollack had been regarding Rayfiel, who, in 1986, was the subject of a very flattering *New York Times* profile titled "David Rayfiel's Script Magic." According to the reporter

Alex Ward, Rayfiel toiled in Hollywood as a "master re-write man. . . . His fee for an original screenplay is about half a million dollars; on rewrites, he is usually paid for his time, earning between $20,000 and $25,000 a week."

After their brief stay at the Beverly Hills Hotel, the two men's relationship only went downhill from there on the ski slopes of Idaho. Stark didn't give Laurents time to return to his brownstone at 9 St. Luke's Place in Greenwich Village before shuttling him off to the exclusive Sun Valley Lodge. The producer warned his screenwriter to bring sports gear with him to California, well aware that Laurents was a skiing aficionado who had even written articles about the sport for *Ski* magazine. The writer came to snow skiing in middle age, having been given lessons by his much younger lover, Tom Hatcher, an expert on the slopes. Every year the couple took a two-week skiing trip to Saint Moritz, Switzerland—even when they considered themselves pressed for cash, despite the not inconsiderable royalties from *West Side Story* and *Gypsy*, as well as the rent from Laurents's many beach properties on Quogue, Long Island. They were a most profligate, free-spending couple.

Since Columbia Pictures would be paying for it, Stark splurged on the accommodations in Idaho. Laurents and Pollack stayed at Sun Valley Lodge for three weeks, from February 1 through February 21. The producer joked that he had booked separate rooms for the two men, but they would have to use "the same ice-skating rink." Pollack took the stint in Idaho as an opportunity to replicate the working relationship he had established with his favorite actor. "We practically live together before a film," the director said of Redford. "Talk, talk, talk. And then no talk."

But Laurents was not Redford. He wanted to write alone and not talk. Besides, he considered Hatcher, who held a degree in architecture from Oklahoma State, to be his best editor. In the beginning of their collaboration, Laurents thought he knew how to handle Pollack: he would listen politely to the director's suggestions and promptly ignore them, just as he had ignored Stark's suggestion that Hubbell be a philosophy student.

The wealthy producer owned a condo nearby Sun Valley Lodge, and he invited Pollack and Laurents to dinner there for their first night in Idaho. Also present was Stark's wife, Fran. The daughter of Fanny Brice and Nicky Arnstein had recently sprained her wrist, which meant she could not be as bejeweled and gaudy as usual. She made up for that uncustomary lack of glittering ostentation by wearing a matching sling for whatever dress, pantsuit, or ski outfit she happened to be wearing. Those rotating slings turned into a favorite, oft-told anecdote as soon as Laurents returned home to New York.

Stark instinctively knew the two men would not get along, because, basically, Laurents got along with almost no one. The writer took umbrage at any perceived slight against his being Jewish or homosexual. Since Pollack was also Jewish, the trapdoor for him would be one of sexual orientation. Laurents had recently lashed out at Arthur Penn's wife, Peggy, when she innocently but ineptly paid him a compliment one night at Sardi's restaurant in Manhattan. She said how much she admired him.

"For what?" Laurents asked the wife of the man who had directed *The Miracle Worker* and *Bonnie and Clyde*.

"Living openly the way you want," she replied.

"Don't patronize me," Laurents shot back. He did go on to admit, but not to Mrs. Penn, that "the Jewish chip on my shoulder [had] been replaced by the gay chip."

In his opinion, an even more egregious insult to his manhood occurred one evening at his beach house on Quogue. Hank Guettel, a good friend, made what Laurents perceived to be a homophobic remark, and it stung because he considered his guest to be a closet case. Taking immediate and swift umbrage, the host of the dinner party asked not only Guettel but also his wife, Mary, the sharp-tongued daughter of composer Richard Rodgers, to leave the table immediately. "Not until I've finished my chicken!" Mary snapped back.

Pollack, for his part, fell into the Peggy Penn trap of paying Laurents a compliment and rather awkwardly linking it to the writer's sexual orientation. During their stay in Sun Valley, after a long day of not making significant changes to the screenplay, Pollack toasted Laurents with an early-evening drink. "You don't know how everybody in Hollywood is amazed by you," he began.

Laurents asked why.

"Because you've written the best love story in years and you're a homosexual," Pollack replied.

Laurents kept any retort about patronization to himself, which did not prevent him from thinking, "What an ass-hole!"

Scott Rudin, who produced the Pollack-directed movies *The Firm* and *Sabrina* and considered both the director and Laurents to be his friends, believed it was the kind of thing Pollack might have said. "Sydney didn't think of it the way it plays now," Rudin said of the remark. "He wasn't a wildly sophisticated person on gay issues, although over the years he improved. He was not an emotional person either. Sydney could be brusque. He could be tough."

In the end, Mrs. Penn and Mrs. Guettel got off easy, as did Mrs. Stark when it came to her array of matching arm slings. Laurents merely lashed out at them in print years after the fact. None of them ever had to work with the guy. He had a reputation in the Broadway community for being an unsparing truth teller who never minced words when he believed he was right, which was always. He also took pride in another reputation: he often provided a kind shoulder for people to cry on.

Laurents was especially considerate with actors, especially female actors, whom he directed. He played the psychiatrist and elicited from them intimate details about their past. It was a directorial technique he had picked up from Elia Kazan and Jerome Robbins; and for performers, it could have the effect of revealing facets of their personality, which, in turn, surfaced in their performances. For friends and acquaintances, Laurents's empathy made them immediately bond to the man. What they revealed to Laurents, however, could often end up being used against them. One person whom Laurents mentored in the theater remembered the two sides of the man. "He could be the wisest person in your life," said the colleague. "You could go and talk to Arthur, and he would listen and offer great advice. But when he turned on you, all the things you confided in him would be thrown back in your face."

In Sun Valley, Laurents listened to Pollack as he extravagantly praised the talent, virtues, and gifts of Robert Redford. He said nothing at the time, but Laurents made note of an Achilles' heel in what the Jewish director said about the Gentile actor. Straight women and gay men weren't the only Jews who doted on their fantasy WASP.

It wasn't enough that Laurents skied better than Pollack and took several opportunities to prove his superiority on the slopes. He also found it necessary to mock the director's ski clothes and gear. "[E]verything Sydney wore was a hand-me-down from Robert Redford. Everything, hat to skis," he critiqued. Like Laurents, Redford was an expert skier. It made for a good, nasty story, but as with so much that came out of Laurents's mouth and pen, it ignored the facts that Pollack had enough money to buy his own clothes, and he harbored no need to derive some fetishistic pleasure from wearing a movie star's hand-me-downs.

Stark noticed the enmity growing between the two men, and knowing Pollack's somewhat less confrontational personality, he saw Laurents as the source of the problem. He called the writer a "genius" but warned he would "kill him" if Laurents allowed his explosive temper to ruin the screenplay they were supposed to be making camera ready there in Idaho. Stark wanted to start filming in August.

In the beginning of his working relationship with Laurents, Pollack appeared to be more than a little stuck in the screenplay of one of his previous movies. In *They Shoot Horses, Don't They?*, there are flash-forwards to a murder trial. Pollack envisioned *The Way We Were* as a HUAC hearing with flashbacks and Hubbell on the stand. The director thought that this structure would put the male lead character in the crosshairs. Otherwise, Hubbell and Katie were merely talking about the political crisis taking place around them in Hollywood. "[I]t was a little bit like two people living next door to Dachau and watching the people being led into the ovens and then having a domestic squabble. It does not directly touch their lives," Pollack explained. He went on to call it "yenta-ism carried to the extreme, it was two neighbors gossiping about the blacklist." Putting Hubbell on the stand would not only make him a participant, it would also tell the story from his point of view, making the film fifty-fifty between Redford and Streisand, if not tilting it slightly to him. And again, he recommended David Rayfiel as the man to help with the rewriting.

Laurents hated Pollack's flashback structure almost as much as he hated Pollack's screenwriter friend, whom he had never met. He firmly believed *The Way We Were* was Katie's story and needed to be told from her viewpoint. Regarding all their disagreements—the film's lead character, structure, and viewpoint, as well as Rayfiel—Laurents would win only two of those four battles: the film remained Katie's story, and Hubbell would not testify before the House Un-American Activities Committee.

During their very unpleasant and equally unproductive twenty-one days together, Pollack also wondered aloud to this Hollywood ex-pat about some of the movie-world characters he had created, namely, the turncoat director George Bissinger, the informer-agent Rhea Edwards, and the two blacklisted screenwriters, Paula Reisner and Brooks Carpenter. He didn't use the word *camp*, as he had with Redford. He instead asked Laurents if perhaps he harbored "too much contempt" for life in Hollywood. Laurents never made any secret about hating the industry town during one of its darkest periods. He even boasted about never wanting to step foot there ever again, much less live there. Pollack mused about whether such "contempt" made it impossible for Laurents to correct what was lacking in the script. With such animosity toward Hollywood, could he ever make Hubbell, as well as all the other Hollywood characters, more sympathetic and less reactive? Laurents did not answer the "contempt" charge, but he remembered it, just as he remembered the director's fulsome praise of Redford and his "homosexual" compliment. It was only a matter of months before he would use those memories to attack the director openly, and with unerring precision, as only a "great" writer can.

After their stint in Idaho, Pollack took the time to write a memo, dated March 10, to Laurents that detailed some of his problems with the screenplay. Pollack wanted to make Hubbell's and J.J.'s girlfriends, Carol Ann and Judianne, less "stereotypical" and more "sympathetic." He suggested cutting a lot of the blacklist "speechifying" from the Hollywood characters. And much more impactful, he wanted changes in the dynamics of Katie and Hubbell's relationship. Or he wanted them explained. Pollack did not understand why she was so committed politically and he was so uncommitted to much of anything, even the writing of his second novel.

Laurents wasted no time rejecting Pollack's criticism. In the margins of the director's memo, he wrote that Katie was "Jewish!" and Hubbell was "Gentile!" In his mind, Jewish and Gentile were shorthand that explained everything.

Despite all the resistance to his suggestions, Pollack continued to assure Redford that Laurents was addressing his concerns. Stark took the actor at his word, however. When it came to who would play Hubbell, he went back to batting around the name Ryan O'Neal.

Chapter 4

Warren Beatty and Barbra Streisand

Since Arthur Laurents hated Ray Stark's idea to cast Ryan O'Neal, he also tried to solve the big Hubbell mystery. After his Idaho trip, he started promoting Ken Howard to play the role. He knew the actor's work on Broadway in *Child's Play* and in the musical *1776*, in which Howard achieved the formidable feat of making Thomas Jefferson come off as sexy. Also, Howard was blond—and a lot taller than either Redford or O'Neal, which Laurents considered a big plus. Laurents even went so far as to arrange a meeting between Howard and Barbra Streisand at the Beverly Hills home of a fellow Brooklynite.

Herbert Ross had worked with Streisand, having choreographed *I Can Get It for You Wholesale* and directed the movie version of *The Owl and the Pussycat*. His connection to Laurents was considerably more complicated. Ross was married to Nora Kaye, a former star ballerina who, back in her dancer prime, had made the rounds of dating such homosexuals in need of a cover as Jerome Robbins and Laurents himself. Neither of those men was alone in believing that Kaye had perfected and solidified her beard status by marrying Ross. Somehow, Mr. and Mrs. Ross remained friendly with Laurents, until—like most people—they had a falling-out with him. Their breakup came when Ross was directing Laurents's screenplay for *The Turning Point* and cut a homosexual subplot from the script that its writer liked a lot.

Before that contretemps took place in 1977, Ross and Kaye accepted Laurents's ploy to play matchmaker for Streisand and Howard. On the tennis court at their home, the doubles match paired Laurents and his old girlfriend against the potential costars, while Ross sat it out to be referee. "You've never seen bad tennis playing until you've watched Barbra on the court," Laurents recalled. The better tennis duo sent a ball directly at the actress's chest. "Don't worry," she joked. "I have another one!"

Despite losing, and losing badly, Howard and Streisand appeared to bond. Then a beautiful woman showed up to drive him home. The next day Streisand phoned Laurents to tell him there was no *there* there. In other words, there was "no sexual tension."

Next up to "audition" was Dennis Cole, also blond, and over six feet tall and very athletic. Unfortunately, his trail of less-than-stellar TV series (*Felony Squad* and *Bracken's World*) took him out of the running when everyone involved happened to catch a few episodes of his latest tube effort, something called *Bearcats!*

Streisand had to wonder, Did Hubbell need to be blond, despite Laurents's description of the character in his screenplay and novel? Even she began to hunt for a leading man, and she looked no farther than her current boyfriend. The talent pool of bankable male blonds in Hollywood appeared much shallower than originally thought. Streisand usually waited until she'd been cast in a Broadway show or a movie before romancing the leading man. She changed course on *The Way We Were*. Even though they were rarely seen together in public, Streisand was already dating Warren Beatty when she proposed that he play Hubbell.

The couple knew each other from summers in the late 1950s, when they both performed at the Clinton Playhouse on the Connecticut shore. Back then, Streisand spelled her first name with the usual number of vowels, as in "Barbara," and even more remarkably, she emerged as one of the few females in the theater company and elsewhere in New England to reject Beatty's sexual advances. Hollywood's most prolific satyr joked about the teenage Streisand, saying, "One of her convictions seemed to be that with the recent loss of my virginity, I might be experiencing too much of a good thing."

Cut to two decades later, and the Streisand-Beatty casting negotiations took place on his turf. El Escondido, a.k.a. the Hideaway, was a vast suite of rooms at the Beverly Wilshire Hotel that Beatty had called home since 1966. Strewn with discarded magazines and books that its occupant had read but never put in their place on coffee tables or bookcases, the penthouse featured both a private entrance and a private elevator, both of which helped Beatty earn the rather baleful moniker "The Phantom of the Beverly Wilshire."

The fans and the press weren't even aware that he and Streisand had been an item for months. "One of my flings" was how she categorized her short tenure with the hirsute star, who was already famous for separating his long, often tangled eyelashes with a small pin before every camera close-up.

Among other things, the couple spent considerable time at El Escondido talking about the remote possibility of his starring in *The Way We Were* and the much more real likelihood of her singing at a fundraiser concert for Senator George McGovern. The Democratic nominee for president had endeared himself to both Beatty and his sister, Shirley MacLaine, and both actors practically gave up their film careers in 1972 to campaign for him. Ultimately, Beatty won both arguments: Streisand sang at his concert, and he did not star in her movie. To add insult to this double whammy for Streisand was Beatty's even newer girlfriend, one whom he did not mind showing off in public. When Streisand finally made her way to the McGovern fund-raiser at the Forum in Los Angeles on April 15 to sing "Stoney End," "Make Your Own Kind of Music," "Sing" and, of course, "People," Beatty entered the venue with Julie Christie, who, as was often the case with this actor's latest paramour, starred opposite him in his upcoming movie, *McCabe & Mrs. Miller*. Streisand had been played.

It was not until after she had performed at the Forum that Beatty leveled with her regarding *The Way We Were*. "Come on, Barbra, you're kidding," he told her. "Why don't I play the girl and you play the guy?" If that wasn't bad enough, he called the Hubbell character "apathetic." Streisand may have been used by Beatty, but she soothed those hurt feelings by stoking her mounting dislike for Nixon. It felt good that she had helped raise $320,000 for McGovern's presidential campaign, even though only eighteen thousand dollars had gone into the coffers of the Democratic Party. The expenses for the concert had been enormous. Regardless of the final pitiful sum raised, McGovern's national campaign director gave Beatty tremendous credit. "He invented the political concert," said Gary Hart, a future presidential candidate, who would be derailed in those efforts when his "Monkey Business" scandal with playgirl Donna Rice hit the tabloids.

Laurents always envisioned *The Way We Were* as Katie's story, told from her point of view. Perhaps if his initial treatment and novel had played it more equal and not reduced Hubbell to a mere love interest, Beatty, as well as

Redford, might have been attracted to the film's politics, especially in light of their mutual support for a true liberal like McGovern and their contempt for an archconservative like Nixon, who had long ago sat on HUAC.

The two Hollywood stars rejected *The Way We Were* in the winter and spring of 1972. How different might they have felt about the project if the Nixon administration's break-in of the Democratic National Committee headquarters at the Watergate Office Building in Washington, D.C., had taken place already and was not a few weeks into the future?

On June 17, 1972, to be exact.

In the novel *The Way We Were*, Laurents makes a very prescient observation, linking HUAC to one of its earliest supporters, US representative Richard M. Nixon, of Orange County, California. He didn't need to stretch events much to have the characters Katie Morosky and her screenwriter friend Paula Reisner chat about the HUAC investigation as "[a] cheap spy novel."

"*Alice in Wonderland*," Katie adds.

Paula proceeds to correct her friend, saying, "Malice in Wonderland—that is Nixon."

The Nixon remark is a bit of revisionism on Laurents's part, although not entirely inaccurate. More likely, Katie and Paula in 1947 would have referenced the HUAC chairman J. Parnell Thomas of New Jersey. A member of HUAC, Richard Nixon was then serving his first term in the House of Representatives and had been in Washington, D.C., only a matter of weeks, if not days.

Prescience, however, rarely sells books. Laurents's novel failed to make any bestseller lists after its March 1972 publication. The reviews were decidedly mixed. Jack Conroy, author of the acclaimed leftist novels *The Disinherited* and *A World to Win*, responded warmly to Laurents's strong condemnation of HUAC in the novel *The Way We*

Were. Conroy wrote in the *Chicago Sun-Times*, "This is playwright and movie scriptwriter Arthur Laurents' try at the novel form, and the result is predictably well-structured and sprightly as to dialogue and other attributes of the stage, screen and TV."

Laurents deeply respected Conroy, whom he knew as a fellow worker-writer who wrote and edited for such leftist publications as *Rebel Poet*, *The Anvil*, and *New Masses*. What difference did it make that concurrently to Conroy's upbeat review, a mere food critic panned his novel?

It was seismic, because that food critic was an editor at the *New York Times*, and Laurents's Broadway crowd of friends never read the *Chicago Sun-Times* and nearly ate the *New York Times* for breakfast every morning. The Old Gray Lady's Raymond A. Sokolov dismissed Laurents's first and only novel when he wrote, "The author never grapples with his real issues. Instead, he has crafted another daytime TV serial . . ."

Laurents took out his frustration over that negative review by quickly attacking Stark for reneging on his promise to support the book. He complained that the producer had bought only a few dozen copies "at discount." Stark apologized profusely and promised to buy more copies at full price in the immediate future. But Laurents never forgot—his memory was a vast storehouse of unsettled grievances, complaints, and resentments—and he pointed to Stark's abandonment of his novel upon publication as the exact moment in which the producer also lost confidence in the box office potential of the movie *The Way We Were*.

Chapter 5

Ryan O'Neal and Ray Stark

Bestseller or no bestseller, Ray Stark continued to insist on an August 1972 start date for the movie version of *The Way We Were*. And still, they had no one to play Hubbell. Sydney Pollack never gave up on Robert Redford. In a way, it became a deal breaker. If Redford wouldn't do the picture, Pollack wouldn't direct the picture. He repeated his opinion that Streisand's past leading men weren't strong. "All of her pictures had been Barbra Streisand vehicles—all of them," he insisted. "I kept saying the only guy I know of who could stay toe-to-toe with her is Redford." Pollack believed Redford possessed the charisma of classic movie stars like Gary Cooper and Spencer Tracy. "They come on-screen and you read in a past with them, you read in more than what's there, somehow."

Meryl Streep adamantly agreed with her *Out of Africa* director in the following decade. "Redford walks on the screen with that—with size. He just has it. That old movie-star stuff. Other actors would need five scenes to make that happen. With Redford, the work's done when he appears in the doorway," said the actress.

The director kept insisting to Stark that "at all costs," they had to sign Redford. "I must say my greatest ally was Barbra, who felt the same way," said Pollack. "I needed the added strength that Redford brings on the screen and Barbra understood that."

Streisand agreed. "I wanted him in that part so badly," she said. "I was hoping and praying, but it didn't look good."

Pollack and Streisand needed Redford, but after the box office sensation of *Butch Cassidy and the Sundance Kid*, Redford didn't need them or their film, *The Way We Were*. He had become much more interested in films that explored his environmentalism, like *Jeremiah Johnson*, or his liberal politics, like *The Candidate*, or that featured complicated characters, like *Downhill Racer*, that is, men who face an existential dilemma regarding the true nature of success, life, and the pursuit of happiness. After Warren Beatty had rejected it, Redford signed to do *The Sting*, playing a grifter in a period piece that had nothing to do with the environment, liberal politics, or existentialism. However, it did reunite him with his *Butch Cassidy* director, George Roy Hill, and, most important, with Butch Cassidy himself. Paul Newman's wife explained the situation best. "Bob and Paul really do have a chemistry," said Joanne Woodward. "Someday they'll run off together and I'll be left behind with Lola Redford."

Streisand and Redford together might have been intriguing, but it was untested. Newman and Redford together guaranteed gold at the box office. Make that platinum.

The problem remained that no matter how much Laurents rewrote it, Redford didn't care for the script. "He didn't like the character, he didn't like the concept of the film, [and] he didn't think the politics and love story would mix. There was nothing about it he liked," said Pollack.

But more than anything else, he did not like the character. "He was shallow and one-dimensional. Not very real— more a figment of someone's imagination of what Prince Charming should be like," said Redford. He even went so far as to call Hubbell a "Ken doll."

Redford kept saying to his friend, "Pollack, you're crazy! What are you doing this for?"

Redford even told his wife, Lola, "Maybe he sees something I don't see."

The pitch continued across the Atlantic Ocean, at the Cannes Film Festival, where in May 1972 the public got its first look at Pollack and Redford's latest effort together, *Jeremiah Johnson*. An American Western had never played the festival, but before any European got the chance to see the film, Stark forced the director's hand. He made him sign a contract to direct *The Way We Were* that May, before Pollack left for France. Otherwise, the producer would get another director.

The fact that he was now committed to directing *The Way We Were* only made it more imperative that Pollack secure Redford. He didn't want to direct Ryan O'Neal.

There in Cannes, under the palm trees and over the red carpets, the Hubbell sales pitch continued. "I went for a vacation, but suddenly Sydney was waylaying me with a new script . . ." Or as Redford referred to *The Way We Were*, "Aw, that piece of junk." The two men went back and forth over the many revisions of the screenplay. "No, it doesn't work, Pollack," Redford said. "I don't know what you see in this." Redford liked neither the romance at the beginning of the picture, which he considered "overly sentimental and drippy," nor the political HUAC blacklist sequences in Hollywood that ended it, which he called "bullshit knee-jerk liberalism—very arch."

Buoyed by good reviews for their new film at the Cannes Film Festival, the two men returned to New York City, where Stark staged Armageddon over which actor was going to play Hubbell. The impatient producer invited Pollack and Laurents to his apartment in the Dorchester Hotel, and it was there that he repeated himself for the umpteenth but last time: "We have Barbra, and what do we need Redford for? Ryan O'Neal will do it." Pollack informed Stark that he and Redford were meeting later that night. "I'm going to give Redford one hour and then fuck it," the producer told his director. "I'm just not going to chase my life around Robert Redford. Who the fuck does he think he is?" For a Hollywood producer, Stark had honed a very soft-spoken persona. He even cultivated a winsome grin to soften his often harsh demands. He was neither soft-spoken nor grinning that night at the Dorchester.

As Pollack opened the door to leave, Stark turned the knife, saying, "Look, I'm not going to wait anymore. I'm not going to be pushed around by Robert Redford. We'll get Ryan O'Neal."

"Ray, don't do it," warned Pollack.

As Pollack shut the apartment door, Stark yelled after him, "You've got an hour!" Pollack would later call it "a real vindictive, ego conversation."

In that final hour, somewhere else on the island of Manhattan, Pollack leveled with his recalcitrant star. "You have to do it. It's really important. I, as your director, want you to do it, and I think you'll be good in it," he said, face-to-face with Redford.

Looking back nearly fifty years, Redford could not remember anything specific Pollack said that night that finally made him agree to star in the film. "My decision was based on our relationship and my trust in him," said Redford.

Streisand got the good news in Kenya, in the Samburu National Reserve. It was where conservationists George and Joy Adamson had raised Elsa the lioness, made famous by the book and movie *Born Free*. Streisand wasn't there to protect the wildlife or do a sequel about Elsa's cubs. She was shooting the movie *Up the Sandbox*, based on Anne Roiphe's feminist bestseller about a young wife and mother who feels trapped in domestic chores. The movie needed the African locale to flesh out one of the many fantasy adventures that Streisand's character dreams up between fulfilling baby duties and being ignored by an unappreciative husband. The breaking news on her next leading man came via a telegram sent by her agent Sue Mengers. It read: *Barbra Redford?*

"I knew Bob had signed," said Streisand.

Denials of Redford's participation in *The Way We Were* continued even after both that telegram and that final hour set by Stark. The drama played out on the front page of the *Hollywood Reporter*, where the chronically unreliable gossip columnist Radie Harris broke the news on June 6 with an otherwise error-ridden page-one story about the film's casting negotiations, which had been in the works for eight long months.

Under the front-page headline ROBERT REDFORD SET IN "WAY WE WERE," Harris wrote, "Robert Redford, whose last two films have been for Warner Bros.—*The Candidate*, opening at the Sutton here on the 25th of this month, and *Jeremiah Johnson*, to be released in October—will report next to Columbia and Ray Stark. Redford has been signed as Barbra Streisand's co-star in Arthur Laurents' screenplay of his current novel, *The Way We Were*, about love and marriage in 1944. Filming, under the direction of Sidney Lumet, starts in New York in August and continues in Los Angeles, when [*sic*] the House Un-American Activities Committee moved in on the movie industry." Harris had heard the name Sidney from her source and assumed it was Lumet directing the picture, and then she went on to mangle a plotline that follows characters for fifteen years, from 1937 to 1952.

And that wasn't all that Harris got wrong: Created in 1938, HUAC didn't begin hearings specific to the film industry until 1947. Then again, if Pollack couldn't keep these facts straight, who could expect someone who wrote a column called Broadway Ballyhoo in the *Hollywood Reporter* to get it right?

Robert Aldrich had already lampooned Harris in his 1968 send-up of Hollywood, *The Legend of Lylah Clare*, casting Coral Browne as Molly Luther, a character, who, like Harris, sports a prosthetic leg. Unlike Harris, Luther is intellectually sharp to the point of diabolical. Harris was merely incompetent, although she did land the Redford part of her scoop.

A retraction in the *Hollywood Reporter* the following day, June 7, flashed the headline SIDNEY POLLACK TO DIRECT "WAY," to correct Harris's major error, but the director's first name was misspelled. The short blurb went on to report unequivocally that "Redford will not be in the film." It was the kind of knee-jerk retraction that stars demanded of producers, who, in turn, demanded it of reporters. The editors at the *Hollywood Reporter* clearly enjoyed having the weekend to fashion their Monday headline, which spun the news that there was now a "Retraction of a Retraction." Published on June 12, the piece revealed that "Ray Stark phoned the *Hollywood Reporter* offices on Friday to retract his retraction on June 7. According to Stark, at 11:30 p.m. on Thursday, Robert Redford closed the deal with Stark to star in 'The Way We Were.'" The article was capped with the announcement "[o]nce again, Radie Harris was right all along."

Except when she wasn't.

Chapter 6

Robert Redford and Arthur Laurents

Casting Robert Redford was, in the end, not good news for Arthur Laurents. It meant he had to be pushed aside or replaced or removed from the project. As of June 27, 1972, the writer continued to work, making changes to please Sydney Pollack and Ray Stark but knowing that the real one he had to woo was Redford, whom he had never met, because Pollack refused to let them meet face-to-face. If Pollack said that Stark had an "ownership thing" with Barbra Streisand, then Laurents believed that Pollack had a "control thing" with Redford.

With his days numbered, Laurents continued to submit not only revisions but also reminders to Pollack and Stark that he'd been hired to write a story for Streisand, not Streisand and a male star of her box office stature. Laurents hoped she'd agree to let Ken Howard play the role. He'd recently seen the actor on a talk show and found him funny and smart and blond and tall, which, in his opinion, was "an enormous help."

Howard would play the role as written and wouldn't

think to ask to make the story "fifty-fifty" with Streisand. "It's Katie's story," Laurents kept insisting, and he didn't stop there in his criticism of the ways in which Pollack and Stark were trying to distort his screenplay. He openly accused the producer and director of creating a cabal to turn Katie into a "shrew," who would end up chasing away Hubbell with all her sociopolitical demands. Back in Sun Valley, Pollack had told Laurents that he held "too much contempt" for Hollywood to write an effective story about the town. Now Laurents had to wonder aloud on paper if Pollack wasn't letting the Hubbell character enjoy his career in Hollywood too much. As Laurents envisioned it, the good life was reason enough for Hubbell not to want to be an activist like his wife, Katie. Unsympathetic? Perhaps a little around the edges, Laurents agreed. After all, he never intended for Hubbell to be "heroic." Katie was the hero of *The Way We Were* and nobody else.

Regarding Pollack's charges of "contempt," Laurents embraced that strong emotion with immense pride. He never played the diplomat. He relished being the provocateur. He told the director and the producer that they were both "twisting" his screenplay, because Pollack and Stark were, in fact, "male chauvinists" who neither liked nor admired strong women. They wanted Katie to be "a little wife," according to Laurents, and for that reason, they could never envision her as the film's sole hero.

Suddenly, in his late-in-the-game correspondence with Stark and Pollack, Laurents found Redford all wrong for the role, even though in publicity maneuvers for his novel only two months earlier, he'd completely dismissed the possibility of Ryan O'Neal. He had told a reporter at the *San Francisco Examiner*, "No, indeed not. As a matter of fact, I think [O'Neal] would be all wrong for the role. I think of Robert Redford or an actor like him."

That was in April 1972. Two months later, Laurents claimed that showing "vulnerability" was beyond Redford's range and talent as an actor. He agreed that Streisand had not shown much vulnerability in any of her screen performances, but he knew that quality could be found in her. He'd witnessed it firsthand during their time together on *I Can Get It for You Wholesale*, when she was deeply in love with her costar and future husband, Elliott Gould.

Laurents refused to build up the Hubbell character and objected to suggestions that the politics of the script be diluted. If Pollack and Stark were ruining the love story because they were "male chauvinists," they were destroying the Hollywood blacklist elements in the script because Pollack was "uninformed" and Stark was "a conservative Republican." In the opinion of Laurents, it didn't get any worse than being a conservative Republican. They were the ones who had inflicted HUAC and the blacklist, not to mention Nixon, on America. Furthermore, he reminded Pollack of his initial interest in *The Way We Were* and why he wanted to direct it. The film would be the "first movie" ever to examine this dark period in Hollywood history, and any "first" carried with it enormous responsibility. If they didn't handle the subject honestly and with complete accuracy, Laurents predicted that the film would be "crucified" by the press.

Laurents saw Streisand as an ally in the preproduction process. Later, she fought to keep some of his material in the finished film. However, regarding how much the screenplay should be altered to please Redford, they were not always in agreement. "I was the one pushing for Redford to play Hubbell from the beginning," she said. "I couldn't imagine anyone else in the role, because I knew instinctively that the dynamic between us would make the picture work. I wanted the writers to do anything they could to make him happy—strengthen the character of Hubbell and give him more scenes."

Which was precisely what her Broadway friend refused to do.

That June, Pollack wasted no time writing a letter to answer Laurents's diatribe. He defended his two stars, saying that Streisand had always wanted the love affair to be told in a way that was "fifty-fifty," and he went on to note that Redford had played a "dumb jock" in *Downhill Racer*. The actor held no qualms about playing an unsympathetic character. What Redford did not want to play was a character that had no second or third act, i.e., the Hollywood section of the movie, in which he is devoid of any noble character traits, including "even wisdom."

Pollack went on to defend himself regarding the film's politics or lack thereof. He let Laurents know that it was not enough to call the blacklist simply "evil." He pointed to the speech Laurents had written for the film's blacklisted screenwriter Brooks Carpenter, a supporting character who lashes out against the blacklist and HUAC at the Thought Control Conference, held at the Beverly Hills Hotel. The scene would eventually be filmed at that iconic pink hotel, with Murray Hamilton playing the screenwriter, but it would also go on to be cut from the movie even before it was screened for preview audiences. From what Pollack revealed to Laurents in late June 1972, it's surprising the scene was ever filmed. Pollack called the scene "dramatic but unmoving."

From there, Pollack managed to infuriate Laurents further by injecting a Broadway competitor into his argument. He revealed that he'd recently spoken to director Arthur Penn, legendary for bringing *The Miracle Worker* to the stage and screen, and that the two of them had discussed the difficulty of making a film like *The Way* We *Were*. At the time, Penn rode high in Hollywood after the phenomenal success of his movies *Bonnie and Clyde* and *Alice's Restaurant*. Penn had told Pollack there were only two ways to deal with large social issues in the movies: either one found a strong personal story to tell or the issue had to be "tackled head-on." Pollack had abandoned the idea of seeing the Hubbell character testify at HUAC hearings and using that as a leitmotif to stitch the film together. Now he strongly preferred that *The Way We Were* tell a good love story. Pollack dug in the knife that Ray Stark tried to plant in his back at the Dorchester Hotel by saying he had "agreed" with Penn on that point.

Even at this late date, the memos and letters flew back and forth between the director and the screenwriter and the producer. Perhaps at this point in the film's stormy development, Laurents would have preferred that Penn direct *The Way We Were*. Or that Stark get Laurents's old World War II "army buddy" George Cukor to direct or even his friend Herbert Ross—that is, before Ross completely heterosexualized *The Turning Point* and the two men stopped speaking to each other.

Regarding hurt feelings, none were more bruised than Laurents's. He'd had his screenplays rewritten before. It always happened when he adapted someone else's play or novel to the screen. In fact, all his previous screenplays relied on source material, whether they were based on plays, like Patrick Hamilton's *Rope* and Guy Bolton's *Anastasia*, or novels, like Mary Jane Ward's *The Snake Pit*, Françoise Sagan's *Bonjour Tristesse*, Elia Kazan's *The Arrangement*, or Libbie Block's *Wild Calendar* (which ended up as the film *Caught*, based on the life of Howard Hughes).

As Laurents saw his contribution to those films, it was

work, and his writing a job for which he received a lot of money, in most cases. *The Way We Were* was different. It was personal, much more personal. It was *his*! "Ray and Sydney started to muck around with it," Laurents explained. "It was really painful because I cared a great deal about that story. Much of it was from my own life and was about the witch-hunt, which they knew nothing about."

In their parting shots with each other, both Laurents and Stark continued to hone their sarcasm to a point where they could have taken their act together on the road. Laurents said the final screenplay credit for *The Way We Were* should include not only his name but also another dozen, including that of Streisand's son, Jason Gould. And he called the producer "chintzy."

Stark responded by pointing out the many screenwriting "bonuses" that he'd paid Laurents over the past twelve months, and he defended himself, calling only his office décor "chintzy."

In his final exchange of words with Pollack, Laurents gleaned something much more significant and substantive than fights over money or window treatments or even screenwriting credit. He saw, finally, that they could never work together, because in the end they envisioned two very different movies. According to Laurents, Pollack conceived *The Way We Were* as a story about two people who love each other but who, all politics aside, break up because they're wrong for each other, witch hunt or no witch hunt, blacklist or no blacklist. He saw the film's romance as a tragedy, one that "collapsed" from within due to its own internal flaws and differences.

Laurents agreed that Katie is committed to the politics of the moment, whereas Hubbell takes the long view, which renders him passive and ultimately cynical. But he and Pollack saw the effect of HUAC on the couple's relationship very differently. The witch hunt had not simply "complicated" their marriage; it had "destroyed" their life together. Pollack thought they were doomed regardless. Laurents believed they could survive, but the blacklist made that impossible. He saw the romance as a melodrama, one that was ultimately destroyed by outside influences. Here, the film's leading lady switched sides to rejoin the Laurents camp.

"I don't agree that their marriage was a mistake and they weren't 'right for each other,'" said Streisand. "For me, the attraction of opposites—the ying and the yang—was very real. Their physical passion as well as their emotional bond was so strong, and that's what makes you root for them as a couple." She went on to explain. "These two people were really in love with each other and that wouldn't go away, even with all their differences. It was only when Katie was informed on that she was forced to make the painful decision to end their marriage, because if Hubbell had a subversive wife it would have ended his career in Hollywood." The real reason for the couple's divorce was yet another issue where Streisand and Laurents found common ground only to be overruled by Pollack and Stark.

Laurents had seen many such lives in Hollywood destroyed and knew only the strong survived. He considered himself one of those survivors. This writer even went so far as to invoke the memory of his parents, whom he called survivors, without actually naming them in his first memoir, *Original Story By*. It was a telling and deliberate omission that would come back to haunt the author late in his life.

In his last letter to Pollack, Laurents included a quote from Eve Merriam's poem "The Coward," about the need to take a stand against tyranny, a stanza from which he quoted in his first play, *Home of the Brave*, and later put in *Original Story By*. From there, Laurents took off the gloves of poetry to chop off Pollack's Achilles' heel, that is, his "fantasy WASP."

According to one of Redford's old high school girl-friends, Pollack enjoyed a healthy envy of his handsome actor-collaborator. "Many people have remarked that Sydney really wanted to be Bob, that all he lacked was the blond mane," said Carol Rossen.

Laurents put into relief the subtext of that attraction. He recalled back-to-back telephone calls with Pollack and then Stark. They went something like this: "One day Sydney Pollack called me up and said, 'I don't know how to tell you this, but Ray Stark is going to fire you.' Then Ray Stark called and said, 'Sydney's going to fire you.' They both fired me. And they hired eleven other writers, none of whom worked out," he said.

In his phone conversation with Pollack, Laurents asserted, "I know how you feel about Redford, but the story is hers. No matter what you do, you can't change that, but you can hurt it."

Laurents always knew how to bring drama to a scene. Whether this phone call ever happened is debatable, but it's almost verbatim what Laurents put in a letter to Pollack. Years later, in his first memoir, Laurents expanded on this phone conversation. He added the following advice: "You're going to build up Redford's part because you're in love with him. I don't mean homosexually, but he's the blond goy you wish you were."

Scott Rudin recalled the director's reaction when *Original Story By* was first published. "Sydney was very upset by what Arthur wrote about him," said the producer.

However, the significance of this exchange is not

whether Laurents's words hurt Pollack or whether they were committed to print in a letter or also spoken over the phone. The significance is what those words "he's the blond goy you wish you were" said about Laurents and his long relationship not only with Tom Hatcher but also with several other men who were his "fantasy WASP."

Chapter 7

The Jew and the Shegetz

Neither his novel nor his screenplay was the first time
Arthur Laurents used the title *The Way We Were*.
Those four words previously graced a stage musical Laurents proposed, one that got no further than his twenty-
page treatment. The story of the first *Way We Were* focuses
on a middle-aged man and woman who meet on a Carib-
bean vacation, and then meet again when she wanders un-
invited into his daughter's outdoor wedding somewhere in
New England. From there, the story imagines alternate real-
ities for the man and the woman: in one story, they go their
separate ways; in another, they marry and have children, as
well as extramarital affairs. Laurents's outline was never de-
veloped into a full-scale musical with songs and a book.

The Way We Were was also not Laurents's first attempt
to write a novel. He wrote a first chapter about a Jewish
boy named David who is enamored of a very attractive
Gentile boy named Frankie, whose major accomplishment
in life is that he comes from a long line of blonds. One lazy
afternoon, with nothing much else to do, the two boys decide to get naked together and fondle each other's penis.

When they are exposing their privates, David suffers pangs of inferiority upon noticing that Frankie has a larger member, despite the two boys being about the same size and age. Even more psychologically debilitating, Frankie takes just one look at David's penis and immediately decides against touching it. He accuses his Jewish friend of having it "fixed." The humiliation emotionally cripples David, who, within very few pages, emerges as a poignant portrait of a boy grappling with deep feelings of inferiority.

Laurents wrote no more than that first chapter, and on a cover page, the word *Novel* is scrawled in ink. The original work titled *The Way We Were* and the chapter of an untitled novel can be found in the more than 150 boxes of photos, datebooks, manuscripts, letters, memos, and other documents that comprise the Arthur Laurents Archives at the Library of Congress in Washington, D.C. Those many papers also include letters to the editor of his first memoir, *Original Story By*, published in 2000. One letter is in response to a query from Victoria Wilson. In the letter, the memoirist responds to apparent criticism from his editor at Alfred A. Knopf that his manuscript contained too much sex. Laurents disagrees. Laurents almost always disagreed when it came to any criticism of his work. He informs his esteemed editor that he included many anecdotes about sexual relationships with men (and a couple of women) in a way similar to how heterosexuals write about their sex life, and in no more detail. Also, he insists in the letter that he incorporated only those carnal encounters that were meaningful to him, and not to titillate or to "out" homosexuals to increase book sales. For instance, he did not write anything in his *Original Story By* manuscript delivered to Wilson about his affair with Tyrone Power.

His mentioning the legendary movie star in his letter to the Knopf editor could be read as a dare on Laurents's part. Wilson wanted less graphic sex in his book? Okay.

Laurents let her know exactly what she would be missing by censoring him with regard to casual, i.e., insignificant, sex with a movie icon. Laurents waited for his editor to recant, to request that he mention his affair with Power in the memoir. Wilson apparently did not take the bait.

Power, the uncommonly handsome hero of such swashbuckling epics of the silver screen as *The Mark of Zorro* and *The Black Swan*, came after the Frankies of Laurents's youth and before Farley Granger, who, as movie stars go, was only slightly less fabulously attractive than Power. Laurents wrote a lot about his love for Granger and his sex with Granger in *Original Story By*. The two men met while working on Alfred Hitchcock's 1948 film, *Rope*, loosely based on the famous Leopold and Loeb murder case of 1924. Laurents wrote the screenplay, adapted from Patrick Hamilton's 1929 play of the same title, and Granger played one of the two lovers, who commit the crime with no other motive than to experience the thrill of it all. John Dall played the other murderer.

In his own memoir, Granger discussed briefly and reservedly his affair with Laurents. "Arthur had been very meaningful to me as a young actor starting again in Hollywood just after the war," the actor wrote in *Include Me Out*. "He was older than I and he was very knowledgeable about the theater and the arts in general. I learned a lot from him and we had some wonderful times together." Granger went on to describe his former boyfriend as having a "cutting" wit and to reveal that "remaining a friend to Arthur has never been easy. . . ." Granger could be writing about a good buddy, not a lover.

Laurents, admittedly far more smitten, was also far more effusive in his descriptions of Granger. He didn't simply write about Granger being handsome. He wrote about his "beauty," which he called "striking and improbable." Regarding Granger's personality and intellect, he used the somewhat more earthbound word "uncomplicated." Laurents worshipped good looks because, as he put it, "I never liked what I looked like." As he aged, Laurents often commiserated with friends, saying, "The good thing about never being physically attractive is that no one will ever call you 'a former beauty.'"

Long before anyone ever called Granger "a former beauty," he and Laurents lived together in the Hollywood Hills, and they attended all the best weekend afternoon parties hosted by Charlie Chaplin and Gene Kelly. They even traveled to Europe together, a trip to Venice, Italy, being especially memorable, since it led to Laurents writing his one and only Broadway hit as a playwright. *The Time of the Cuckoo* tells the story of a single middle-aged woman, Leona Samish, who visits the city of canals and tacky glass figurines to find love there with a handsome Italian man. Since he is married and Roman Catholic, Leona does not find commitment with him. She returns to America sadder but wiser, as they say. The play opened on Broadway in 1953, and its star, Shirley Booth, won the Tony Award for Best Actress in a play.

"Arthur was a lot like Leona," said the playwright's longtime assistant, Ashley Feinstein. "He had this thing in his mind that he was not good looking. And when he went to Europe, he probably thought of himself as plain and single, and he liked good-looking people. He wouldn't admit it, but he certainly did like good-looking people."

Before *The Time of the Cuckoo* opened, Laurents ended his affair with Granger and resumed a short-lived one with the equally handsome ballet dancer Harold Lang, who shared the ex-boyfriend's extraordinary black Irish good looks. Having left Ballet Theatre (later to be renamed American Ballet Theatre), Lang scored a major success in 1952 in the first Broadway revival of *Pal Joey*, the musical that made Gene Kelly a star in 1940. Laurents claimed that the dancer was "the best sex I'd ever had," and he went on to enthuse, "How could the answer to 'What is art?' compare to Harold Lang's ass?"

Before reacquainting himself with the dancer's backside, Laurents split with Granger when the actor departed Los Angeles to do some location work on his new movie, a film noir titled *Side Street*, in New York City. It was a big city, unless you were gay, and then New York could be a very small town indeed. Even before Granger returned to the West Coast to finish *Side Street* on the Metro backlot, Laurents had already heard about the affair between his boyfriend and a famous conductor-composer whom he considered a friend. Besides being "uncomplicated," Laurents described Granger as "[g]uiltless, gorgeous and gentile" with regard to his having sex with Leonard Bernstein.

The only word missing in all that glorious alliteration is the word *golden* to describe the man who replaced Granger and Lang in the arms of Laurents. Tom Hatcher got around in Hollywood, despite being an out-of-work actor who worked first as a truck driver for Pabst Blue Ribbon and then as a manager at William B. Riley, a high-end men's clothing store in Beverly Hills. "Tom almost admitted that he was a hustler in those years," said Feinstein. The twenty-four-year-old men's store manager counted the author of *The Berlin Stories* and his young artist partner as close friends.

"I don't know how Chris [Isherwood] and I first met Tom," said Don Bachardy. "Probably we met at cocktail parties. Tom was so incredibly handsome."

Gore Vidal was yet another famous homosexual bedazzled by Hatcher's looks, and knowing Laurents's taste in handsome Gentile men, the author of the novels *Williwaw* and *The City and the Pillar* recommended that his fellow writer friend pay a visit to William B. Riley to check out the Blond. That meeting led to Hatcher becoming Laurents's boyfriend, and it was only a matter of weeks before the one introduced the other to the most famous same-sex couple living in Santa Monica Canyon or, perhaps, the whole world in 1955. Laurents believed he was being asked to meet Hatcher's "foster parents."

Bachardy rejected that description. "That suggests Tom needed parents," he said. "He had his own parents. He was very together. He didn't need us. Tom was very young and very beautiful and he had charm. He was wonderful looking. I never asked him to sit for me. I wish I had." Although Bachardy went on to call Laurents "a fascinating personality, a wonderful conversationalist," he mentioned nothing about wanting to paint a portrait of Hatcher's far more famous partner.

"There was an electrical current between them," Bachardy said of the couple. "They weren't just two men together. Something was going on, very high energy."

By comparison, the thirty-year difference in age between Isherwood and Bachardy turned the twelve years separating Laurents and Hatcher into a mere blip. But it wasn't a blip, and as with so many relationships involving lovers of vastly different ages, it is the older person who often provides the security, stability, and wisdom, as Granger described the situation in *Include Me Out*. Unlike that affair with the movie star, Laurents also provided the money, as well as the career opportunities, for his newer and younger boyfriend.

For Hatcher, his dreams of becoming a movie actor ended abruptly when he refused the sexual advances of his agent. Henry Willson, notorious for keeping the longest running gay casting couch in town, had already bedded and made Rock Hudson (né Roy Fitzgerald) and Tab Hunter (né Arthur Gelien) stars. Hatcher thought he could do the same for him, and it helped that Willson liked his name, Tom Hatcher. It fit the agent's rule of one syllable followed by two syllables and exuded those bland Middle American values popular at the time. As if his blond hair, emerald eyes, pinned-back ears, perfect teeth, eager smile, and extremely fit body weren't enough to beguile Willson, Hatcher made sure to dress appropriately for his first interview with the rapacious agent. "I left on my truck-driver outfit," said Hatcher, referring to his job at Pabst Blue Ribbon beer. "I was pretty sure Henry Willson would like that."

Willson signed Hatcher on the spot. The sexual attraction, however, was not reciprocal. The young truck driver turned actor did not find the fiftyish, balding, overweight, and slack-jawed Willson up to his bedroom standards. A few days later, when Hatcher refused to have sex, the agent shot back, "I've got better-looking men than you." And to prove his point, he drove the soon-to-be ex-client to an apartment in West Hollywood, where, using his own key, he entered the bedroom of an Italian American teenager. Throwing off the covers, he pointed at the rudely awakened boy and told Hatcher, "He's better looking than you!" Willson left the apartment with John Saxon (né Carmine Orrico) in tow, leaving it to Hatcher to find his own way home that night.

Almost as effortlessly, Hatcher soon found his way to New York City as the boyfriend of the man who was writing the book for this great new Broadway musical. During rehearsals for *West Side Story* in 1957, Grover Dale played the role of Snowboy, a member of the Jets gang. The future choreographer of *The Way We Were* recalled seeing Laurents and Hatcher only occasionally at that time. "Jerome Robbins never allowed anyone to attend the rehearsals," said Dale. According to the director's dictate, even composer Leonard Bernstein, lyricist Stephen Sondheim, producer Hal Prince, and the show's book writer had to wait until Robbins was satisfied with his cast's performance. "Only then did he allow others to see our work," said the actor-dancer.

Dale saw much more of Laurents and Hatcher on the beach on Quogue, where Robbins rented a house and invited some members of the *West Side Story* company for weekends there. "Tom and Arthur were partners. They were a couple," Dale recalled. Later, he noted that "Tom and Arthur were part of the limousine and treasure hunts that Sondheim had in the city."

At the time, Hatcher was an out-of-work actor. Early in 1957—the year *West Side Story* opened on Broadway, on September 26—Hatcher made his New York stage debut in a small role, credited as the Boy, in an experimental play. It featured one female character who was identified alternately as Ginna, Jigee, and Virginia, and performed by, respectively, Joan Lorring, Barbara Myers, and Kim Stanley, whom many believed to be the greatest stage actress of the 1950s. Years later, Edward Albee would take that same structure of one character and three actresses to write *Three Tall Women,* which won the Pulitzer Prize in 1994. Too adventurous for Broadway audiences in 1957, *A Clearing in the Woods* closed after only a month of performances, despite Stanley's box office draw. Laurents wrote *A Clearing in the Woods,* and it was his influence that secured a Broadway debut for his boyfriend. Hatcher had to wait three years for his second Broadway credit; it came when his lover wrote and directed *Invitation to a March.*

Doing double duty as playwright and director, Laurents hired Ashley Feinstein to be his assistant on that follow-up play, a dark comedy about a woman who extracts a Dürrenmatt-style revenge for having been abandoned with an illegitimate child years before. Good friend Stephen Sondheim put aside his musical-theater career for a moment to write incidental music for *Invitation to a March*, and the play opened in 1960 with Broadway stalwarts Celeste Holm and Eileen Heckart in the lead roles. Familiar names also filled the supporting roles, although James MacArthur and Jane Fonda were better known in the movies than onstage at that early point in their respective careers. Laurents cast Hatcher in a smaller role, as the anodyne boyfriend of Fonda's character, and he had to dye his glistening blond hair a dull brown to distinguish his character from the foundling Adonis, or "fantasy WASP," being essayed by MacArthur. In between his two stage assignments, Hatcher landed three small TV jobs in drama series, such as *The United States Steel Hour*. His two Broadway roles weren't demanding, but they posed problems, especially *Invitation to a March*. "Tom had a lot of trouble with the part," Feinstein recalled. "Arthur did everything he could to help him, but Tom wasn't much of an actor. I think he was happier when he gave it up."

Laurents and Hatcher kept their relationship a secret from the *Invitation* cast. Only one actor among them possibly knew. Shelley Winters had originally been cast in the role played by Holm. "Shelley had had an affair with Farley Granger, and so she knew about Arthur and suspected he was having an affair with Tom," said Feinstein. "She wanted Tom fired from the production." Instead, the show's producers fired Winters when she refused to learn her lines for out-of-town engagements of the play.

Not long after *Invitation* closed three months into its run, Hatcher ended his affair with Laurents to return to Los Angeles, where he booked a small role on a classic episode of *The Twilight Zone*. In "It's a Good Life," he is one of a few guests held hostage at a bizarre birthday party hosted by a young boy, played by Billy Mumy, who exerts extraordinary powers over the frightened adults. Cloris Leachman costarred.

Deeply in love, Laurents didn't wait long to follow his ex-boyfriend to California and, as he explained it, put his pride "in cold storage" to bring Hatcher home. It was not a difficult rapprochement. Laurents facilitated it by making Hatcher the manager of Arthur Laurents Enterprises as soon as the couple returned to New York together. One of his first managerial responsibilities was to fire a publicist hired to promote Laurents's work on *I Can Get It for You Wholesale*. If Laurents could be brutal in his attacks, Hatcher showed himself to be the master's equal in letters not only to the flack but also to others who dared to disappoint.

It was during this period that Laurents also bought 9 St. Luke's Place, which led to Hatcher's career as a renovator of houses. How much he contributed to that renovation of the Greenwich Village brownstone is debatable. A letter dated July 15, 1962, written by the architect Eugene R. Branning and addressed to Laurents, makes no mention of Hatcher. The letter does detail the hiring of a new contractor, Morris Green, to complete the renovation of the Italianate four-story brownstone, built in 1852. Another construction company, the Everglades, had walked off the job on June 29 for undisclosed reasons.

After the St. Luke's Place purchase, Hatcher encouraged Laurents to buy other old buildings in need of repair, and soon the couple owned several properties near their beach house at 220 Dune Road on Quogue, Long Island. Hatcher took full charge of those renovations, although some wags in the couple's set of friends disputed that fact. Mary Rodgers ruefully asked her memoirist, Jesse Green, "Did you ever see any of those houses he renovated?" Rodgers, who wrote the music for the musical *Once Upon a Mattress*, expressed what might have been a minority opinion.

"Tom's work was extraordinary," said Feinstein. He recalled a party that celebrated the completion of Hatcher's renovation of a mansion that had been in severe disrepair on Dune Road. Guests included Lee Remick, Stephen Sondheim, and Hank and Mary Rodgers Guettel. "Everyone remarked how beautiful [the renovation] was, including Mary," said Feinstein. Hatcher divided the mansion into two beach rentals. "And Clinton Wilder rented the barn on the property for several summers," Feinstein said of the theater producer who had brought *Who's Afraid of Virginia Woolf?* and other Edward Albee plays to Broadway.

The cluster of buildings owned by Laurents and renovated by Hatcher would eventually cause the town of Quogue to rename two of its streets Laurents Way and Hatcher Road. Even earlier, that complex inspired an autobiographical play that Laurents wrote concurrently with his *The Way We Were* screenplay.

The Enclave marked a return to his first love, playwriting, and the story Laurents chose to tell details the same-sex relationship between Bruno, an architect in his late thirties, and a young man, Wyman, in his early twenties, who manages a coffee shop. Bruno plans to develop an enclave of houses in a mews somewhere in Greenwich Village, and he has engaged three heterosexual couples to join him in the project. As the drama progresses, it is difficult to tell what bothers the straight friends more: Bruno's nascent relationship with Wyman or the difference in their ages or the fact that Bruno may end up "keeping" his younger lover. One distraught character tells Bruno, "I don't intend to have my kids look and pretend we don't see you playing house with a kid young enough to be your son."

In the ensuing brouhaha, the play's youngest character gradually emerges to be the sage as well as the drama's moral compass. Wyman tells Bruno, "I don't want to be put up with."

The heterosexuals' dismissal of Wyman in *The Enclave*

reflects what Laurents felt was his own friends' negative attitude toward Hatcher, and that included married friends, like the Guettels; homosexuals, like Stephen Sondheim; and lesbians, like Liz Smith.

Laurents would complain that his Broadway colleagues never fully accepted Hatcher as their equal. In 1969, correspondence between Laurents and Smith exposed the double standard that existed among many same-sex couples, especially when the less famous or less financially secure partner ended up being viewed as a kind of trophy. Before she became a nationally syndicated gossip columnist, Smith had worked as the entertainment editor at Helen Gurley Brown's *Cosmopolitan* magazine, and her social path often crossed with those of several other famous gay men and lesbians in New York City. At one such party, she made a crack about Hatcher being "kept," and Laurents took immediate revenge by referring to Smith's current girlfriend as being on the "rebound."

The year before this war of words, Zvi Howard Rosenman met Laurents through his friend Stephen Sondheim. The future film and TV producer walked into the brownstone at 9 St. Luke's Place one spring morning and quickly took a step back. "Wow, this house is incredible!" he exclaimed. His first impression of Hatcher was somewhat less enthusiastic.

"When I first saw Tom, I thought, typical 'shegetz,'" he recalled. Rosenman explained, "You know what a 'shiksa' is? A 'shegetz' is a male 'shiksa.' It's Yiddish. It's taken from the Hebrew word 'shikootz,' which means 'bug,' which gives you an idea of what some Jews think of a 'shegetz.'"

The shegetz became a romantic constant for Laurents. "Arthur had a lot of Jewish friends. He didn't have Jewish boyfriends," Feinstein noted.

Rosenman went on to describe the Laurents-and-Hatcher relationship, which is the story of Katie and

Hubbell in *The Way We Were*. "The Jew is the dynamic one, and when you fall in love with a vapid 'shegetz,' it's because he's the one you want to be, the beautiful one. That's what attracts some Jews to Gentiles, the vapidity. There's no drama," said Rosenman.

The shegetz throws the stereotypical American concept of the woman as sex symbol or love object on its head. Now it's the man who is shown off as a trophy, turned into a thing of beauty, a love object.

What Rosenman thought when he first met Hatcher was something Feinstein never dared express to his boss. "Arthur did not want to face anything but that Tom was God's gift to the world," said Laurents's assistant. "I wouldn't say anything bad about Tom, because Arthur had put him on a pedestal, although Arthur started realizing that all his fancy friends treated Tom shabbily." It was just one of the reasons that Laurents began to use the name "Chernobyl" to describe the Broadway community that he used to love so much.

Laurents admitted it, noting, "For years, people were cruel to Tom as the less notable half of a couple. At least they lusted after him, so there was that." He gloated when his friends were "lusting after" Hatcher. It was a pride reflected in the novel *The Way We Were*, when one of Katie's wartime buddies wonders aloud, "How did Little Red Riding Hood get Prince Charming?"

William Inge, who rented summer properties on Quogue from the writer, was not alone when he posed a question about Hatcher and all the other handsome lovers in Laurents's past. "How does Arthur get them?" asked the author of *Picnic*.

Besides Little Red Riding Hood, Laurents refers to Katie in his novel *The Way We Were* as Sleeping Beauty to Hubbell's Prince Charming. Feinstein saw similarities between the two fictional characters and the real-life couple. "Arthur was always doing more to keep the relationship going, and [regarding] that dichotomy, Robert Redford is more like Tom, and Arthur is more like Barbra. There's something about Tom being Gentile and Arthur being Jewish. Redford is more dashing. Tom was not dashing. He was a hunk. The Ken doll thing is there," Feinstein observed. As with Katie's pursuit of Hubbell, Laurents never stopped working to energize his real-life relationship, and that commitment created tension in the couple. "Arthur was afraid Tom was going to leave him, because he did leave him a few times," said Feinstein.

Chapter 8

Alvin Sargent and David Rayfiel

Whether Arthur Laurents was "fired" from *The Way We Were* is a subject of interpretation, especially in the byzantine world of Hollywood screenplay writing, where it's not unusual for a dozen or more writers—not to mention actors and the director and anyone else who happens to wander onto the set—to tinker, add bits of dialogue, or completely rewrite a script at their whim. Always ready to add drama by casting himself as the victim, Laurents often told the story about the competing phone calls from Sydney Pollack and Ray Stark, the ones when both men supposedly told him that the other one was about to fire him. The word *fired*, however, is never used in Laurents's last go-to-hell letter to Pollack, dated June 26, 1972. The letter does refer to his knowledge that a "new writer" is being brought on to the project.

Pollack explained the problem with Laurents's many rewrites of his original script. "It was about a relationship [between Katie and Hubbell] complicated by HUAC, but those vivid subtexts were lost. It's not that he didn't understand HUAC, but he didn't contextualize it properly. There had to be a kind of education curve for the audience, and Arthur was bad at that," Pollack said.

Among the many people who would eventually be hired to rewrite, edit, or offer suggestions to improve the original screenplay, there was only one woman. New to Hollywood, Judith Rascoe worked as a script consultant for Ray Stark on *The Way We Were*. "It was my introduction to the movie business," said Rascoe, who would go on to write the screenplays for, among other films, *Havana*, directed by Sydney Pollack and starring Robert Redford, and *Endless Love*, directed by Franco Zeffirelli and starring Brooke Shields. At Rastar Productions, Rascoe often found herself the only woman in the conference room, and when it came to the screenwriting process, she called herself "a script gofer, a fly on the wall. I had a desk in Ray Stark's secretary's office. I traipsed around productions, reading and reading rewrites of scripts. My essential job on *The Way We Were* was, when they had a meeting, I would be asked, 'What is the scene where Hubbell goes to the top of the stairs and Katie goes into the room?' I was the one who was supposed to keep track of this. It was all pre-computers."

Rascoe wrote a few memos detailing her problems with Laurents's script, and at the top of her concerns was Hubbell's likability, or his lack thereof. "I thought that it wasn't the romance it could be," she recalled. "Laurents was more concerned with the political story. Romantically, maybe it did limp. Hubbell subverted the marriage too quickly and it felt like [he and Katie] never had a moment of happiness or fun when they got to L.A. I wound up not liking Hubbell, so Katie seemed a fool to love him so much." Katie's apparent masochism was something all the men in the conference room had failed to notice. When they finally signed the actor whom Pollack wanted to play Hubbell, Rascoe relaxed a little. She thought, "It's good they have Robert Redford."

Regarding the script consultant's "fool" comment, it was good they had Barbra Streisand. By his presence alone, Redford would make Hubbell likeable. By her presence alone, Streisand would make Katie strong.

But more than two magnetic stars were needed, and Pollack made good on his threat to bring on his friend David Rayfiel to rewrite Laurents's script. And he didn't stop there. He also enlisted Alvin Sargent, who would go on to win Academy Awards for his screenplay adaptation *Julia*, as well as *Ordinary People*, which marked Redford's directorial debut. The two writers rewrote *The Way We Were*, their first collaboration together, and surprisingly, their initial changes did not drastically affect the scenes regarding the Hollywood blacklist. They instead took Rascoe's advice to make Hubbell more likeable and give the couple a moment of happiness and fun.

In Laurents's novel, as well as in an early draft of his screenplay, Hubbell and Katie stumble upon the news of their pregnancy when he says, "I threw up again," and she says, "It's just morning sickness, my dear, oh Jesus!" They stare at each other and then embrace at the realization of their dream. Sargent and Rayfiel rewrote that exchange, having Katie learn French and Hubbell asking if the word *enceinte* means "incensed." When Katie tells him "pregnant," he realizes the truth about her condition.

Later, the two men revised the scene a second time, and it was this version that ended up being filmed. Katie delivers one of the movie's most famous exchanges when she tells Hubbell, "This loudmouth Jewish girl from New York comes to Hollywood, California, and tells her gorgeous goyish guy—"

Hubbell interrupts her. "Good alliteration."

Katie continues, "That she's pregnant."

In the rewritten script, Hubbell's response, "M-m-m-mazel tov?" is crossed out and replaced with "Are you kidding?" The directions have him running around the kitchen counter to hug her. It is a prime example of what two people on the production said were changes that brought "life" to the screenplay.

"I can describe the difference from what Laurents had on the page and what Sargent was able to do," said Hawk Koch, the first assistant director. "Sargent made it a movie. It came to life. The characters came to life in a different way. You understand the love story. And that was Alvin and then David."

The movie's associate producer agreed. "Alvin really was a great screenwriter," said Richard Roth. "He was able to express emotion. He gave the script life."

Sargent and Rayfiel also hacked away at Hubbell's marital infidelity to make it far less chronic. Laurents had envisioned a months-long affair between Hubbell and director George Bissinger's wife, Vicki. Katie becomes aware of an affair when she enters a dark projection room on the studio lot and sees a naked Hubbell and a woman performing oral sex on each other. Later, when Bissinger is called to testify before HUAC in Washington, D.C., Hubbell takes over second-unit work on their film and flies to New York City to do location work there. A pregnant Katie calls his hotel room repeatedly one night and gets no answer. When he returns to Malibu, she confronts him, suspects the affair is with Bissinger's wife, but Hubbell tells her, "What's wrong between us has nothing to do with Vicki or any other girl." The line was taken from the novel version of *The Way We Were*, and it is spoken in the final film, but with the Vicki reference dropped.

Sargent and Rayfiel radically reduced that full-blown affair to a one-night fling with Carol Ann, whom they gave a second act. Instead of disappearing in New York City, the female character migrates to Hollywood to be J.J.'s girlfriend there. In one scene, the three college chums watch old home movies taken in 1937 on the campus of their alma mater; and in another scene, set outside the projection rooms on the studio lot, Hubbell and Carol Ann make plans for a rendezvous after she and J.J. have broken up. "I'm going back to New York," says Carol Ann.

"New York," says Hubbell. "When are you leaving?"

"Not until tomorrow."

In a memo dated July 11, 1972, Stark thought the screenplay needed even more help. To make his start date of late August, he brought on a virtual army of writers. He sent the most recently revised screenplay to the respective writers of *Marty* and *A Thousand Clowns*. Paddy Chayefsky and Herb Gardner refused the assignment, remaining faithful to their Broadway colleague. Another recipient, Francis Ford Coppola, made minor suggestions, as did Charles Grodin, an actor whom the producer had heard great things about from a close writer friend. Neil Simon had been raving about Grodin and considered him not only a great actor, having worked with him on his upcoming movie *The Heartbreak Kid*, but also an equally talented writer. Grodin would later go on to write a number of best-selling humorous memoirs.

Most auspicious among the new gang of writers was the erstwhile leader of the Hollywood Ten. Stark even made a visit to the home of Dalton Trumbo, and his script consultant accompanied him there. "Ray wasn't a stickler for historic accuracy. He didn't mind altering the facts a little bit to make the story work," Rascoe recalled. During their summer visit to Trumbo's home, the legendary screenwriter said one thing that impressed the young script consultant. Looking back at his one-year incarceration, the

Academy Award–winning screenwriter told Stark and Rascoe, "We believed in the Constitution. It never occurred to us that we could be sent to jail. We might not have done as we did if we knew we might end up in prison."

Trumbo, despite his firsthand knowledge of the blacklist, would have little impact on the final screenplay. "I remember reading Dalton Trumbo's additional dialogue," said Hawk Koch. Pollack had advised his first assistant director to read everything he could about the blacklist. "I read all the letters between Trumbo and Ring Lardner and all that played into it. That didn't end up in the film." Indeed, Pollack had long abandoned making the blacklist "dead center to the drama," as he had initially envisioned the story. *The Way We Were* was now on track to be a romance, not a political diatribe.

Pollack admitted, "I was hung up on Dalton's views, because I felt that historical veracity was the way to persuade Bob to play the role. I thought that this was a huge story—a love story, yes, but so much more in the representation of Morosky as the do-or-die Marxist and Hubbell as the jock-novelist who doesn't need to face the moral issues, but is faced with the demands imposed by love and the compromises that come with love." The director rejected Laurents's charge that he was being manipulative, but he did own up to making Redford's role bigger. "I did it because I had a hunch Bob and Barbra would be magical together, and I knew I had to engage Bob's intelligence."

Ultimately, it would be Sargent, working in tandem with Rayfiel, who most reshaped the Laurents screenplay. Starting with *They Shoot Horses, Don't They?* Rayfiel became a constant presence on Pollack's sets. "Can you doctor this?" Pollack would ask him.

"If we needed a tweak on a scene, that was David," said Koch.

Roth agreed. "David was Sydney's person. He would express on the page what Sydney wanted," said the movie's associate producer.

Sargent and Rayfiel collaborated to make Hubbell less static as a character. In the script, they circled a bit of dialogue that Laurents had borrowed from his novel—"Katie, I am what I am." Sargent and Rayfiel did not like the paralysis suggested by the line and crossed it out, writing in the margin that it was "leftover" from the old Hubbell. The two writers didn't make Hubbell a HUAC informer, which was Pollack's initial concept, or a passive love object, which was Laurents's. The edict that they had to please Redford led to Sargent's writing the Union Station scene. It's here that Hubbell angrily welcomes home Katie when she returns from Washington, D.C., after protesting the HUAC hearings. The scene does not exist in Laurents's novel or in any of his versions of the screenplay.

"What emerged out of the rewrites were glimpses of the dark side of this golden boy character—what his fears were about himself," said Redford. The Union Station scene delivered what Redford wanted: a stronger, more active Hubbell. But Redford had to trust his director. The pages for that scene would not be delivered in full to any of the actors until that morning in November when *The Way We Were* cast assembled outside the historic train station in downtown Los Angeles.

That August, Sargent's first draft of the Union Station scene came up short. Upon Katie's return from the HUAC hearings in Washington, D.C., Hubbell tells her why his agent, Rhea Edwards, did not join with Paula Reisner and George Bissinger in their protest: Rhea had informed on Brooks Carpenter and eight other former communists. But the scene still lacked the requisite drama. Over the next three months, Sargent continued to rework and expand the scene, adding the characters Reisner and Bissinger and lifting dialogue that would eventually be cut from other scenes.

Meanwhile, Redford could assuage his ego by knowing that he would receive a little more money for his acting services than Streisand. She got top billing; he wound up with more money, two hundred thousand dollars more, to be exact, than her cool one million dollars. She asked for the customary first meeting before production began. She asked and she asked, and finally, Streisand asked Pollack, "Why can't I sit and talk with Bob Redford? I'm going to act with him in the movie." The director had to tell Streisand that her new costar preferred the spontaneity of not rehearsing, of not meeting her beforehand. The news did not sit well with the notoriously punctilious performer.

"Finally, it started to get destructive," Pollack said of Redford's refusal to meet Streisand, and he had no choice but to tell his leading man, "You've got to go, because she's starting to take it personally."

The long-delayed meeting was set on Streisand's turf, at her Holmby Hills estate. Redford left his wife, Lola, at home in Utah but insisted that Pollack accompany him to the dinner. He had heard the stories about Streisand's penchant for having an affair with her leading man. He wanted to keep this strictly professional. Pollack understood Redford's method beyond the mere fact of his not wanting to sleep with his next leading lady.

"He believes very strongly that the strangeness contributes to the chemistry in a movie," said Pollack. "Strangeness" accurately describes the first scenes in *The Way We Were* shooting schedule, where Streisand played a college student five years younger than herself, and Redford was a good decade older than his character. It was that stage in Katie and Hubbell's relationship, as Pollack described it, "when she was supposed to be awkward with him."

According to Pollack, Streisand became infatuated with

Redford at that dinner. "Barbra was delighted because she had a crush on him, even before we started," said the director. "It was hard for women not to have a fixation, because he was everywhere, like Elvis. He was the golden boy long before Hubbell came along."

For perhaps the only time, Laurents agreed with Pollack. "She was simply mesmerized by him because she found him so beautiful," said the writer. "She was infatuated with Robert Redford, who handled it well, neither encouraging her nor using her crush to his advantage."

When it came to being infatuated with Redford, Streisand was not unique among actresses. Jane Fonda had fallen under his spell while making *The Chase* in 1965. "The only problem with working with Bob is that I just look into his [eyes] and I kind of fall into his eyes and forget my dialogue," the actress admitted. According to her assistant Howard Jeffrey, Natalie Wood "fell head over heels for Redford" while making *Inside Daisy Clover* in 1964.

And the Redford charm continued even into the next decade, when he filmed *Out of Africa,* again with Pollack directing. "I had a big crush on him. He's the best kisser I've ever met in the movies," said Meryl Streep, who had already appeared on screen opposite such strong leading men as Kevin Kline, Robert De Niro, Jeremy Irons, and Kurt Russell before making the 1985 film with Redford.

While prepping for *The Way We Were* in the summer of 1972, the actor remained happily married to his wife of fourteen years, Lola Van Wagenen Redford. He left it to Warren Beatty and other Hollywood lotharios to feed the gossip columns with their affairs. Over dinner at Streisand's home, Redford wasted no time setting the parameters with his newest costar. As he was quick to learn at that first dinner, she liked to ask questions, too many questions, in his opinion. He told her, "Barbra, if we're going to be able to work together, you have to keep in mind that anything I tell you about myself will be volunteered because I want you to know it. Not because you think you have some kind of right to know it."

Streisand liked strong men. She liked Redford.

According to Judith Rascoe, not everyone at Rastar Productions instantly fell in love with the much-bally-hooed pairing of the two stars. "It seemed strange to me and others," she said. "Is this going to work? Redford and Streisand?" Her opinion changed after the two actors got together for a table reading.

Even though it was a rehearsal of sorts—Redford hated any kind of rehearsal—there were no other actors present. Stark introduced his two stars to his script consultant. "Streisand and Redford were sitting across from each other, talking and looking at each other. It was like a lightning bolt," Rascoe recalled.

The script consultant later told her boss, "This is really going to work!" She also confessed, "It was the first time I understood the concept of chemistry. It was something about their looking at each other, a feeling. They were curious about each other."

The second assistant director on the film saw another dynamic at work among the two stars, one that would come to be replicated in the Katie-and-Hubbell relationship and one that Jerry Ziesmer documented in his memoir *Ready When You Are*. One day during preproduction, with the El Morocco set being built on Soundstage 21, Ziesmer met with Pollack to look at some costume sketches given to them by designer Dorothy Jeakins. The director wore his usual jeans, sports shirt, tennis shoes, and corduroy jacket with leather patches at the elbows, despite the summer heat in the San Fernando Valley.

Jeakins had been working on the costumes with an equally legendary designer, Moss Mabry, responsible for giving

James Dean his iconic red jacket in *Rebel Without a Cause*. Jeakins made her own contribution to the fashion history books: she had designed Marilyn Monroe's skin-tight dresses for the 1953 thriller *Niagara*. For *The Way We Were*, she designed the costumes for the college section of the picture, and Stark instructed Mabry to come up with some "cute" outfits for Streisand to wear for the Malibu beach scenes. (Several beach volleyball scenes were written and filmed, but most were subsequently cut.) Despite his long résumé, Mabry relished the challenge. "I haven't been this excited about a film in a long time. Barbra wears sixty-two changes of wardrobe ranging in feeling from 1937 to 1952. If this isn't a designer's dream—I don't know what is," he said.

Mabry, like a lot of gay men and Laurents before him, found Streisand to be very sexy, and he went on to rave about the beauty of her skin, bosom, and buttocks.

The El Morocco set incurred an expense Ray Stark had wanted to avoid. His production team had negotiated to film those World War II scenes in the real El Morocco on East Fifty-Fourth Street in Manhattan. The owners of the nightclub, however, gave the filmmakers a narrow window in September, before their patrons returned from vacations in Saint-Tropez and the Hamptons. Script difficulties and Redford's "personal problems," as the producer referred to them, forced Stark to push back the film's start date. Those nightclub scenes, now being constructed at enormous cost, would have to be filmed in October on a Warner Bros. soundstage.

In the El Morocco scene, Hubbell wears a formal white navy uniform when Katie spots him on a barstool. The two have not seen each other since college in 1937, and he is drunk and half-asleep. There, amid the half-completed nightclub set, its signature zebra-skin upholstery not yet installed, Redford modeled the navy uniform. Jeakins brushed some lint off his shoulder. Since the actor's outfit that day wasn't actually "designed" by her, its fit and historical accuracy fell under the jurisdiction of Pollack's brother, Bernie, one of the movie's costume supervisors. The inspection crew that day also included cinematographer Harry Stradling Jr., and he declared the uniform "a good white" for the camera.

"Is the jacket too tight?" Bernie Pollack asked Redford. There seemed to be some disagreement between the costume designer and the costume supervisor regarding the jacket's fit. Finally, Bernie asked the star, "What do you think?"

Redford may have been chewing gum, but even with a lump of spearmint in his mouth, he looked regal, privileged, Ivy League. He shrugged his shoulders to the question, as if to say, "It's fine."

The conversation on the subject would have ended there if Redford's costar had not entered the soundstage with her longtime manager. Marty Erlichman, like Laurents, was a Brooklynite who had been with Streisand since her early days at the Bon Soir in Greenwich Village. There on Stage 21, Streisand was much more interested in Redford's navy uniform than Redford was. She wanted to know, "Are those medals right? What's this one for? The red and blue." She had to point. "No, this one."

Bernie Pollack had done his homework, fortunately. "That's the good conduct [one]," he replied.

Satisfied that the medals weren't bogus, Streisand looked around the unfinished set and wanted to know the final color of the El Morocco nightclub and whether she'd be wearing the blue outfit or the outfit that was blue *and* white.

Bernie confirmed, "Yes, Barbra, the blue with white and your hat."

She also wanted to know if she wore that blue-and-white outfit in any other scene.

"In the cab," said Bernie. "You and Hubbell go with . . ."

"I know the cab!" Streisand snapped. "When we meet again, what do I wear?"

Bernie said she would be wearing her office outfit. Katie is coming from work when she and Hubbell meet that second time in New York City.

Since they were all gathered to check out Redford's costume and not to get a rundown on Streisand's extensive wardrobe for the picture, Sydney Pollack turned the talk back to the subject at hand. "What do we think of Bob's uniform?" he asked.

Impatient, Redford let everyone know, "Guys, it's fine. A uniform's a uniform." He was in a hurry to get out of there, to do something else, anything else. "Okay? What's next?" he wanted to know.

Streisand ignored his question. "Your first uniform is dress white, but the second has to be tan because it's spring . . ."

And so it would go for the next three months of production.

"When we started on *The Way We Were*, she wanted me *to be* Hubbell," said Redford. "That was how she conceived me." Later, "she reoriented herself," he believed. But how much that reorientation progressed, Redford never knew. "Was I—am I—a Hubbell figure in her mind?" Redford said he never knew, but in his commitment to spontaneity on the set, he thought that "some of that tension made our chemistry on-screen."

The two stars could worry about their many costume changes, or not. Pollack had the much heavier lift of having to deal with Columbia Pictures. In the end, the executives there wanted another Barbra Streisand movie. They had done phenomenally well with *Funny Girl* and *The Owl and the Pussycat*. In 1971, however, Columbia boasted only one hit, Peter Bogdanovich's *The Last Picture Show*, and when it committed to *The Way We Were*, the studio was in the process of bleeding over two hundred million dollars in the red. Stanley Schneider headed the studio and worried about a film that looked to expose one of Hollywood's darkest periods, which both he and his father had been party to.

Journalist Nat Segaloff described the dilemma. "Everyone knows the Hollywood 10," he wrote. "But what about the Hollywood 48, who disavowed their colleagues and cut deals with HUAC? These were the guys—Louis B. Mayer, Samuel Goldwyn, Harry Cohn, and others—who invented the blacklist."

Abraham and Stanley Schneider had spent their entire professional lives at Columbia Pictures, first working for Cohn, who had founded the studio, and later serving as its concurrent presidents.

From the beginning, "The pressure I was getting was just unbelievable," said Pollack. His daughter Rebecca Pollack vividly remembered "all the difficulties," many of the problems having to do with Columbia Pictures top executives, who feared what might be exposed and relived in *The Way We Were*. "The studio was very nervous about the political part of it," she recalled.

It was 1972. The blacklist in Hollywood had been broken only twelve years earlier when producers Kirk Douglas and Otto Preminger gave Dalton Trumbo full screenwriting credit for their respective films, *Spartacus* and *Exodus*, both released in 1960.

The perpetrators of that blacklist, however, continued to be major industry players. Chief among them was the William Morris Agency, the largest talent agency in the United States, which had vigorously enforced the blacklist. Its top agents, men like Nat Lefkowitz and Lou Weiss, were still active in Hollywood and did not want to be reminded of their past sins. Columbia Pictures's Harry Cohn had been dead for more than a decade, but Jack Warner, another HUAC-friendly witness and one of the architects of the blacklist, had retired from his eponymous studio only three years earlier. In 1972 Ronald Reagan continued in his second term as governor of California, and as the president of the Screen Actors Guild, he had testified before HUAC in 1947 to give a stirring endorsement of the committee's activities. "We have done a pretty good job in our business of keeping those people's activities curtailed," he said of communists. "We must legally recognize them at present as a political party. On that basis, we have exposed their lives when we've come across them."

And, last but not least, there was the man in the White House. Back in 1947, during his first year in Congress, Richard M. Nixon had sat on the House Un-American Activities Committee. Laurents had attacked Nixon in his novel *The Way We Were*. Would the film version do the same?

Hollywood's old conservative political guard of stars like James Stewart and John Wayne maintained enough control to award Duke his first and only Oscar in 1970. Even before HUAC set its sights on the movie business, Wayne had founded the archconservative Motion Picture Alliance for the Preservation of American Ideals. Hollywood had changed, but its younger and more liberal generation actors, like Paul Newman and Jane Fonda, had not yet transformed the place from a HUAC-obeying citadel into the Republican-hating town that it would soon become. And even more important than his shiny new Oscar, Wayne consistently found himself cited as one of the top ten box office stars in the early 1970s.

For his part, Stark worried that Laurents's original screenplay contained back-to-back scenes in which Katie harshly condemns George Bissinger and Rhea Edwards, two characters that were essentially stand-ins for John

Huston and Meta Rosenberg, respectively. Rosenberg had gone through a major transformation since the 1950s. Her friendly witness testimony in 1951 had left friends feeling devastated. "Meta was a great person," said Bess Taffell, a blacklisted screenwriter. "It was a shock to all of us that she cooperated . . . We were very good friends." Undeterred by past sins, Rosenberg expanded her résumé in Hollywood to produce TV series in the 1960s and would go on to have a big hit with *The Rockford Files* in 1974. More personal for Stark, he had recently produced Huston's film *Fat City*, which had garnered rave reviews and resurrected the legendary director's film career after a decade of decline. Stark didn't want to offend Huston or any of his Republican friends in high places.

Political concerns comprised only part of the mounting pressure for Pollack. Equally crucial were the script changes Redford wanted, and those rewrites took time and money. Then the unthinkable happened. Redford got attacked by a bat on his Utah ranch and had to undergo a series of painful rabies shots. Memos back and forth between Pollack, Stark, and others in the company kept referring to the star's "personal problems," which became code for the producer's suspicion that Redford simply wanted a longer vacation before starting work on a movie he never really wanted to make.

And there were other problems for Pollack, especially when Stark rejected his choice of a film editor on *The Way We Were*. He wanted Fredric Steinkamp, who had edited *They Shoot Horses, Don't They?* Stark rejected that choice, using the editor's demand for an extra $250 a week as the excuse. The producer instead hired John Burnett, who had edited Stark's production of *The Owl and the Pussycat*.

"Sydney didn't have any choice. Ray wanted me on the movie. That was that," said Burnett.

Being one of Stark's chosen people, the editor heard gossip emanating from the producer's office. "The week before I came on to the movie, apparently there had been a lot of problems with the script," he recalled. "People were not happy with the script."

Stark set down the law, finally. "We're going to shoot on Monday. This is Friday. I want a brand-new script on Monday," he ordered.

"I don't know how many writers there were. A fleet of them," said Burnett.

Chapter 9

The Director and His Two Stars

Shooting did not begin in late August, as originally planned, on the Williams College campus in Williamstown, Massachusetts. Shooting began on Monday, September 18, on the Union College campus in Schenectady, New York.

"The preparation was all in Williamstown for two weeks," Richard Roth recalled. Then someone at the college reminded the movie's associate producer, "No, you can't be here when the students come back. You have to have finished."

The stipulation forced Roth and the movie's location scouts to find another suitable institution of higher education. Fortunately, the far less prestigious Union College, with its far less bucolic grounds, needed the publicity and welcomed the attention a major movie would bring the place.

The drama started even before shooting began in Schenectady. While Barbra Streisand and Robert Redford made their own flights eastward from the West, seventy members of the cast and crew flew together, with Sydney Pollack and some of the supporting actors being seated in first class.

Donald Cash Jr., the chief makeup artist, underwent total shock when he discovered that his ticket put him in coach. "I am now crew?" he rhetorically asked Jerry Ziesmer. Also upset with her coach ticket was a hairdresser, who insisted, "We are with Barbra. It does not matter if she is on the plane or not! We are with her and we should be in first class."

Ziesmer counted *The Way We Were* as his first major gig as a second assistant director, but regardless of his inexperience, he had the facts on his side. First class was sold out. The makeup and hair people could take their seats in coach or stay in Los Angeles. In the end, they swallowed their second-class status and got on the plane.

In many ways, Ray Stark could be a very hands-on producer, one who wrote a plethora of detailed memos, a practice not seen since the days of David O. Selznick, the producer of *Gone with the Wind* and other movie classics. Stark even cautioned costume designer Dorothy Jeakins to make sure that the college had enough ROTC uniforms. He also wanted to know if the students practiced with real guns. Jeakins might need to add firearms to her wardrobe list.

At other moments, Stark appeared to have little knowledge of what film he was making. In an interview with Earl Wilson, he told the nationally syndicated columnist that they were shooting in Schenectady to replicate the look of a campus in 1943. Had he forgotten—or did he never know—that those particular scenes were set in 1937? To everyone else's relief, Stark made only one visit to *The Way We Were* during its entire production on both coasts. It came during the first workweek, in Schenectady, when he walked on the campus of Union College to have his photograph taken with Pollack—it documented the start of production—and he quickly ran into a lurking piece of sound equipment. The area around his left eye slightly injured, he never returned in person to oversee the shoot. He remained in control from afar instead.

Schenectady boasted of being "the city that lights and hauls the world." That motto didn't refer to the present but rather to the past, when the Edison Electric Company and the American Locomotive Company dominated the local economy. It also didn't translate into the kind of Four Seasons–style hotels that movie people like Redford, Pollack, and Stark typically holed up in during an on-location shoot. They had to make do with the local Holiday Inn, while Streisand rented a Victorian mansion for herself and her five-year-old son, who had entered a difficult stage of development. The boy wanted people to call him Jason Streisand.

Before being attacked by film equipment, Stark did manage to welcome the company of *The Way We Were* by cooking dinner for a few members of the cast and crew. "He was an extraordinary cook," said Judith Rascoe. Stark's choice for the entrée? "It was very thinly sliced liver. It's a standard recipe. It was delicious."

Williams College looked leafier and more bucolic, but an advantage of shooting at Union College was its student body. Classes were in session, and students could work as extras on the film at fifteen dollars a day. David Rayfiel lived nearby, and according to his future wife Lynne, several of his stepchildren, other relatives, and friends were "thrilled" to be hired as extras. Unfortunately, there were not enough of them. Casting director Jack Saunders had to advertise for "short-haired, clean shaven males and females with shorter hairstyles of the 1930s" to meet his quota of 150 movie extras.

Saunders found his extras but no surplus of them. In 1972, in the waning days of long hippie-style hair, most men did not want to espouse the politically conservative style of the crew cut. It symbolized the army at the height of the very unpopular Vietnam War, when most male students still feared being drafted. A different problem arose regarding the female extras. Many coeds found their costumes "ugly" or "out of fashion," and each of them wanted to look her best alongside Redford.

In the end, the movie's hair and makeup artists had better luck convincing the extras to replicate the year 1937 than the two stars. Despite playing a communist waitress, Streisand refused to cut her long nails, and Redford, despite playing a navy officer, refused to get a butch haircut. Pollack remained philosophical on the subject of movie actors and their unwillingness to alter any physical trait they consider part of their iconography. "You can go only so far with these things," he mused.

Even with anachronistic hair and sideburns, Redford dazzled. Once he arrived on campus for a simple jog across the grounds to film the movie's title sequence, and the 150 extras stood stunned and immovable, gawking. They would not clear a path for him to do his work. Redford pointed to the stationary throng facing him and told the second assistant director, "Look, I can't run through that." Many students and relatives of David Rayfiel had never seen a real-life movie star before.

"That was typical wherever Bob went in any film production," said Michael Britton, the uncredited second assistant director on the film. "Extras would just naturally gravitate towards him."

Streisand usually arrived two hours ahead of schedule for hair and makeup. Redford often arrived ten minutes before the cameras rolled for a far less extensive makeover. Eventually, the second assistant director found a way to part the sea of starstruck humanity threatening to block the leading man. Ziesmer held a mass therapy session so that Redford, playing the college's star athlete, could jog past Streisand and yell, "Katie, what're you selling?" It was a simple shot but it wasn't easy to get. "Bobby needs your help!" Ziesmer began. "Act like you're all in college with Bobby back in 1937, you know?" Apparently, calling Robert Redford "Bobby" endeared him to the student actors. But it didn't always work, and after a minute or two of watching 150 people barely budge, the assistant director ended up having to beg, "Spread out! Please, make me look good!" It was, after all, his first second-assistant-director job.

With the film's title sequence, Pollack wanted to establish, as Katie hands out political pamphlets, Hubbell's incredible prowess at every sport known to the summer Olympics. It was here, as Redford whizzed by Streisand, that they both met a young actor who had made his film debut only a few weeks earlier. Arthur Laurents may have been discharged from working on the screenplay, but he had enough clout to recommend and get James Woods cast as Katie's communist ally on campus, Frankie McVeigh.

"Arthur had seen me perform onstage in East Hampton," Woods recalled.

While Laurents wrote in his novel and screenplay that Katie and McVeigh enjoy a sexual relationship, rewrites by Sargent and Rayfiel quickly reduced them to mere comrades.

The big-budget *The Way We Were* could not have been more different from Woods's debut effort. In Elia Kazan's penultimate film, the low-budget independent feature *The Visitors*, the twenty-four-year-old actor played a Vietnam War veteran. A few weeks later, Woods found himself in Schenectady, performing opposite Streisand and Redford, and no one had bothered to introduce him to the Hollywood royalty.

She did those honors by asking him, "Are you afraid of me?" Streisand repeated the question. "Are you afraid of me?"

"Fuck—no," Woods finally replied.

She wanted to know why not.

He told her, "When they say 'action,' it is just you and me and the camera. No star, no billing, no credit, no nothing."

Everyone within earshot froze. Except for Streisand. She didn't flinch before shooting a glance at Pollack. "I like this guy—he stays in the movie," she said. Until those words were spoken, Woods hadn't realized he needed to continue auditioning for the role.

Woods found it far less stressful getting along with Streisand than Pollack did. She peppered her director with questions and qualms and concerns, and while Pollack found her intuitiveness and curiosity and work ethic very admirable, he also wanted to tell her, "Will you just relax?"

Redford put it more bluntly; he believed that his co-star "talked everything to death." Her obsession with Redford's navy uniform was only the beginning. By far the most logistically difficult scene to film on the Union College campus took place the day of the big peace rally. As president of the Young Communist League, Katie has demanded it be called a peace "strike" instead. She stands on a platform in front of a dismissive student body: her fellow students have assembled on the campus grounds essentially to mock her commitment to stopping General Franco's Nationalist forces during the Spanish Civil War.

The scene's shoot took place less than a week into production, and all the extras were again assembled after having spent two days watching Hubbell's run across campus to taunt Katie. According to the local newspaper, the students had already broken up into two camps: pro-Redford and anti-Streisand.

"Streisand is hard to work with," one student told a reporter at the *Post-Star and Times*. "She disappears often and we have to wait. She'll never mingle with us and always leaves at lunchtime." Another student noted, "Redford will talk with us and he fools around quite a lot."

Maintaining her usual safe distance from the extras, Streisand also indulged in her usual perfectionism by questioning every detail of the production. The peace strike was a case in point. Ziesmer arrived at Streisand's trailer to let her know that the scene would begin with her standing on the Communist Party's platform.

"Why am I on the platform?" Streisand asked. "Shouldn't I make an entrance?" Concerned, she wanted to know, "Where's Sydney? Have him see me, please."

Pollack hadn't planned for Katie to make an entrance. If he filmed one, he knew it would be cut out. No matter, one of his stars wanted an entrance, and when Streisand realized that her director didn't agree, she looked elsewhere for support. Streisand asked Redford, "What do you think?"

Redford pretended not to know what scene they were shooting that day. The rally, after all, was basically Streisand's scene, her first big moment of extended dialogue on the shooting schedule. Redford had no lines to speak that day. The scene required nothing more of him than standing there in the crowd to watch her. Off camera, Pollack would tell him when to smile and when to applaud and, finally, when to look concerned. Only Hubbell and Frankie McVeigh are on Katie's side. Everyone else in the throng of students laughs at her.

"What do you think?" Streisand repeated.

"Sure . . . yeah, good," Redford replied finally.

Streisand wanted to know where her costar would be standing. Redford didn't have a clue. Pollack answered for him. "In the crowd watching you," he said.

"You happy there?" she asked Redford. "Why aren't you on the dais? Or over there?"

Redford gave another shrug.

Finally, Pollack tried to explain that Hubbell was not a communist. Redford would be there in the crowd with Lois Chiles, playing the coed Carol Ann, and Bradford Dillman, playing Hubbell's best friend, J.J. They are all watching Katie, reacting to what she tells them about Franco and the civil war in Spain in the year 1937 and why the Russians, despite being communists, are not evil for supporting the Spanish freedom fighters in their quest to maintain democracy in the land of Picasso and Lorca and overdressed bullfighters. On the dais, Katie asks her fellow students, "Are you so afraid of freedom?"

The important thing for Redford was to show genuine concern when all the other actors playing students laugh at Katie; that big moment arrives when five college clowns raise signs that read NO PEACE BUT KATIE'S PIECE, one sign for each word.

Redford didn't know where he would be standing. It wasn't his scene.

"Is that right?" Streisand wanted to know regarding his position on the campus lawn. "Yeah, that's right," he said.

The peace strike scene took fourteen hours to shoot. After all the logistics were sorted out, Streisand found it one of her easier assignments in the movie. "I could relate," she said. "It was a typical situation for me, to be made fun of. It felt natural."

The next scene on the shooting schedule called for only Streisand, Redford, and a few extras. It took place in the college library and showed for the first time in the film that Katie might have some romantic interest in Hubbell.

When Woods didn't see his name on the call sheet, he approached Pollack the morning of the shoot.

"About the library scene," he began.

"What library scene, Jimmy?" Pollack wanted to know. "It's Bob and Barbra."

"Yes, and me," Woods added.

Pollack stepped back. "Hold on, and you *what*?"

"I should be in that scene."

Pollack didn't pause. "Let me explain why you'll never be in that scene. You have a small part, this gnat. This is the scene about the two biggest movie stars falling in love for the first time. The answer is no," he said.

Undeterred, Woods approached Streisand. He explained, "Katie and Hubbell need an obstacle."

"An obstacle?" she wanted to know.

"You are attracted to the other guy but furtively look back at your boyfriend, and he catches what's going on. I become the obstacle that gives the love play between Katie and Hubbell much greater intensity," he explained.

Streisand thought about it, then turned to Pollack. "Sydney, the kid's in the scene."

"I'll kill you," Pollack told Woods. He also thought a moment. "Okay, but I'll never use it."

Whether or not this anecdote is hyperbole on Woods's part, his Frankie McVeigh character is not present in the library in any version of the screenplay, but he's very much there in the finished movie.

Woods spent most of his time in Schenectady rehearsing a dance, to be performed in the big prom scene with Streisand. Grover Dale had been hired to choreograph, and he brought with him Anita Morris, an actress-singer-dancer who had some free time between Broadway gigs of *Jesus Christ Superstar* and *Seesaw*. Dale was supposed to choreograph the Andrew Lloyd Webber stage musical, but he got the axe as soon as Tom O'Horgan replaced Frank

Corsaro as the show's director. Dale received *The Way We Were* assignment, as well as the fleeting *Superstar* gig, thanks to rave notices he got for choreographing *Billy*, a Broadway musical based on Herman Melville's novella *Billy Budd*. Dale couldn't believe that a flop like *Billy* landed him his first job choreographing a major movie picture.

His agent explained, "The show closed in one night, but you got great reviews!"

In addition to teaching dozens of extras how to do 1930s-style dances, like the Lindy and the mambo, Dale rehearsed and rehearsed and rehearsed with Woods. He wanted the actor to be more than ready when he had to perform with La Streisand. Anita Morris played Katie Morosky to Woods's Frankie McVeigh for two intense days of rehearsals. In between those dance sessions, "we followed Barbra for two days," said Dale. "But they wouldn't schedule it, the rehearsal with Streisand." Finally, on day three, the star deigned to look at Dale and Morris. She snapped her fingers to announce, "Show me what you've got!"

Dale had performed under the direction of such towering show-business figures as Jerome Robbins and Gene Kelly. Somehow, Barbra Streisand was different. "There was royalty about her. I felt she was the royalty of show business, [so] it was scary," said the choreographer.

Morris threw Dale an "Everything's under control" look, then grabbed Woods to show Streisand the twenty-five seconds of the Lindy the two of them had perfected over two days of intense rehearsal.

"The extras applauded and hooted," Dale recalled.

Everyone's attention then switched to the star. Did she approve?

"Okay, I'll do it. Show it to me," said Streisand. Dale squeezed a gold coin he carried with him always—a good-luck charm given to him by his former boyfriend Anthony Perkins—and took five minutes to show the steps to the star.

"Streisand said she'd do it because Anita made it look so great and so easy," said Dale. "Everybody was satisfied with the dance because the star was satisfied."

Dale did his job, and an hour after teaching Streisand how to Lindy, Dale and Morris climbed into the limousine provided by Columbia Pictures to take them on their three-hour drive back to Manhattan. The chauffeur came well prepared and quickly poured his exhausted passengers two glasses of Dom Perignon.

Morris toasted Dale, saying, "We survived Barbra Streisand and *The Way We Were*!"

That night the terpsichorean couple was back in Manhattan, where they shared a brownstone with Perkins and his current girlfriend, Berry Berenson. "Anita and I really bonded over that *Way We Were* experience," said Dale. A year later the couple married. Perkins and Berenson also wed in 1973.

Dale and Morris never got to see, much less meet Redford, whose dance with Streisand was shot the following day. The two stars were to perform a simple slow dance at the prom, one that follows the more rambunctious Lindy performed by Woods. Pollack believed the two stars could handle a slow dance without help from Dale and Morris.

Again, Streisand didn't agree with her director. Even though her slow dance with Redford was far less difficult than the Lindy, she suddenly wanted to rehearse. With Woods, she ultimately decided not to Lindy much, and instead, Katie winds up applauding her friend's skills on the floor, saying, "Frankie McVeigh, you've got the moves!" With Redford, it was different. Streisand thought they needed to practice. A lot.

Except for his jog and her rally, the two stars had not

really performed together in the film, much less even touched. There had been no exchange of dialogue, except for that moment in the title sequence when he asks, "Katie, what're you selling?" And she snarls back, "Fascist!"

Streisand's request for a dance rehearsal forced Pollack to make a trip to Redford's trailer. "Can you do me a favor? She's nervous. [S]he's taking some chances," he said. "Talk to her, calm her down."

Redford refused. "Let's do it on the set, from scratch," he replied. "We'll meet on the set in the scene. Let's just do it on the set and start from scratch and see where it goes."

In the prom scene, Katie and Frankie McVeigh are dancing when Hubbell taps him on the shoulder so he can also slow dance with her for a few seconds. Pollack instructed Woods, "As soon as Bob taps you on the shoulder, just get lost."

Woods, again, did not do as told. He made Redford tap twice—"I made him work for it"—and then threw him a dirty look. Cinematographer Harry Stradling Jr. even rewarded Woods with a reaction shot that stayed in the film.

Making only fifteen dollars a day, many of the extras had grown tired of being stuck in a gym for the second day in a row, and more than a few had started to leave before Pollack ever got around to shooting Redford and Streisand's brief dance together. He had planned to have the camera circle around them 360 degrees, but suddenly there weren't enough extras to make the gym look full. The extras had glommed around Redford on his jog across the campus. That was six days ago. Now they were bored looking at him.

"Sydney had to recycle the extras," said Woods. That conversion process required the extras to run behind the camera as soon as they were out of range and retake their dance positions behind Streisand and Redford a second and third and fourth time.

What was never filmed is the prom scene as Laurents wrote it. In his version, Hubbell dances with many coeds but not with Katie, much to her disappointment. Sexually frustrated, she then proceeds to seduce Frankie outside the gymnasium. They are both virgins, and Katie pulls him down to "do it" right there on the campus grass. Hubbell's dance with Katie at the prom was to become a major point of contention as soon as Laurents saw rushes of the nearly finished film a few months later.

Pollack had more immediate problems with the prom scene. When the director yelled, "Action," Redford noticed that Streisand didn't move; she froze, her feet stuck to the floor. "I was in my place, doing just fine. But she wasn't dancing. It was awkward," he recalled.

Pollack had to pull him aside to whisper, "C'mon, man, she's uncomfortable." He told Redford to change positions with his costar.

"Okay, whatever works," he said.

Only later did Redford learn of the problem. "Apparently, she had a side she favored, right or left. A discomfort about her nose from one or the other angle."

Streisand was typically not so deferential to her fellow actors. Stradling Jr. described her maneuvers with leading men not named Robert Redford. "Always automatically, even when they start to rehearse a scene, when the director's looking, she'll get herself into a position where only the left side of her face is showing," noted the cinematographer.

From *Funny Girl* onward, Streisand had been photographed on the left side of her face, except for rare, brief, and very long-distance moments on-screen. There were some people on the *Way We Were* set who thought this caused a problem, because Redford also favored the left side of his face. Three moles to the right of his mouth presented a visual problem. At least that was what the makeup artist on the film claimed. "[Those three beauty marks] sort of pop out on camera. Very distracting," said Donald Cash Jr. When the two stars shared the same shot, such as in the dance scene, Cash maintained that it forced Stradling Jr. to use "some sort of soft light behind them so there were no harsh shadows on their faces."

Michael Britton, who worked on a number of Redford films, disagreed that the actor had a preferred side of his face. In fact, a quick perusal of Redford's previous movie, *The Candidate*, shows that the right side of the actor's face is often featured, moles and all.

Britton believed that Redford's initial positioning of Streisand for the prom dance might have been done for a different reason. "To play with Barbra's head," said the assistant director. "I'm not familiar with Bob having a favorite side. He was always into practical jokes, besides being habitually late. He would set all these traps for people. Knowing Barbra had a favored side, Redford would set it up so it would not be her favorite side. Just for fun. A lot of actors need to get rid of their anxiety in some way. A few actors scream and yell. Bob plays jokes."

Britton apparently knew the star better than any makeup artist. "She was fun to kid," Redford said of Streisand. "I remember liking her energy and her spirit. It was wonderful to play off of. I also really enjoyed kidding her."

Chapter 10

The Memo Writer
and the Accused

The 1937 college sequence of *The Way We Were* became known as act one among the company. By far the most challenging scene for Barbra Streisand in this first act took place after Hubbell's short story, "A Country Made of Ice Cream," is read aloud in class by their instructor, Dr. Short. Distraught that her writing is not considered the absolute best, Katie runs outside to rip up her manuscript and throw it into a trash barrel. Between the two scenes, Arthur Laurents had written another; it was shot but never used. He lifted it from his novel *The Way We Were*: Immediately after class, Katie meets with Dr. Short in his office, and he commiserates with her for "not being a writer." To soften the slap to her ego, he goes on to mention that his wife is an editor at a university press. Maybe that's what the future holds for Katie—being an editor, not a writer. It's a moment that sets up the character's future career: first as a producer at a radio station in New York City, and later as a reader at the movie studio in Hollywood.

Laurents borrowed here from his own college days. He

had taken a writing class at Cornell University in 1937 from a professor named Dr. Raymond E. Short, and like Hubbell, he enjoyed having his short story proclaimed the best and read aloud in class. In college he also wrote plays, and Katie- and Hubbell-like characters are already present in these early works, each of which sets an activist into conflict with the prevailing complacency surrounding them. In his one-act play *You All Want Something*, a student joins a worker's strike, and his parents fear that he might be mistaken for a communist. The student wants to change society; his parents want him to play it safe and not be arrested or beaten up in a protest. In another one-act play, *The Young Go First*, a Katie-esque newspaper publisher takes on the conservative town establishment to defend a political radical living among them. Here a Hubbell-esque character takes the long view and wants to capitulate to the public pressure in order to save the newspaper from losing essential advertising.

Ray Stark hated the scene between Katie and Dr. Short as soon as he saw how Pollack had filmed it. The producer may not have been visiting the set, but he did watch the rushes, and he threw a fit over the "incompetent" performance of Robert Gerringer, the actor playing the professor. The producer also complained about the "lack of response" from the extras cast as students in the classroom scene.

Pollack vigorously defended his work. He pointed out that the "students" in the scene were not professional actors; he had not been given the money to hire a couple dozen professional actors to fill up the college classroom. Pollack knew from experience working with nonprofessionals that it was better not to have them "respond." The director knew how bad amateurs could be when they over performed. Pollack fully agreed with Stark regarding Gerringer's performance but reminded the producer that the

THE WAY THEY WERE   115

film's associate producer, Richard Roth, a Stark protégé, had hired the actor. Pollack believed that the film's casting director, Marion Dougherty, would have done a better job if it had been left to her—or if Pollack himself had cast the role. Blaming Pollack for the Gerringer mistake would not be the last time a Stark attack wounded the wrong person.

Director and producer agreed that Dr. Short's moment alone with Katie in his office could not be salvaged and immediately designated it for the cutting-room floor. From there, Stark's initial problems with the production only grew and intensified. There had already been warnings from the editing supervisor about Harry Stradling Jr.'s "washed-out" photography and, more significant, Streisand's appearance in the college scenes. Those pronouncements did not originate with the producer; rather, they came from a legend in Hollywood. Margaret Booth boasted a career as a film editor that went back to the silent era, with stops along the way to edit George Cukor's *Camille*, starring Greta Garbo, and William Wyler's *Ben-Hur*, starring Charlton Heston. "Maggie Booth was very tailored, and she was not afraid of Ray Stark at all," said Judith Rascoe.

Booth, with Stark's full approval, took it upon herself to bring some needed color to the campus photography, much to the cinematographer's dismay. "It affected Harry Stradling Jr.'s confidence, since it was an effect we both wanted," Pollack complained.

Stark lashed out, letting his director know that if he had wanted that kind of "white sky" effect, the producer would have talked him out of it. According to Stark, the cinematographer Conrad Hall had overused this sepia effect in recent films, turning it into a cliché. The producer knew firsthand what he was talking about. Most recently, Hall had worked as cinematographer on his production of John Huston's film *Fat City*, and the questionable results there also incensed Stark. Once was enough. Twice, he would not allow. Stark had always thought the college scenes in *The Way We Were* should look "green and verdant." Booth made sure they were going to look very green and very verdant in the final film.

Regarding Streisand's appearance, word got around to the star that she wasn't looking her best in the rushes. If she had her way, Streisand would have hired Harry Stradling Sr. to be the cinematographer on *The Way We Were*. She loved his work on her films *Funny Girl, Hello, Dolly!, On a Clear Day You Can See Forever*, and *The Owl and the Pussycat*. Unfortunately, the veteran of more than 130 movies had passed away in 1970. Streisand bet on his son to be the cinematographer on *The Way We Were*, but their new relationship took some getting used to—for both of them.

After one especially difficult camera setup, Streisand told the younger Harry, "Your father never did it like that!"

The son replied, "That's because I never showed him how."

It was the kind of sharp retort that endeared the actress to Redford and James Woods and now Harry Stradling Jr. Streisand, in the end, found her "appearance" appropriate for the period and her character—she was playing a proletarian college girl, after all, the so-called "ugly duckling" of the story—and she even went so far as to phone the son of her favorite cinematographer to compliment him on his work. Her courtesy call ended that problem and restored some of Stradling Jr.'s confidence in the wake of Stark's various complaints. The college scenes, however, remained full of color.

Stark did find something to like in those college-scene rushes. In fact, everyone who saw them raved about Streisand's intensely dramatic moment when she rips up Katie's manuscript and tosses it into the trash barrel. She had worried out loud about the scene in what had already become a late-night ritual between her and Pollack: she phoned him at eleven o'clock most nights, and since they'd arrived in Schenectady, this crying scene had especially haunted her.

The morning of the shoot, the first assistant director approached Pollack even before Streisand was called before the cameras. "I think Barbra's a little uptight about scenes like this," said Hawk Koch, who had worked with the actress on her previous film, *Up the Sandbox*. "On the other picture, she needed the makeup man for the artificial tears, because she can't cry."

Pollack, the erstwhile acting coach, refused to believe Streisand could not shed tears on demand. "Anyone who can sing like she does can cry," he thought.

Pollack, the crew, and his leading lady began rehearsing the shot, and as they blocked the scene, Pollack saw an actress in front of him who was "getting more and more upset in anticipation of the scene." He mused, "She's supposed to cry and thinks she can't. Now, that's like a stew that's cooking."

Pollack let her stew for a few minutes, but he knew if she could relax, "the tears will come." Streisand went back to her starting position, behind a big sycamore, to get ready for the first take. Pollack took Koch aside to tell him, "Okay, you wait here. I'm not going to say, 'Roll it,' and I'm not going to say, 'Action.' When I give you a wave, turn on the camera." He then joined Streisand behind the tree. As expected, she asked for the makeup man, with his can of camphor and his tube to blow the substance, with its strong aroma, into her face.

"No, he's not here, and you don't need that," said Pollack. "Just a minute." He remembered giving her a hug.

"It wasn't a hug," said Streisand. "He just put his arms around me. Sometimes words are not even needed. It was Sydney's compassion and caring when he held me that made me cry."

When the tears came, Pollack waved his hand to roll the camera, and gently pushed his leading lady into camera range.

"She did the scene beautifully in one take," Pollack recalled.

Afterward, Koch ran up to ask, "What did you say to her?"

Pollack couldn't really explain it. Acting, in his opinion, was not a rational process. He could have talked about the character's motivations to Streisand—that Katie had just suffered the second worst humiliation of her life, second only to the peace strike debacle, and now her whole life felt like a failure. "All that would have done is given her cramps of tension," he was convinced. "But for the rest of the picture, I didn't have to say or do much in similar scenes, because once she knew she could do it, then she could do it."

Streisand explained the Pollack effect. "A lot of directors don't know what they want or how to communicate what they want," she said. "But Sydney knows ways to talk to actors that somehow make them feel they're arriving at a new place by themselves. There's a creative way to talk to actors and there's a clumsy way, and Sydney knows the creative ways."

Pollack called directing actors a "kind of double-talk," or, in this case, a double embrace. "[T]rying to make actors comfortable, which I think is ninety percent of getting a good performance," he said. It worked for Katie's big scene ripping up her short story, and it would work again for an even more emotional scene to be shot on the Warner Bros. lot in Burbank the following month.

On one of the film company's last nights in Schenectady, the local Teamsters invited the principal actors, Pollack, and a few others in the company to a home-cooked Italian dinner. It was an invitation *The Way We Were* troupe could not refuse. There had been reports of movie equipment being destroyed or going missing after the film's location manager did not obey a request to hire more union drivers, for example.

Koch remembered that unusual invitation to dinner. "The Teamsters were young guys and their fathers and uncles, who were great Italian chefs, and they wanted for Redford and Barbra and their hair and makeup people and about eight or ten of us, to make dinner, which was sweet," said the assistant director.

He and Streisand rode in the same car, driven by one of the younger Teamsters. It wasn't a short trip across Schenectady to a part of town neither of them wanted to visit.

"Where are you taking me?" asked Streisand. "The food better be good!"

The car finally turned into a very dark street and stopped in front of a building with a neon luncheonette sign. Hawk remembered it "looking like something out of an Edward Hopper painting."

Streisand asked, "Are you sure this place is safe?"

Koch lied, "Of course it is!"

That night the diner housed not only the dozen or more Teamsters working on *The Way We Were*. Also crammed into the small space were the men's wives, children, parents, and various and sundry other relatives and friends. About fifty Polaroids came out of hiding as soon as Streisand, and later Redford, entered the diner. Despite all the flashing lights and inconvenience and other brouhaha typical of fans' autograph and photo requests, everyone agreed it was a great Italian meal, which included lobsters flown in from Maine.

"What I didn't know," said Koch, "is that they kept all the Teamsters' cards until after this ten-course Italian dinner finished at one in the morning." Columbia Pictures wound up paying for a very, very long workday. "And we thought it was a free dinner!"

From Schenectady, the production moved sixty miles east to Pittsfield, Massachusetts, where they filmed a few seconds of rowing on Onota Lake. While Williams College had forfeited the honor of its campus being immortalized in *The Way We Were*, thirteen members and two coaches from the school's rowing team joined Redford to film a brief moment in the title sequence, which shows Hubbell to be an all-star athlete as competitive with the javelin and the pole vault as he is with the oars. Union College, alas, did not have a rowing team. "The water looks beautiful," claimed Chuck Austin, although the film's photography director went on to add that he would have liked more sun.

That water imagery would cause problems a few months later, when Alan and Marilyn Bergman wrote the lyrics "water-colored mem'ries" for the movie's title song. It was one battle the two lyricists would not win.

From there, the production moved back to New York State and a town a half-hour drive south of Schenectady. An early fall mist in Ballston Spa, New York, softened the artificial light just enough to give the street and sidewalk the moody, glistening wetness that movie directors love when it comes to shooting outdoor night scenes. Over the years the local *Democrat and Chronicle* had printed numerous editorials regarding the lack of urban development in this town of fewer than six thousand people. The upside of that neglect was that neither Pittstown nor Schenectady could boast the time-capsule quality of Ballston Spa, with its many historic buildings and streets. It was what attracted location scout Chris Hoene to the place, which he praised as a "just beautiful town," with its "excellent preservation," even if the charming old facades owed their existence to a stalled economy more than civic pride.

Barbra Streisand receives ovations for her funny Miss Marmelstein turn in *I Can Get It for You Wholesale*, 1962. *(Photofest)*

Streisand rehearses with her *Funny Girl* songwriters, Jule Style (at piano) and Bob Merrill, 1964. The Broadway musical, costarring Sydney Chaplin as Nicky Arnstein, follows her debut LP, *The Barbra Streisand Album*, 1963. *(Photofest)*

Elliott Gould and Streisand have a
son, Jason, in 1966. The couple
divorces five years later.
(Photofest)

After starring with Streis
in *What's Up Doc?*, 1
Ryan O'Neal becomes the fallb
choice to play Hubbell Gard
(Photo

Julie Christie and her new boyfriend
Warren Beatty, another Hubbell contender,
attend the political fundraiser for
Sen. George McGovern, which features
a performance from Beatty's former girlfrien
Barbra Streisand, 1972.
(Photofest)

Jon Peters is Streisand's date for the Academy Awards in 1974. Here, the couple attends the premiere of *Funny Lady*, her last collaboration with Ray Stark, 1975. *(Photofest)*

Regretting his appearance in the Natalie Wood film *Inside Daisy Clover*, 1965, Robert Redford turns down *Who's Afraid of Virginia Woolf?*, starring Elizabeth Taylor, 1966. George Segal takes over the rejected role of Nick. *(Photofest)*

Streisand and Redford aren't the only ones who have chemistry. Redford and Paul Newman heat up the screen in *The Sting* and even earlier in *Butch Cassidy and the Sundance Kid*, 1969. *(Photofest)*

Hubbell and Katie enjoy a brief dance at the prom The role of Frankie McVeigh, played by James Woods (center), is radically reduced from the novel and original screenplay. *(Photofest)*

Producer Ray Stark makes one visit to the shoot, in Schenectady, NY, before injuring himself. He never returns to the set, much to the relief of director Sydney Pollack. *(Photofest)*

Hubbell and Katie's first night
in bed requires two days to film.
Streisand asks for take after take
with Redford atop her.
(Photofest)

The Way We Were ends
at the Pulitzer Fountain in front
of the Plaza Hotel in 1952.
A scene cut from the film shows
Hubbell and Katie making an earlier
visit to that site during World War II.
(Photofest)

Pollack plays referee in Malibu when Streisand and Redford wage a contest to see who can follow whom to the set each day. *(Photofest)*

After meeting a decade earlier on *The Tonight Show*, Groucho Marx and Streisand reunite for the film's big party scene. Redford eschews a photo op with the comedy legend. *(Getty Images)*

Having been the *Funny Girl* rehearsal pianist, Marvin Hamlisch ̃es on to write the film's theme song, "The Way We Were," on spec; he and his lyricist collaborators, Marilyn and Alan Bergman, become Streisand's close friends. *(Photofest)*

Streisand attends the Los Angeles premiere of *The Way We Were*, October 30, 1973. Redford skips the event, as he does the earlier premiere in New York City. *(Getty Images)*

Patrick O'Neal (left) joins Streisand and Redford
the pivotal Union Station mob scene.
O'Neal's character is based on director
John Huston, who faced real protests, 1947.
*(Left photo, Getty Images;
photo below, Photofest)*

Humphrey Bogart, Lauren Bacall,
Danny Kaye, and other Hollywood
notables stage a demonstration against
HUAC at the National Capitol, 1947.
(Photofest)

Several Hollywood stars support
HUAC and testify at its hearings,
including Ronald Reagan and
Robert Taylor, who is greeted
by the committee chairman
Rep. J. Parnell Thomas, 1947.
Sterling Hayden identifies
Communists for HUAC,
only to regret his 1951 testimony.
(Photofest)

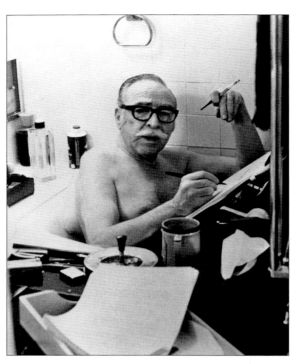

Dalton Trumbo, shown here in 1968, is the most famous of the Hollywood Ten and one of many uncredited screenwriters who make contributions to *The Way We Were*. *(Photofest)*

Like Katie, Arthur Laurents works in radio during World War II, 194[ ]. Like Hubbell, he enlists in the armed service[ ]. *(Photofes[ ]*

Laurents (second from left) writes the book for *West Side Story*. His collaborators on the Broadway classic include (from far left) lyricist Stephen Sondheim, producers Harold Prince and Robert E. Griffith, composer Leonard Bernstein, and director Jerome Robbins, 1957. *(Photofest)*

Sondheim and Laurents, shown here in 1964, are friends and frequent collaborators until, late in life, they stop speaking to each other. *(Photofest)*

Tyrone Power is one of Laurents's many "fantasy WASPs," as he called them. More committed is his years-long affair with Farley Granger, shown here with the actor's official girlfriend, Shelley Winters, in 1951. *(Photofest)*

Katie isn't the only female character that Laurents reveals to be drawn from his own life. Others are Leona Samish in *The Time of the Cuckoo* (Shirley Booth, 1952) and Rose in *Gypsy* (Ethel Merman, 1959). *(Photofest)*

Gorgeous and golden, acclaimed ballet dancer Erik Bruhn (left) becomes a brief fling during Laurents's decades-long relations with actor-turned-developer Tom Hatcher.
(Photo of Erik Bruhn, Getty Image photo of Hatcher, Photofest)

Laurents (far right) greets actors James MacArthur, Jane Fonda, and Hatcher, his cast for *Invitation to a March*, 1960. Hatcher performs with Cloris Leachman in a classic *Twilight Zone* episode, "It's a Good Life," during the 1961–1962 season.
(Photofest)

Hatcher gives up his acting career to become a successful real-estate developer on Quogue in the 1960s.
(Ashley Feinstein)

His fantasies continue:
Laurents originally praises
Matt Cavenaugh in his
West Side Story revival, 2009,
but later calls the performance
"too preppy." When Jeremy Jordan
replaces Cavenaugh, Laurents
duplicates that love-hate dynamic.
*(Photo of Matt Cavenaugh
Getty Images; photo of
Jeremy Jordan, Photofest)*

"I think a lot of people realize it but don't appreciate it, what this town looks like," said Pat Hodsoll. He stood there on Front Street with more than three hundred other local residents who wanted to see a couple of movie stars in the flesh. Finally, "There she is! There she is!" spectators gasped as Streisand left the Good Whip restaurant to saunter down the town's major commercial street for less than a block. She performed the walk three times, after which Pollack yelled, "That's a good one!"

The film's location scouts worked with a local lawyer to secure the needed permissions from all the store owners. "It was absolutely not difficult to get them to sign the waivers," said the lawyer, Harry Seibert. "Bang! Bang! Bang!"

On Front Street, the local barber received the full Hollywood treatment. "They used my barbershop, but they wouldn't let me in. They had a guard outside the door," reported Ted Della-Porte. "I'm so excited about their being here and proud that they will use my shop that I forgot to ask about specific amounts of money."

Pollack rented six vintage cars—Stark wanted him to rent only one—and the town removed parking meters on Front Street. It had taken over three hours to set up the twenty-second shot of Streisand's walk, which would eventually be cut from the movie.

At around eleven o'clock, Streisand walked a little farther down the street to take her canvas-chair seat in front of one of the town's oldest buildings. The Medbery Hotel dates back to the early 1800s and was renamed the Old Dutch Hotel for the movie. About a dozen off-duty employees of the Medbery gathered on the second-floor balcony to watch Streisand as she discussed the next scene with Pollack. Redford, as usual, arrived later.

It was their first significant scene together with extended dialogue in the film, and Streisand wanted to go over the scene with her leading man. Redford, however, refused.

Again. Although he'd never been a devotee of the Method, taught at the Actors Studio—the young actor attended the far less prestigious American Academy of Dramatic Arts in New York City—he employed that revered acting technique here. He wanted to replicate as much as possible what Hubbell and Katie would be feeling at this moment when they engage in their first real conversation together. If Streisand was nervous and on edge, it was just the way Redford wanted it. He wanted spontaneity, especially for a scene in which his and Streisand's mutual awkwardness and discomfort would work to the scene's advantage.

For Pollack, there was one big benefit to shooting so late at night. It meant that Streisand would not be phoning him at eleven o'clock to discuss everything that had happened that day and what would be taking place tomorrow. It was only the ninth day of the shoot, and already Pollack felt exhausted. It wasn't easy to chat with his leading lady on the phone until midnight and then get up four or five hours later to go over the day's camera setups with his cinematographer.

"She called me around eleven o'clock almost every night," Pollack revealed. "She called out of compulsive worry. 'Should I do this? What do you think if tomorrow, I . . . suppose, maybe I should wear my hair down?' "

Regarding her incessant late-night calls, Pollack told friends on the set, "It's not a problem. It is just time-consuming."

Redford's extreme nonchalance and Streisand's chronic anxiety were only two of the problems confronting the production that late night on Front Street in Ballston Spa.

Jack Solomon, the sound mixer, felt compelled to give Jerry Ziesmer a quick lesson in crowd control; otherwise, if those three hundred people gathered on the town's main street didn't shut up, he could not get anything usable on tape. As the second assistant director described the situation in his memoir, he was about to tell the crowd to be absolutely quiet and move behind the camera. "No, you're not," warned Solomon. "You go out there and talk about their weather, their town, their kids. Be country with them and be yourself. When they're all with you . . . all your friends, you tell them what's happening and why. Then you mention how it'd be nice if they joined you over behind the cameras. And remember to say, 'Please?' "

The film's set decorator had fashioned a sidewalk café in front of the Medbery Hotel. None existed there before, and when he saw the rushes months later, Laurents would complain that no such outdoor café ever existed in Ithaca, New York, the home of his alma mater, Cornell University. No matter, this wasn't Ithaca. And it wasn't Cornell. It was a movie. Pollack knew it was simpler to have Katie and Hubbell meet by chance at an outdoor café, where she's exhausted, having just left work at the local newspaper, and he's enjoying a celebratory beer, having sold his first short story. Quicker is better in the movies, and Laurents had fashioned a far more complicated situation that saw Katie running into Hubbell unexpectedly as he celebrates his good news with Dr. Short and his editor wife.

Before Streisand and Redford could begin the scene, Ziesmer grabbed a bullhorn on Solomon's strict instructions to address the crowd. "Good evening, ladies and gentlemen," he began. "Welcome to the filming. As you can see, that's Robert Redford and Barbra Streisand about to begin an important scene in this outdoor café. They'll be speaking so softly you won't be able to hear, so let me tell you what's being said."

He read the scene from the script in which Hubbell offers Katie a beer and she accepts awkwardly. Katie then signals her nervousness when she makes a non sequitur about the Duke of Windsor having just married Mrs. Simpson. She knows this breaking news because of her part-time job in the Linotype room at the newspaper.

Hubbell asks, "Do you always work?"

She asks, "Do you smile all the time?"

Hubbell then tells her a story about that smile.

Laurents took enormous pride in the scene. He called it the Tony Blue Eyes scene, because it was based on a guy he knew who had incredibly blue eyes. Laurents always knew how to tell a good story, and he claimed that even Elizabeth Taylor would have been envious of this guy's eyes. "Their extraordinary color had ruined his life ever since he was a little kid in grade school, when his homeroom teacher sent him to another teacher with a note," said Laurents. "That teacher read the note, looked at Tony, sighed, kissed him, and sent him on to another teacher, who read the note, sighed, gave him a kiss, and sent him on to another teacher, who sent him on to another and another, until he opened the note and read, 'Did you ever see such fantastic blue eyes?'"

That was the way Laurents described the inspiration for a speech that was intended to explain Hubbell's curse that everything comes so easily to him. Left out of his story was that the real Tony Blue Eyes supplied marijuana and other recreational drugs to Laurents. That omission didn't prevent the writer from further altering the facts, and for Hubbell's anecdote, told to Katie, he changed the "beautiful eyes to a fantastic smile." It played off the short story that Hubbell has written and Dr. Short reads aloud in class, which in Laurents's novel is titled "The All-American Smile." For the movie, it got changed to "A Country Made of Ice Cream."

Ziesmer read Hubbell's "fantastic smile" speech to the crowd assembled behind all the lights, the cameras, and the crew. The citizens of Ballston Spa were touched. They sighed. They applauded. "So you can understand why it's essential we have absolute silence," the second assistant director told them. "Your cooperation will be deeply appreciated."

To everyone's surprise, even the babies obeyed the absolute silence edict. Ziesmer had to wonder what little kids were doing up past midnight.

The crowd gathered outside the Medbery Hotel eventually stopped "oohing" and "aahing" over Ziesmer's reading of the fantastic-smile anecdote. They couldn't hear it coming from Redford's own lips. More important, those sensitively written sentences would not make it into the final film. After Katie asks if he smiles all the time, instead of telling her his grade-school story, Hubbell simply deadpans, "No!" Then he breaks into a fantastic smile.

What did remain in the scene was something Laurents never put to paper. Alvin Sargent gave Hubbell a line, the one where he tells Katie, "Put your foot up here," and he takes her right shoe, puts it on his left knee, and ties its loose laces. He then places his hand on the shoe before letting her go and saying, "Go get 'em, Katie."

"Sargent added that gesture of tying her shoelaces," Streisand recalled, "but it was Redford who gave her shoe that pat, which wasn't scripted."

In December, when Laurents looked at the rushes, he didn't like the shoe and the extra pat any more than he liked Hubbell dancing with Katie at the prom. But those fights were to come. Some of them he would win. Almost all of them he would lose.

The following night in Ballston Spa, the *Way We Were* production moved inside Front Street's Good Whip restaurant, where Streisand donned Katie's waitress costume. The scene begins with her wielding a pen to make changes in her short story, the same one that will soon be rejected by Dr. Short. Frankie McVeigh asks why that writing assignment is so important to her. A pen in one hand and a jelly donut in the other, she explains that nothing's more important to her. She wants to be a writer.

Also participating in the restaurant scene was the real owner of the Good Whip, Cornelius Goodwin, who nurses a cup of coffee behind the counter for a few seconds of screen time. Mrs. Goodwin had been told to stay in the back room during the shoot. The production did not want too many cooks in the place. The restaurant is not named in the film, but a painted sign on the restaurant window reading THE GOOD WHIP is visible in the finished film.

After Katie and Frankie's confab over her short-story ambitions, Hubbell and three of his college friends enter the restaurant, sit at a booth, and start talking about such innocuous Joe College things as how they want to decorate the gym for the upcoming prom. Ziesmer noted, "Robert Redford seemed above it all," not only in the Good Whip but throughout the shoot. "Like his character in our film, everything seemed too easy for him."

Typically, Redford disarmed the other actors, not to mention his director, when he sometimes approached a scene as if he were not absolutely sure of what anyone expected of him or, for that matter, what scene they were filming. Just as typically, when it came to rolling the cameras, Redford invariably knew his lines word perfect, where to hit his mark and, most important, how to act and behave. That night in the Good Whip, he not only knew where he was and precisely what to say and do, he even gave a directorial tip to his nervous costar. It came after the awkward moment when Katie tries to take the food order from Hubbell and friends and they make bad jokes about the "Stalin Shuffle" and "the college grad meets the Leningrad," at which point Katie walks away in a huff and Hubbell follows her to the counter. There's a close-up of Streisand when Katie says, "I think you're all disgusting." (In Laurents's novel, Katie levels this charge in response to a favorite cause of Hubbell and his friends: they want to legalize marijuana.)

Off camera, when the cinematographer readied a second take, Redford told Streisand, "Don't look at me. Have a hard time looking at me. Look down first."

On that second take, Streisand did as Redford had instructed her. She looked down, said her line, and then slowly lifted her gaze to lock eyes with his. Streisand would later say it was what made Redford a star. "He's a man of depth who has what it takes to be a great movie star: mystery behind the eyes," she said. "You wonder, 'What is he really thinking?'"

James Woods watched the scene, amazed not at Redford's eyes but at his expertise at coaching other actors, even though his directorial debut was eight years away, with *Ordinary People.* "Bob knew it was vulnerable to have her eyes down. She started in this humble position," said Woods. "This guy also knows how attractive he is. Bob was aware."

The actor's longtime publicist, Lois Smith, remarked that the young Redford had a penchant for looking at himself in storefront reflections. Regarding his scene with Streisand in *The Way We Were,* there was something else at work beyond how great he knew he looked. "Barbra had a massive crush on Bob," said Woods.

Three weeks into production, Streisand and Redford had performed only two major scenes together, but already Pollack could see he was dealing with two extremely different actors. "Barbra wanted precision; Redford, spontaneity. Barbra likes lengthy rehearsals and multiple takes," he said. "Redford is better in his early takes. After that, he just gets bored."

Michael Britton would notice a similar dynamic at play a few years later, when he worked as Redford's assistant on *All the President's Men*. "Dustin Hoffman liked to re-hearse. Bob didn't," he said. And David Ward, screenwriter for *The Sting*, noted the same acting process between that film's two stars. "Paul [Newman] was a Method actor who loved to worry the character out. He needed to talk and talk and talk," said Ward. "Bob's working style, on the other hand, was 'Let's get it over with.'"

In that respect, Pollack's direction style was more in sync with what Redford wanted than what Streisand needed. "I don't . . . lock them in," he said of directing ac-tors. "You surprise them. You put them somewhere differ-ent, or you change something in the other actor, restage the scene quickly somehow. Or you say, 'We've got that one. Now let's try something different.' You need a little bit of fear on film. Or, at least, adrenaline."

Streisand, for her part, did not find what she wanted all that different from her costar's. "I like a rehearsal basi-cally for technical details like where to stand, where the light is coming from, but I always want to be open to whatever happens in the actual take," she said. "I want to be completely in the moment when we're shooting the scene, and Redford and I both enjoyed working off each other. If actors are good, they are really listening to each other and reacting from moment to moment, so each take is different."

Despite her multiple-takes reputation, Streisand found that "my first take is often best. It's the most sponta-neous . . . the most original . . . and the last thing I want is to lose that spontaneity with too many rehearsals." (In fact, it was her *I Can Get It for You Wholesale* director who complained that, once the show opened, she never gave the same performance twice. "You're too undisci-plined," said Laurents.)

When the production moved to New York City on Oc-tober 1, the memos from Stark to Pollack went from frequent to blizzard force. Perhaps even Stark realized he was pulling another David O. Selznick. That month Random House published a collection of memos written by the *Gone with the Wind* producer, titled *Memo from David O. Selznick*. The book featured a mere fraction of Selznick's written directives to writers, actors, editors, and others working on his films. Despite judicious editing, the tome weighed in at 640 pages, and to show he had a sense of humor, Stark got his hands on an early copy of *Memo* and sent it to Pollack with a short note. Even though Selznick died in 1965, Stark's note to his director read:

> *Dear Sydney,*
> *If you think Stark sends out memos, you should have worked with me.*
> *David O. Selznick*

Stark's many memos specifically focused on the 136-page script, which continued to undergo massive revisions. Those rewrites were adding pages, not subtracting them, and the producer estimated that each page translated into more than one minute of screen time. He wanted a two-hour movie, not something approaching two and a half hours. He immediately ordered his two film editors, Margaret Booth and John Burnett, to put together a rough cut of the college section to see where they were time-wise on *The Way We Were*.

It was why Booth and Burnett immediately emerged as a double festering wound. It was bad enough that Stark had not hired the director's preferred editor, Fredric Steinkamp. "What film has two editors?" Pollack griped.

The director always complained that Stark had an "ownership thing" regarding Streisand due to *Funny Girl*, and his control of her now extended to the way she looked and performed in the college scenes of *The Way We Were*.

Stark liked that Pollack had been able to wean her from some of her "shtick," as he put it, but he found that her overall acting in the Ballston Spa scenes lacked "energy and appeal." He also thought the lighting lent her "premature maturity," especially bad since she was playing a college-age student. In one important respect, Stark's criticism of Streisand's acting seemed to preclude his having any understanding of the Katie character. A fan of Streisand's comedic performances in his films, Stark wondered why her portrayal in *The Way We Were* did not possess humor or any kind of "self-deprecation." He missed the point completely that Katie's political intransigence as a hard-core communist ruled out a lightness of tone in her performance similar to what she had achieved in *Funny Girl* or *The Owl and the Pussycat*.

Surprisingly, the producer liked what he saw from Redford in the rushes, despite their mutual animosity, or as Pollack put it, "Bob didn't get along with Ray Stark, and neither did I." That issue aside, Stark found the character of Hubbell to be "clearly defined." In memos to come, the producer would never find the character of Katie to be even remotely defined.

To kick off the production in New York City, Pollack eased into it by doing a few easy setups. New York City did not cooperate. Historically, it had been one of the most difficult places in which to film, especially when it came to shooting stars like Streisand and Redford in a period film on busy streets filled with modern cars and eager onlookers wearing equally contemporary clothes.

Seeing the first rushes from New York City, Stark immediately put the production designer's head on the chopping block. The producer called Stephen Grimes's location work in New York City a "disaster." Those supposedly easy setups featured no dialogue and showed Katie shopping for steaks, flowers, and fruits and vegetables in a variety of shops. The character looks forward to preparing dinner for Hubbell after their first impromptu night together, and Katie even has a new door key made to give to her fantasy WASP. She plans for what will be their first date, since their first encounter in bed was not technically a "date." Stark complained that much of her shopping should have been filmed in outdoor markets to show off the city. He especially disliked that her visit to the butcher shop did not "read" as New York. It could have been shot on any backlot in Hollywood. Ditto the scene between Streisand and Redford filmed in the East Fifties, outside what is supposed to be Katie's apartment. Again, it could have been shot in Hollywood.

The film was clearly going over its five-million-dollar budget, but since Streisand and Redford together were receiving $2.2 million, it didn't leave Pollack that much money to replicate New York City in the year 1945. Pollack had already fought for renting five more antique cars in Ballston Spa than Stark wanted. The producer continued to flip-flop on the budget. When he saw that Pollack had put only two rowboat loads of people in Central Park, he wanted to know why he had not used a dozen.

Grimes fought back against Stark's "disaster" attack regarding the locations. The street in front of Katie's apartment had been chosen because production dictated that it be near Beekman Place, the scene of Hubbell and Katie's first big fight in front of J.J. and friends. "A condition that was surely met," Grimes noted. There was also the little "obvious precondition" of getting a street that could be cleared of modern cars. Especially galling for Grimes, as well as Pollack, was Stark's "disappointment" with the Beekman Place apartment itself. After seeing rushes, the producer suddenly wondered if art deco was appropriate for 1945, unaware that some apartments built in the 1920s and 1930s in that sleek architectural style would still be in existence at the end of World War II. Grimes insisted that the apartment fit the period and also that it needed to "contrast dramatically" with Katie's far less opulent apartment and lifestyle. (That October the interior of Katie's apartment was being built on Stage 21 at Warner Bros.) Grimes became so incensed that he asked Stark if he might be happier with a "change of production designer."

Criticism of the Beekman Place apartment outraged Pollack for another reason, and he had to remind Stark that the producer himself had handpicked that location, and that due to its small size, the actors barely had room to perform in front of the cameras.

"J.J.'s apartment had to be a real location in New York City because we wanted to see the East River traffic and all the city outside the windows," Jerry Ziesmer reported in his memoir. The scene begins with a showdown between Katie and Hubbell's friends shortly after the death of her hero, President Franklin Delano Roosevelt. Filming actually took place in three locations to simulate the one apartment. Some of the interiors were shot in a real apartment on Beekman Place, the one chosen personally by Stark. It's where a guest at the party remarks that "a fourth term was too much for the old man" and Judianne (performed by Susan Blakely) adds jokingly, "The third was too much for my old man." Katie explodes when Hubbell's college friends go on to joke about Eleanor Roosevelt going into a coal mine and emerging with her face blackened and "those big white buckteeth."

Katie and Hubbell then retreat to a glass-enclosed terrace with views of the East River. "What are you doing?" he asks. And she asks in return, "Why did you bring me here?" It's where Katie also tells Carol Ann (performed by Lois Chiles) that she has "friends in Harlem," and Carol Ann replies, "I'm sure you do." That scene had to be reshot later on the Warner Bros. lot in Burbank, but originally both scenes on the terrace were shot in Manhattan, at a historic hotel near the Beekman Place apartment and located on the corner of First Avenue and Forty-Ninth Street.

"The Beekman Tower. It is the most marvelous place on the East Side, with this art deco bar at the top," Judith Rascoe recalled. "They used it mostly for the views through the window. It's good movie magic."

Besides the magnificent views and the equally stunning interior design, what impressed Rascoe were the number of huge cables on the street that ran into the hotel, all the way up to the twenty-sixth floor so that the penthouse bar there could be properly lit and photographed. "God, this is a lot of money!" she thought.

Stark's memos continued to replay a familiar leitmotif. After watching the Beekman Place rushes, the producer once again found the Hubbell character "clearly defined." Regarding Katie, he continued to be confused, unable to see "a consistent characterization."

Photographing stars like Streisand and Redford on the busy streets of New York City demanded lots of security control, a big expense; and in a period film like *The Way We Were*, it also required that physical anachronisms, like modern parking meters and post office boxes, be removed or camouflaged, again at great expense. And looking beyond issues like crowd control and 1972 objects showing up in a scene set in 1945, there was the added problem of shooting Streisand outdoors anywhere, much less in New York City. In conversations with Stark, and in his written memos to the producer, Pollack practiced the utmost diplomacy with regard to photographing this particular star outdoors in the sunlight. He mentioned the many "planes and angles of her face." The sunlight often played unflattering tricks.

Harry Stradling Jr. was more blunt. "Whenever there

was an outdoor scene, we had to build a canopy to shade her, because with direct sunlight on her nose, it looks terrible," opined the cinematographer.

Even the brief moment in front of Katie's apartment took an eternity to set up. In the scene, when it appears that Hubbell may not stay for dinner, Katie frantically mentions all the food—steaks, baked potatoes, chives, salad, and pie—that she bought on saved-up war rations. She's desperate until Hubbell lets her know he's staying for dinner. He asks, "What kind of pie?"

The exchange between the two actors was brief, but Stradling Jr. had to get the lighting just right for one of them—and that took time. "Every now and again, Robert Redford would get a little grouchy, because every shot was always lined up to suit Barbra," the cinematographer noted.

Chapter 11

Groucho Marx and the Hollywood Ten

Robert Redford didn't like to wait around. Then again, he didn't mind making others wait around for him. As early in Redford's career as *Butch Cassidy and the Sundance Kid*, Paul Newman noted the chronic lateness of his far less famous costar. It would come to be known as "Redford time" on set after set, even when the actor put on his director's hat. That lack of punctuality surfaced most chronically on *The Way We Were* as soon as the production moved to the West Coast on October 10.

One of the first shots there required nothing more of Redford than to arrive in Hubbell's sports car at dawn in front of the Beverly Hills Hotel. The operative words here were *at dawn*. Redford did arrive shortly before dawn, but this gave hair and makeup mere seconds to ready him for the big shot as the sun rose over the skinny palm trees lining Sunset Boulevard.

According to Ziesmer's memoir, Redford apologized profusely, but in a backhanded sort of way. "I'll help you guys out, but no one told me," he began. "Honest. You never told me, Jer. Sorry, but you didn't. You know I'd have been here if you had."

Pollack ordered his star, "Get in your sports car. Hurry! The sun is coming up! We've got to get this shot at dawn!"

Fortunately for "Jer" Ziesmer, even Pollack wasn't buying the fake apology that put all the blame on the second assistant director. "Jer, didn't you tell him?" Pollock asked, mocking Redford's overly sincere tone of voice. Pollack then smiled. "No, you told him," he added. "You must have told him. Why else would he know to be here? Before six in the morning."

Having now worked together for nearly a month, the film's two stars had already entered into a contest to see who would follow whom onto the set. Barbra Streisand had a plan. She asked Ziesmer, "Why don't you call Robert first, and then when I see him coming, I'll rush out to the set, okay? By the way, how you doing?"

This may have been Ziesmer's first big job as an assistant director, but he knew enough to realize that he was in trouble whenever a superstar asked him about his personal well-being, posing such questions as "By the way, how you doing?" He knew that the famous restricted themselves to two topics of conversation. "The first topic, they talk about themselves. The second topic, you talk about them," he noted in his memoir.

In *The Way We Were*, Katie and Hubbell share a small cottage on the beach in Malibu. It held special significance for the company due to its owner, Bruce Campbell, who was Dalton Trumbo's son-in-law. A big fireplace in the living room displayed an unusual only-in-Hollywood iron plaque embedded in the granite. It read THE HEART OF HIS AGENT WAS THE SIZE OF A GNAT.

Streisand's and Redford's respective motor homes were parked equidistant from Campbell's cottage at 23940

Malibu Road. "So that neither star was given preferential treatment," explained Ziesmer. The assistant director thought he had a foolproof plan to foil either of them from delaying their entrance when he called. "I took their walkie-talkies and set them to an isolated channel," he reported. "I placed one in Barbra's motor home and the second in Redford's, and I kept the third. I asked both Barbra and Redford to please come to the set when they heard me over the walkie-talkies."

Streisand did as told when Ziesmer phoned. The door to her trailer opened, and out she walked. Likewise, the door to Redford's trailer opened—and then out came the walkie-talkie.

Ziesmer did not hold much respect for one of the film's stars. "Many times Redford would enter a set and ask questions as though he was not sure what movie we were doing, let alone what scene. I learned to ignore this," he noted. Again, the assistant director Michael Britton chalked this up to Redford's way of relieving tension before performing.

Redford's lateness and Streisand's micromanagement emerged as minor difficulties for Pollack and his crew to overcome. Much more problematic was the fact that, while the bulk of the movie would be shot on the West Coast, the bulk of what would eventually be cut out of *The Way We Were* was also shot there. Ray Stark warned his director on day one in Los Angeles that they now had a 138-page script, up two pages in a week. One week later it had ballooned to 144 pages. The powers that be at Columbia feared they were making a three-hour movie!

Stark cautioned that they could no longer trim the movie simply by cutting a minute here and there; instead, whole scenes needed to be removed. To save money, the producer wanted to omit those scenes *before* they were ever committed to film. The pressure on Pollack grew, especially when John Veitch, a senior vice president at Columbia, started to complain about the amount of film being used, as well as the many additional printed takes. The latter would eventually come out of Pollack's salary to the tune of twenty-five thousand dollars (only to be reimbursed).

Stark dealt with the situation by making up a list of questionable scenes, ones that should be saved until the very end of production in case he found them superfluous to the story. Only two of them, a wedding and honeymoon montage, and a "mogul scene," in which the head of the studio fires Hubbell, were never filmed. Stark liked the "mogul scene" as written, but thought it would take too long to introduce the character of the motion-picture executive. In the end, no such studio tycoon was ever cast. Money, more than screen time, scuttled the couple's wedding.

One scene that got pushed back on the shooting schedule features Hubbell and J.J.'s nostalgic chat on a sailboat off the coast of Malibu. It was written by David Rayfiel. Stark worried it would be expensive and difficult to film, as all scenes on the water are. Here Hubbell and J.J. play a game of the "best afternoon, best month, best year." Pollack fought for the scene. "It works so well at the end, when [Hubbell] can't think of a year that's the best year anymore," he said. The director had an ally also pushing for the sailboat scene even though she wasn't in it. Streisand recalled, "I thought it would make sense structurally and dramatically that after the UCLA scene—where Katie is on her own and stops to listen to the student—there should be a scene with Hubbell on his own, and that became the scene in the boat with J.J."

It's a moment in the film when J.J. tells Hubbell, "It wouldn't be like losing . . . you know, somebody. Katie. That's . . . a loss!"

It embodied the kind of nostalgic, heart-tugging sentiment that Rayfiel proved expert at delivering and Laurents never wrote and, in fact, despised.

Of the crucial scenes yet to be filmed was one that Streisand had read in Laurents's original treatment and loved. "That [phone] scene was about verbatim in the treatment, and when I got to it, I knew I wanted to do the picture," she recalled. It was also the most demanding for her as an actress: after Katie and Hubbell have a fight on Beekman Place, they break up at the radio studio where she works. Katie then telephones him from her apartment. As he did back in Schenectady, Pollack either hugged or held Streisand for a few seconds beforehand on Stage 21. She then sat down at the telephone, and Katie begs Hubbell to take her back, with the excuse of not being able to sleep.

"She did it beautifully in one take," Hawk Koch recalled.

As with the peace-strike scene, it came naturally to Streisand. "The telephone scene is one of the most important moments in the film, and so beautifully written by Arthur that I didn't need any direction," she recalled. "I just said, 'Roll the camera.' The one thing I wish, looking at it afterwards, was that Sydney had asked me to do another take, without my hand and the handkerchief in front of my face. But he liked the first take."

Some improvisation on her part, however, was needed. Streisand had to say, "Wait a minute," while she went into the pocket of Katie's pink robe to pull out a handkerchief.

Equally anticipated for Streisand, but for different reasons, was her first love scene with Redford. "Barbra Streisand was a star who reportedly had had affairs with many of her leading men," said one member of the *Way We Were* team. A notable exception was Walter Matthau on the set of *Hello, Dolly!* The two stars famously loathed each other from almost the first day of production on that movie musical. Unlike Elliott Gould in *I Can Get It for You Wholesale*, or Sydney Chaplin in the *Funny Girl* stage musical, or Omar Sharif in the movie version, or Ryan O'Neal in *What's Up, Doc?*, Redford was a happily married family man with four children when he signed to do *The Way We Were*. To protect himself in more ways than one, he wore two athletic supporters for his love scene with Streisand, who chose to don a bikini.

"It was a pretty G-rated scene," Michael Britton recalled. Indeed, Stark had already cautioned that he didn't want even "a heavily shadowed nude scene." *The Way We Were* was going to be PG rated, just as it was going to be two hours long and not a minute more. Stark had already deleted a "fuck" in the script for the same reason: he wanted the largest audience possible, and a dreaded R rating wouldn't give him that.

While Pollack called for a closed set, with only him and the cinematographer present, the special assistant to both the director and the leading man managed to be present for the two-day shoot in Katie's apartment on Stage 21. The scene required Redford to act like he either was very drunk or was sleeping or both. It required Streisand to act both nervous and thrilled as she slowly undresses to slip under the bedcover next to her costar. From there, Hubbell rouses himself enough to move on top of Katie. In the finished film, it's not clear whether he actually inserts himself, and most definitely, neither character achieves orgasm.

In the novel, there is no doubt. Laurents wrote, "[T]hen he threw back the coverlet and rolled on top of her, and then he was inside her." The passage goes on to reveal that the sex is very quick: he climaxes, and she does not, and the only kiss she receives from him is on her neck. In both the novel and the movie, when it's clear that

Hubbell has fallen asleep on top of her—in the movie, his sudden narcolepsy is cued by a minor key shift in the music—Katie says, "Hubbell. Hubbell. It's Katie. You do know it's Katie?"

It was a simple scene. But "[t]here were a lot of takes," Britton recalled. Finally, Redford eyed Pollack, giving him a look that said he'd had enough. Redford tended to do his best in the first take, maybe the second, rarely the third, never the fourth. From there, he tended to lose energy and concentration. Since this scene required little from him except the back of his head, Redford lost patience and Pollack had no choice but to inform his female star, "I think we've got it." Even editor John Burnett was amazed at how much footage he had to work with to put together the simple lovemaking scene.

Rumors circled that Streisand was not at her most relaxed for the two-day shoot. Pollack defended her treatment of the minuscule crew that day. "If Streisand has been in makeup since 6 a.m. and she walks on to a set at 8 a.m. and is asked to take her clothes off, get under the covers, and do a love scene, and she's shivering and self-conscious and she gets under the covers, and her mind is on the scene, and some guy comes over and shoves a light meter in her face, she is liable to say, 'Get the hell out of here!' "

In Pollack's opinion, that kind of verbal explosion did not make Streisand "impossible." He added, "She's bound to blow up. Then you hear people saying, 'Gee, what a bitch she is.' "

For his part, Redford liked to joke about the love scene. He paraphrased what Marilyn Monroe had said back in 1953, when her nude calendar surfaced in the first issue of *Playboy*. "I had nothing on but the radio," she teased reporters. To the question about what he wore in bed next to Streisand, Redford told a *Newsweek* reporter, "Aramis."

Sometime between the first love scene and the second love scene with Redford, Streisand made a quick trip up to San Francisco to attend the first preview for her new film. The audience there seemed mystified by *Up the Sandbox*, which featured scenes that were a "fantasy within a fantasy within a fantasy," according to its director. Irvin Kershner involved Streisand in the editing process; he had no choice since she was also the movie's producer. Post-preview, the two of them quickly whacked out about twenty minutes of celluloid, trimming specifically all those expensive fantasies shot in Africa. They both hoped for the best. *Up the Sandbox* would open before Christmas but after *The Way We Were* wrapped—or was supposed to have wrapped, on November 30.

When she returned to the Warner Bros. lot on Monday, Streisand fed Redford grape after grape in front of a crackling fireplace on Stage 21. It was the film's second love scene, and it follows the moment when, on the street in front of Katie's brownstone, he delights her with his "What kind of pie?" question.

Redford recited the "What kind of pie?" line in New York City in early October. It was now late October, and the problem of continuity arose. When the couple enters Katie's New York apartment on Stage 21, everything has to match what took place on the street back in the real city. The script supervisor told Redford, "You have the [grocery] packages in your left arm and hand. Your jacket is buttoned, but your tie is undone."

Redford didn't remember it that way. "Left arm? No . . . I had them in my right," he insisted.

Did he not remember? Or was it another Redford joke? Another thing he enjoyed doing on the set was asking how long a setup would take and then asking, "When will I be needed?"

"In half an hour," he'd be told.

"No, I don't need to be back for three hours. Give me half an hour."

And so it would go.

In that second love scene, Hubbell tells Katie about his "drawing her face in the sand" at the beach one day after college graduation. He also muses about imagining himself a high-flying "American eagle." Laurents wrote neither of those speeches—not the face in the sand, not the American eagle. They came courtesy of Sargent and Rayfiel, which may have been one reason why Redford expressed no problem repeating such stuff for the camera. Never spoken was a line that Laurents had put in both his novel and his screenplay, and it was a line that he wanted to cap the scene: Hubbell looks into Katie's eyes after their orgy of grapes and tells her, "It'll be better this time."

Only, Redford refused to say the line. He even made sure to have it crossed out in the working script.

His refusal here replicated what had happened on his previous film. In *The Candidate*, when his politician character, Bill McKay, tries to woo some voters, he makes the embarrassing faux pas of donning an indigenous people's ceremonial headdress. The film's screenwriter, Jeremy Larner, tried to explain that all those feathers on top of his head would show how low a politician would stoop in order to win a few votes, and so he "loses his integrity here."

Despite Larner's explanation, Redford refused to wear the headdress. He didn't care what the colorful but ridiculous plumage said about the character. He thought it might offend his friends in the Native American community, with whom he had bonded on several environmental issues.

It was the same thing regarding the line "It'll be better this time." Redford was never bad in bed. So how could Hubbell be?

Stark exploded when he saw the rushes for the two love

scenes. In the first scene, he strenuously objected to a teakettle shrieking in the kitchen. He called it "shtik" and wanted it taken out. It was not taken out. Pollack defended it, saying it added "humor" to a scene badly in need of it. Not mentioned by the director was another reason for keeping the noisy teakettle: It momentarily awakens Hubbell from his drunken stupor, and he believes the whistling sound is an attack signal at sea. By rote, he recites orders to take command. More than humor, the scene brings home the horrors of war and how it never leaves a soldier's consciousness, even in sleep.

Stark approved of one thing: he liked that Streisand did not appear nude. Pollack had followed his instructions there. But he found that the two stars' lovemaking lacked emotion. Somehow he found the description in the script of Katie finding Hubbell naked in bed, "half-covered" only by a sheet and snoring, far more exciting than "anything" he saw in the rushes. Again, the producer appeared not to have a clear understanding of the movie he was making. Hubbell's lackluster performance in bed is part of what makes the moment so poignant for Katie.

Much more disappointing for Stark was the second love scene. He wanted to know, Where was the line "It'll be better this time"?

In the novel *The Way We Were*, the second love scene begins with Hubbell telling Katie that she does not wear the right clothes. "Don't you know you're beautiful?" he asks her.

She replies, "You are."

The movie kept the "beautiful" exchange but left out any mention that Hubbell might be a closet subscriber to *Vogue* magazine.

Laurents delivered his most graphic moment in the novel for the second love scene: "He ran his hands lightly over her body, then ran his lips over her, then stood up and quickly shucked off his clothes, and as he slowly came down to her, he whispered, 'It'll be better this time.' "

Stark and Laurents felt the line was an apology that established the fact that the couple had actually made love the first time around, and that Hubbell is now showing some humanity and maybe even some regret for the way he treated Katie in his previous drunken state of lovemaking. The producer believed it was in no way an indictment that Hubbell, i.e., Robert Redford, was ever bad in bed. It showed an awareness of their first time. It showed that he remembered. Stark went on to call it not only romantic but also "chivalrous" of Hubbell to mention the first time. Stark admitted to Pollack that he had actually cried when he first read it, and he went on to reveal that others who'd read the script told him the same thing. It had made them cry.

The line turned into an albatross for both Stark and Pollack. The producer would go on to reference it at least a dozen times in as many memos. Especially upsetting to Stark was that Pollack had strongly agreed with him about the significance of the line—until Pollack realized that Redford wouldn't say it, at which point the director considered it "superfluous." Stark resented that Pollack called him "stubborn" on the subject, since his position, unlike the director's, never changed. Suddenly, Stark didn't care about the money. He wanted the scene reshot regardless of the cost.

The great controversy of "It'll be better this time" wasn't the only time Redford defied Stark's orders. Sargent and Rayfiel took much of Laurents's dialogue regarding the first days of the Hollywood blacklist and cleverly inserted it into a party to which everyone comes dressed as one of the Marx Brothers. It was one of the oldest tricks in Broadway musicals, and now the movies: if there's a book problem, distract the audience with costumes.

Stark absolutely loved the party concept. He thought the serious political comments could be injected "glossily," and the fun and color of the theme party would predominate. They could even end the scene with Redford's Groucho mustache sticking to Streisand's Harpo face after he kisses her. He also fantasized that the party could be goosed up if they hired a four-piece band of "big-boobed dames" made up to look like Groucho's female sidekick, the patrician and pretentious Margaret Dumont.

Stark's imagination didn't stop there, not that his ideas were always carried out. The properties person quickly brushed off his suggestion to embellish the party with a parrot wearing a tiny pair of Groucho glasses and sporting a cigar. Later, when he saw the rushes minus any parrot, Stark severely reprimanded Richard Rubin for his disobedience. Pollack also did not shoot the Dumont combo or Groucho's mustache sticking to Streisand's face. Stark did get his way when it came to getting some free publicity out of the Marx Brothers party. He invited the real Groucho Marx to the shoot, even though he would not be part of the action. The eighty-two-year-old comedy legend came for publicity purposes only and would be photographed with Redford and Streisand dressed, respectively, as Groucho and Harpo.

Marx had a couple of reasons for wanting to attend. Back in 1947 he had been an original member of the Committee for the First Amendment. Also, it would be a sentimental reunion in a different, less fraught way. Streisand's second appearance on *The Tonight Show* had taken place on August 21, 1962, when Groucho guest hosted. She had appeared earlier that year, right before host Jack Paar left the talk show. Temporary hosts like Groucho held down the famous desk until Johnny Carson made his debut on October 1. Three days later Streisand made her third appearance on *The Tonight Show*, only to have Carson mis-

pronounce her name. He made the common but unforgiv-
able error of stressing the first syllable of "Streisand" instead of the second.

Her appearance with Groucho on *The Tonight Show*,
however, stood out as the one that most helped her crusade to be cast as Fanny Brice in *Funny Girl*. Regarding
that ongoing casting controversy in 1962, the most famous Marx Brother could not have been more supportive.
Before she sat down for her interview, Streisand sang
"Much More" from *The Fantasticks*. She performed that
night ostensibly to promote her current Broadway show, *I
Can Get It for You Wholesale*, but Groucho kept bringing
up the subject of "the Fanny Brice story." He told the
Tonight audience how he had just spoken to composer
Jule Styne, who told him that Barbra was up against such
established stars as Anne Bancroft and "the actress who
appears on *The Garry Moore Show*" to play Brice.

"Carol Burnett," Streisand whispered in his ear.

The usually acerbic Groucho continued to play starstruck fan, calling his guest such "an extremely big success
at such a young age . . . You're in the big league. You're a
big hit. If not this one"—he meant *Funny Girl*—"then it's
only a matter of time."

Never one to take a compliment sitting down, Streisand
burnished her wacky, very Brooklyn girl persona by wise-
cracking that if she was such "a big success," why did *The
Tonight Show* just introduce her as "*Stree*-sand," and why,
when she went into department stores, "They still don't
wait on me!" In other words, she was still just this ordinary Jewish girl from across the East River who needed to
fight for everything she ever got—and *The Tonight Show*
audience loved her for being gutsy.

Not everyone was entranced. The following week, writing about Streisand's appearance on the talk show, columnist Dorothy Kilgallen wrote in her syndicated gossip

column, "Friends of the sensationally talented Barbra Streisand wish she'd shed that 'angry woman' attitude. She's successful enough now to be relaxed and pleasant." Kilgallen wrote those words in late August 1962. On July 22 of the following year, she broke the news that Streisand would be starring in *Funny Girl* on Broadway.

Regarding her career, it didn't hurt that Streisand, at age twenty, was appearing in a big Broadway musical like *Wholesale*, but more important to her meteoric rise to stardom were those three *Tonight Show* performances in 1962. It helped, too, that Burnett recused herself, believing that Fanny Brice needed to be played by a Jewish actress, and Bancroft (née Anna Maria Louisa Italiano) pulled out when the lyricist Bob Merrill played her a few songs from the gestating musical. She said she couldn't relate to them. Maybe she also couldn't sing them.

On Stage 21 Streisand beelined to Groucho as soon as he appeared at the Marx Brothers party. He came escorted by a girlfriend or nurse at least a third his age.

Suddenly, everybody forgot about Streisand and Redford. "There was all this hubbub about the Groucho scene, and that was just to see Groucho!" said Michael Britton. "Here are two of the top movie stars working on a picture together and Groucho comes in and blows them away!"

Everyone wanted his or her photograph taken with the star of *A Night at the Opera* and *You Bet Your Life*. In a little over a year, Groucho would receive an honorary Oscar, and all the actors and crew on the Warners soundstage wanted to be photographed with him. Everyone wanted Groucho's autograph. Everyone except the other star of *The Way We Were*, the one who, at that very moment, sported a Groucho mustache and cigar.

"I don't like Groucho," Redford announced. "I don't think he's funny." With that declaration, the actor left it to

Streisand to be photographed with the octogenarian comic. After thirty minutes of flashbulb pandemonium, Pollack called for everyone to get back to work. Exhausted, Groucho did not stick around to see Redford and others attempt to imitate him: he quickly disappeared from Stage 21 and went home to take his afternoon nap.

Redford's recalcitrance didn't stop there. He, together with Streisand and Pollack, decided it was not such a terrific idea to end the scene with Hubbell kissing Katie and his Groucho mustache sticking to her face. There were limits to how much *The Way We Were* principals wanted to indulge Stark's questionable taste. He was, after all, the man who named the Thoroughbred horses in his stable after dead movie stars. (The producer's daughter, Wendy, defended the horses' famous names. "They were named after friends, not movie stars," she said.)

At least the Marx Brothers party scene ended up in the final film. Far more expensive was an elaborate musical production number with six gaudily costumed female dancers. "It was a number supposedly in Hubbell's movie," Judith Rascoe recalled. "He sees what they have done to his book, with all these ladies dancing in tights."

In the scene, written by Sargent and Rayfiel, Hubbell complains about those chorus girls, who have nothing to do with his screenplay. Unpersuaded, the film's director, George Bissinger, dismisses his criticism, telling Hubbell that the film based on his novel needs the razzle-dazzle and glamour provided by the scantily clad women. J.J., the film's producer, tells a distraught Hubbell that the dancers give the movie "production value." In the script, Katie then pantomimes throwing up.

Ironically, it is the same thing that Stark would eventually tell Laurents when he complained about the Marx Brothers party scene, as well as two scenes shot off the coast of Malibu with Hubbell on a big sailboat, first with

Katie and then later in the film with J.J., when the two men discuss the best year ever. Stark told Laurents that *The Way We Were* needed those two sailboat scenes for their "production value."

Fortunately for Laurents, he never had to contemplate the production value of the six dancing girls. The scene got cut from the movie even before an early rough cut was screened for him in December. Judith Rascoe, thinking back to the many big cables running up East Forty-Ninth Street into the Beekman Tower, could not help but calculate the enormous expense of the musical number. "It was amazing to spend all that money and then toss it out. You would have to be Ray Stark to do that," she noted. Those dancers, however, were not completely discarded. In the finished film, they are referenced at the Marx Brothers party when Hubbell complains to Bissinger about a line being cut "that's the point of the whole scene!"

Bissinger tells him, "The point is better made by those insane dancers in red, white and blue."

To this Katie replies, "There are no dancers in his book. You can't have dancers just to have dancers!"

Slightly less expensive aspects of the screenplay were also quickly deemed unnecessary and cut. The blacklist confused Stark, and if it confused him, he knew it would completely baffle audiences. He continued to be "bugged" by the Hollywood screenwriter characters Paula Reisner and Brooks Carpenter whenever they mentioned the "Thought Control Conference." The term popped up several times in Laurents's original screenplay, most prominently when the Carpenter character delivers a blistering speech against the House Un-American Activities Committee at the Thought Control Conference, held at the Beverly Hills Hotel. In the novel *The Way We Were*, Katie has to explain it to Hubbell, and she tells him, "[T]hat's the real objective of the Un-American Committee . . . thought control, censorship, stifling dissent . . ."

Stark understood that a movie is not a novel. Explanations took time, they weren't dramatic. Also, he did not understand what the Thought Control Conference had to do with the blacklist. Plus, he found the name off-putting. The Thought Control Conference sounded "confusing." He admitted it was "factual," that back in 1947 the confab became the kick-off point for John Huston, Humphrey Bogart, Lauren Bacall, and other stars in Hollywood to go to Washington, D.C., to protest against HUAC. "Factual" didn't make it any less "confusing," however. He wanted to substitute mentions of the Thought Control Conference with references to the First Amendment. Better yet, since some moviegoers might not even know what the First Amendment actually protects, Stark wanted the characters to mention "the right to free speech."

Those changes meant minor jiggers in the screenplay. One exchange the producer wanted cut featured Katie saying, "The real objective is thought control. Shut everybody up. One big silent movie." Paula Reisner agrees, adding, "The Nazis used the very same . . ." Laurents lifted the exchange from his novel.

In the end, most of Stark's problems with the Thought Control Conference were taken care of when Pollack cut the two major scenes featuring Murray Hamilton, who played the blacklisted screenwriter Brooks Carpenter.

Far more significant rewriting was required to please Redford, and Pollack made good on that promise to his actor friend by having Sargent create the Union Station scene for *The Way We Were*. It appears in neither Laurents's novel nor his original screenplay.

Back in 1947, when Huston, Bogart, and the other stars returned from Washington, D.C., they flew back on an airplane, utterly defeated and demoralized in their attempt to thwart HUAC. Stark may have been no stickler for accuracy, but he did wonder why the characters in his movie were returning to Los Angeles by train. Stark, rather late in the production process, questioned the Union Station locale and asked his production designers to check out historic-looking air terminals. He wanted to see photos of all the extant "1943-type terminals" in the Los Angeles area. He had forgotten that the Union Station confrontation takes place in 1947, but Stark never could match up correctly the exact dates of the many scenes in his movie. When no suitable air terminals were found, Union Station, built in 1939, became the locale by default. All that had to be removed or covered were a few Amtrak signs to make the place read 1947.

Other changes were also made. In a last-minute cost-cutting move, Pollack reduced the number of extras in half, with only one hundred being hired to mob Katie and the others returning from Washington, D.C.

"Alvin Sargent wrote the scene," said Hawk Koch, and the actors did not receive those pages until the morning they all assembled in front of Los Angeles's art deco train station. In the scene, Hubbell greets Katie upon her return from Washington, D.C., where she, Bissinger, Reisner, and others have protested the HUAC hearings. It's obvious from their immediate conversation that Katie and Bissinger have parted ways politically. Sargent took John Huston's statement from 1947 about the Hollywood Ten—"They had lost a chance to defend a most important principle"— and paraphrased it to have Bissinger tell a reporter, "I'm afraid they're headed running toward martyrdom and to their own destruction."

Infuriated by his response, Katie says, "Jesus, George! Standing up for a principle doesn't make you a martyr!"

In 1947 Huston, Bogart, and others on the Committee for the First Amendment were unaware that some of the people they were defending had been members of the Communist Party. When they learned the truth about men like Dalton Trumbo and actor Sterling Hayden, they felt duped, and Screen Actors Guild president Ronald Reagan even went so far as to attack them as "suckers." At the time, the B-movie star labeled the Committee for the First Amendment "one of the most successful operations in the domestic history" of the Communist Party.

Sargent established the battle between Bissinger and Katie at the Union Station as one drawn in stark black-and-white terms: he had sold out, and she remained courageous. Any nuanced thought of someone being duped or compromised was lost. As written, the scene gave Patrick O'Neal, playing Bissinger, his best chance to go full Huston.

"He's a very theatrical person," the actor said of the real-life director. "I think Huston is very easy to play. My problem isn't how to play him but how to keep from playing him too much." Sometimes, O'Neal didn't take his own advice and turned Bissinger into a caricature. It forced Pollack to caution, "A little less John, please."

In Sargent's scene, a fistfight breaks out when a protester yells at Katie, "Shut your mouth, you commie bitch!" and Hubbell slugs him. The police separate the couple from the protesters by pushing them into an empty cafeteria at the train station.

Sargent understood that Hubbell could not remain passive. The character also needed to act or, at the very least, react. In his argument with Katie, Hubbell declares, "We don't have any free speech in this country!"

She insists, "We never will if people aren't willing to take a stand for what's right!"

And he yells back, "I'm telling you that people are more important than any goddamn witch hunt. You and me. Not causes! Not principles!"

Redford liked the scene. Sargent gave him the opportunity to get angry, fight back, and he even let Hubbell go so far as to throw over a tray of dishes. "Hubbell isn't a victim anymore," said Redford. "He's his own man, and that strength gave him a weight in the romance that made the final split with Katie dramatic. The questionable nature of true free speech was a provocative notion, and I attached to that." It's what also attracted him to the screenplay for *The Candidate*.

While Sargent conceived and wrote the scene, he left in a glimmer of what Laurents had originally written. Before Hubbell upsets all the dishes in the cafeteria, he tells Katie what's really important: "You and me. Not causes! Not principles!"

Katie lashes back, saying, "Hubbell, people are their principles!" That line was pure Laurents, and it was a line that Streisand had to fight to keep in the film's final cut.

Shooting the scene, Redford relished the moment. If he wasn't downright happy, he was definitely no longer unhappy.

Chapter 12

The Outcast and the Songwriters

Ray Stark, for his part, continued to fret about the Katie character's arc in the film. He worried so much that he did the unthinkable. He brought back Arthur Laurents to the production. No one had been a greater defender of Katie. No one understood the character better. Maybe Stark knew that Laurents was Katie. Certainly, the script repairs that Stark wanted from the suddenly former outcast had little or nothing to do with Hubbell.

Back on board in early November, Laurents delivered a rewrite of a scene for Viveca Lindfors and Barbra Streisand, one in which the Paula Reisner character reveals she has been blacklisted. He also delivered new lines for Streisand and others in the projection room scene when Hubbell's movie receives lukewarm reviews from the assembled players. "So true to life," says Reisner, paying a backhanded compliment. Hubbell later calls her a "dyke," a bigoted nod to the real-life Salka Viertel. Laurents also wrote two new scenes at the beach, ones where Katie, Paula, and others complain about HUAC in between games of volleyball. The new beach scenes were shot, but only one ended up in the finished film.

Stark remained torn. He didn't "understand" the Katie character, so he kept asking for new scenes that would explain her. Then again, Columbia Pictures was a movie studio on the edge of bankruptcy, and its president, Stanley Schneider, had already gotten into screaming matches with Stark about *The Way We Were* turning into a bloated mess.

"Columbia was going under at the time," Pollack recalled. "They hadn't had a big hit in years, and [our] picture was going over budget."

Stark wanted new scenes, which cost money, took time and, ultimately, did nothing to help explain Katie—or, at least, they did not explain Katie to Stark's satisfaction. In a flurry of memos, the producer defended himself by explaining to Schneider that, while he had made Columbia his home base, starting with *Funny Girl*, he had delivered all those films "on budget." He also stressed that none of those films harbored "the problems" of *The Way We Were*, and he placed blame on Redford's "personal reasons" (the rabies shots) and "bad weather" for pushing back production, which lost them Williams College and El Morocco nightclub. Somehow the producer had mixed up "bad weather" with script problems.

In his fights with the Columbia president, Stark purposefully did not blame Pollack. He saved those brutal attacks for Pollack himself. Among the director's greatest crimes, in Stark's opinion, was his coddling of the movie's male star.

Pollack refused to take the Redford bait; instead, he pointed to a more basic problem for the film's difficulties. He had originally agreed to shoot the movie in fifty-eight days, but even before the cameras rolled, Stark cut out six of those days. Pollack called it a "bullshit practice" to deceive people like Schneider and other executives at Columbia into thinking they were making a far less complicated movie, hence, a far less expensive movie. Even on a fifty-two-day schedule, Pollack had fallen only two days behind schedule: one day in New York for scenes that were never in the original schedule (and were eventually cut) and one extra day filming the bedroom scene, which, he explained, had been extremely "difficult." He diplomatically left out any mention of Streisand's requests for take after take of Redford spread out on top of her as she whispered, "Hubbell. It's Katie," over and over and over again.

In the end, Pollack believed he was doing something completely "cockeyed." He was making a film for which he claimed 70 percent of the budget was above the title and 30 percent was below. (His math was only slightly off.) And for the umpteenth time, he stressed that you cannot "just grab" a shot of stars like Redford or Streisand in a city like New York. Last but not least, Pollack could think of no movie made for five million dollars that was shot in only fifty-two days "without a finished screenplay."

Ultimately, that ever-expanding and morphing screenplay emerged as the greatest problem dividing the two men, and it only got worse in November. "We were rewriting all the time," said Pollack. "While we were shooting, we were rewriting." As he explained the basic difficulty facing them, "We didn't know how to mix the politics and the love story and make it work. There were just a lot of problems."

It deeply distressed Stark to learn that David Rayfiel was still working on the picture. When he demanded the writer's two-thousand-dollar-a-week salary end immediately, a contretemps between the producer, Columbia Pictures, and the writer's agent erupted over petty disputes regarding the cost of Rayfiel's long-distance telephone calls made from his room at the Beverly Hills Hotel.

What incited that expense-report explosion was the most recent rushes, filmed in early November. Worried about Katie's "confusing" arc in the film, Stark believed it could be clarified by emphasizing her return to political action. He focused on a scene set at the Beverly Hills Hotel, where Brooks Carpenter (Murray Hamilton) delivers an indictment of HUAC before the Thought Control Conference. Katie becomes impassioned, and Hubbell fears her actions will jeopardize his career. He screams at her, "You're back on the barricades!" a line lifted from Laurents's novel. Stark fumed when he saw the rushes. The scene had not been shot as "agreed to."

Hawk Koch remembered Rayfiel being "a fixture" on Pollack's movie sets. "David used to make last-minute changes when the dialogue or scene required it," said the first assistant director. "You would come in the next day, and the script would be marked with David's pencil."

One of those last-minute changes had to do with omitting "the barricades" line. Pollack dismissed what Stark thought everyone had "agreed to." As Streisand and Redford performed the scene, he didn't think the "barricades" line made sense "without Barbra being back on the barricades," he insisted. Sometimes changes needed to be made on the set to make a scene work. Pollack let his producer know that he and his actors were doing their best. It may not be what was absolutely required, but it was far better than what was concocted "by you and Arthur in a room," Pollack shot back.

Which brought the director to his newest, biggest beef. He refused to apologize for keeping Rayfiel on the payroll; Rayfiel and Sargent had worked "in tandem" on the script from the beginning. He would continue working with his two writers, Sargent and Rayfiel, and Stark could continue working with his own writer, Laurents. Pollack called the multiple-writers situation "impossible" and blamed Stark for creating such a mess.

Pollack also argued that the shooting had gone better in Schenectady and New York City, where the script was more set. He did not agree with Stark that things improved in Los Angeles when Laurents rejoined the writing team. He also took no responsibility for the assemblage of rushes that Margaret Booth and John Burnett were putting together for Stark's perusal. It was difficult enough working with one editor, "much less two," neither of whom knew his "concept" for the film.

Pollack made it clear. He refused to be "the fall guy" for a film that Stark had purposefully under-budgeted and under-scheduled from its conception.

As the production wound down in November, the film's makers began to tackle the theme song and whether Streisand should be singing it. Stark would have preferred if *The Way We Were* were another Streisand musical. His original concept for the film was "to have Barbra teach handicap children in Brooklyn," said Laurents, who recalled a Stark-inspired hodgepodge that glommed *The Sound of Music* to *The Miracle Worker*. One way or another, Stark was going to get Streisand to sing, and to that end, he hired the rehearsal pianist from a show he had produced on Broadway about his mother-in-law.

"I knew Ray Stark through *Funny Girl*," Marvin Hamlisch recalled. The composer had recently scored the producer's movie *Fat City*, and while that John Huston–directed film required little music, Hamlisch observed, "[M]y name was on Stark's mind." The producer told the twenty-seven-year-old composer, "On spec, we'd like you to write a song for Barbra. Then you'll get the job to do the whole movie." That was, if both Stark and Streisand liked the theme song Hamlisch wrote for *The Way We Were.*

Hawk Koch didn't know about the Hamlisch-Stark connection. When Pollack told him that a young composer was coming in to show him what he had written—"Let's see what he's got to say," Pollack told Koch—neither man expected much. The impression the very nervous and very awkward young man gave these more experienced moviemakers was that of a "rookie," Koch recalled.

"I'm happy to meet you," Hamlisch began. "I'm so excited. I don't have a lot of money, so I taped my piano playing." Even less impressive, he went on to reveal, "Now, I'm using my mouth to sing the part of the horns."

"Sure," said Pollack, taking a deep breath.

Hamlisch turned on the recorder, the piano accompaniment started, and the composer made horn sounds with his hands and mouth.

Koch sat up, immediately impressed. "It was a pretty good horn sound, and then I got the chills," he said.

When Hamlisch finished, Pollack thanked him. "What's your name again?" Pollack asked.

"Oh, it's Marvin, Marvin Hamlisch."

Alone with his assistant director, Pollack asked him, "What do you think of the song?"

Koch didn't take a breath. "It is brilliant," he replied.

Hamlisch originally wrote the song in a minor key but later switched it to major. "If I'd left it in the minor mode, it might have told you too much in advance that Katie and Hubbell were never going to [stay] together," he said.

The melody was so catchy that Pollack's brother started humming the tune on the set even before any lyrics were written. "That's when I first heard it," said Michael Britton. "Bernie's humming it."

Stark may have been wrong about certain things having to do with *The Way We Were*, but his Hamlisch gamble was not one of them. "The Way We Were" ended up being as tightly linked to the film as "Over the Rainbow" is to *The Wizard of Oz*, as "As Time Goes By" is to *Casablanca*, as "Moon River" is to *Breakfast at Tiffany's*. The difference is that none of the titles of those classic songs are movie titles. The eponymous song "The Way We Were" remains an instant advertisement for the movie *The Way We Were*.

"It's a wonderful title, so you're way ahead with a title like that," said the lyricist Marilyn Bergman.

Stark put Hamlisch together with Alan and Marilyn Bergman, who the year before had won an Oscar for their song, written with composer Michel Legrand, "The Windmills of Your Mind" from *The Thomas Crown Affair*. Hamlisch and the Bergmans wrote the theme song for Streisand to sing, obviously. "But there was discussion of Barbra not singing it, because she was the character," said Richard Roth.

Streisand had flatly turned down Stark's request to sing a title song for *The Owl and the Pussycat*. "How many singing prostitutes do you know?" she asked rhetorically.

Alan Bergman recalled the contretemps. "They weren't positive she should sing it in the picture. That was another decision. Sydney, they all were in doubt about it," said the lyricist. "That it would take away from the drama if she was the singer and the character. But in the final analysis, it was decided she should sing it."

Ex-communists, unlike prostitutes, were well known for singing in America.

"The song had a function in the movie in two places," said Alan Bergman. "It was a corridor back in time with the title sequence. The song took you back to when they were in college. And at the end of the film, it reminded you of their whole life together. It had a dual function, and it was written with that dual function in mind."

The composer and the two lyricists played the song for Streisand at her home. Her first reaction was, "Wait, this is going to be an endless song. We don't have the time."

Hamlisch admitted, "There was a very long A section to get to the lyrics 'The Way We Were.'" He shortened it. Streisand hummed along.

"She made a few suggestions," said Alan Bergman. "Not all of them taken."

But two suggestions did alter the song. In addition to shortening the A section, Streisand substituted a word. The lyricists had originally written, "Daydreams like the corners of your mind." Streisand changed it to "mem'ries like the corners of your mind."

At first, the lyricists were leery of the word change. "We had the word 'daydreams' at the top of the song. Barbra suggested 'mem'ries.' The word 'mem'ries' appeared a couple of lines later, in the phrase 'water-color mem'ries.' We weren't sure we should use the same word again, but she was right," said Alan Bergman.

Streisand could not explain why she wanted the word changed. "It just didn't feel right. The word 'mem'ries' was so distinctive," she said.

Since Streisand would not be recording the song for three months, "[i]t was thrilling to think of writing another song. It could be a tango or a waltz," said Alan Bergman.

Not so thrilled was Hamlisch. "I knew I couldn't beat this melody." He told the two lyricists, "I don't have another magical one in me." Regardless, they wrote what came to be known as "The Way We Were 2."

Hamlisch would tell the story that Streisand originally

found the first song "too simple." He told her, "So is 'My Funny Valentine.'"

Hamlisch reported that Streisand's response was "I hate 'My Funny Valentine,'" and so he wrote a more complicated version of the song, which ended up on the singer's album *The Way We Were*.

Alan Bergman rejected that story. "Everyone loved the song, and that included Ray Stark and Sydney Pollack. The only reason Hamlisch wrote a second version was because we [the Bergmans] had asked him to."

Streisand's longtime manager liked "The Way We Were" so much, he predicted it would be a number one single. "When is the movie being released?" Marty Erlichman asked. He was told October. "It will be number one in January."

"How do you know that?" Alan Bergman asked.

Erlichman couldn't explain his reasoning. "I am not a song person, but I am a Barbra Streisand person," he said. "I just knew it."

Regardless, there was some dispute regarding which version of the song to use for the film. Pollack came up with an idea to help make that decision. He asked that both songs be put up against the title sequence. "I needed a road map badly," said the director. "The song was in and out, it threaded throughout the titles, so I needed time when no lyrics were being sung for the dialogue 'Hey, Katie,' and she calls him a 'fascist.'"

Streisand, Pollack, and the three songwriters watched and listened as first the original song and then the second song, written in a minor key, were played against the images of Katie and Hubbell on the college campus in the year 1937.

"There was no doubt," said Hamlisch. "Even though the second song is more complicated and possibly more unique, there was something magical about the film, the voice, the lyrics, and the melody of the original."

"You feel it when it's working," said Alan Bergman.

"And when it's wrong. Like that second song was wrong," said Marilyn Bergman.

Had Pollack put both versions of the song against the title sequence to convince Streisand? "It's not true that I preferred the second version of the song," she said. "They were both very good, but it had to do with which worked best for the film. One played beautifully with the film, and one didn't, but they were both well-written songs." The lyricists asked for only one change. The word *watercolor* in the song is heard at the exact moment that the film's title sequence shows Hubbell and his crew rowing on the lake. "Can you move it?" the Bergmans pleaded.

No, Pollack could not.

Redford held definite opinions about his costar singing, or not singing, in the movie.

"Sydney Pollack told me that Redford was against my singing a song in the movie," said Streisand. "Maybe he didn't realize how seamlessly Marvin Hamlisch would integrate the song with the film, to the point where they're irrevocably linked to this day. It happened to be the perfect melody and the perfect lyrics. Sydney loved it and wanted it in the movie. And the song definitely didn't hurt the film. It only enhanced it."

At the end of November, the production moved back to New York for the final scene. "They wanted a change in weather. They wanted to feel the coldness and [have] a dissolve of years," said Hawk Koch. Laurents had written it as two scenes, one that begins near Fifth Avenue, outside Bonwit Teller, where Katie and Hubbell meet unexpectedly after five years apart. Moments later, he reappears at the Pulitzer Fountain in front of the Plaza Hotel, where he is staying, and she is handing out "Ban the Bomb" pamphlets. At the fountain she invites him to meet their daughter and her new husband, and he refuses, and she brushes a lock of hair off his forehead for the final time. Sargent and Rayfiel combined the two scenes, making it all play out in front of the hotel. And they dropped a flashback near the end of the original script, also employed in Laurents's novel, in which the college-age Hubbell asks, "Katie, what're you selling?"

Pollack decided against the flashback and ended the film more simply, with Katie and Hubbell in 1952 in front of the landmark hotel and fountain.

If Stark had gotten his way and not been dissuaded by any number of circumstances regarding permits and other logistical problems, he would have set the scene in front of the United Nations Headquarters. He asked researchers to check to see if the iconic Wallace Harrison–designed U.N. Building had actually opened by 1952. In fact, it completed construction on October 10 of that year. However, the difficulty of getting permits to film there made the Plaza Hotel more convenient, despite its location at a very busy intersection in Midtown Manhattan.

In the many revisions of that final scene, Stark noticed that Katie's reference to her current husband's name had been omitted. He wanted her "David X. Cohen" comment reinstated. He also mused that instead of Hubbell working in television (as Sargent and Rayfiel envisioned it) or going off to Africa to make a movie (as Laurents envisioned it in his novel and original screenplay), maybe the character should be drafted into the Korean War. Stark reasoned that many men were fighting in that Asian conflict in 1952. What the producer forgot to consider was that men Hubbell's age were not being drafted. And would a thirty-three-year-old married man like Hubbell consider enlisting? Again, wiser minds prevailed.

Stark remained incensed over reports of Redford's continual lateness and fretted about shooting the scene in front of the Plaza Hotel. The shoot needed to be accomplished in two days. He knew not to worry about Streisand; she rarely showed up late, and besides, she would be staying at the Plaza Hotel for those two days and nights in Manhattan. They scheduled the scene for November 28, with the twenty-ninth reserved for close-ups. But Stark feared inclement weather. He asked Hawk Koch, whom he called "Howie," to add chauffeur duties to his first-assistant-director responsibilities and not let Redford be left to his own devices to get to the Plaza Hotel on time. Koch would pick up Redford wherever he happened to be residing in New York City and drive him to Central Park South and Fifth Avenue. They had only two days to shoot an intensely dramatic scene. Nothing could go wrong.

Michael Britton remembered it being a relatively easy shoot, with crowd control not being a problem. "It was an intimate little scene. There wasn't a big banner 'Here's Streisand and Redford.' We weren't there long. It wasn't noticed much by the public," he noted.

Koch remembered it more vividly for another reason. His wife, Rita, was pregnant and unhappy that he had decided not to stay with her for the delivery. "I can't! I can't!" he told her. "I can't *not* finish the film." Besides, the baby wasn't due for another two weeks. But Emily Anne Koch did not wait. On November 28, at eight in the morning, a bellhop rushed out of the Plaza Hotel to inform him, "Mr. Koch! Mr. Koch! You just had a baby girl!"

On the shoot's second and last day in front of the hotel, Streisand pushed back the bangs on Redford's forehead for the penultimate time. (A new scene, shot in May, would require her to do it the fourth and final time.) "I wanted to find some gesture that I could do that I could repeat at certain times of the film," she said. "That's why I did that in the first scene, because I thought I would re-create it later, when it would have more meaning."

Streisand liked to take credit for key bits of business in her performances, beginning with her wanting an office chair on wheels in *I Can Get It for You Wholesale*. Regarding her signature gesture in *The Way We Were*, the direction for Katie to push back Hubbell's hair found its inspiration in Laurents's novel. He wrote, "In the sunlight she could see flecks of gray in that very blond hair. She wanted to touch where it was gray."

Sargent and Rayfiel took that moment from the novel and wrote directions for Katie to brush aside Hubbell's hair. More than a month before shooting began, on August 14, 1972, the two screenwriters added that bit of business about Katie touching his bangs. Hubbell then says, "Gray." To Streisand's credit, she did take that direction on the final page of the rewritten screenplay and used it at three previous moments in the film: first, when Hubbell's drunk and sleeping on a barstool at El Morocco; second, when Katie is beside him in bed for the first time; and third, when the couple is riding in a convertible to George Bissinger's croquet party in Beverly Hills, which was the new scene shot that May. For years to come, female strangers would attempt to brush the hair off Redford's forehead, much to his horror.

Only, Redford never said the word *gray*. If Hubbell was not ever bad in bed, he also was not ever going to go gray.

Chapter 13

The Stage Director and His Next Fantasy WASP

Barbra Streisand commemorated the completion of principal photography by giving Sydney Pollack a gold watch engraved FOR ALL THOSE 11 O'CLOCK PHONE CALLS.

That December Robert Redford reported to Paramount Pictures to do some tests for one of his upcoming pictures, in which he would be woefully miscast. As the film critic David Ehrenstein pointed out, "Producer Robert Evans failed to realize that the title character of Fitzgerald's novel *saw himself* as Robert Redford, while he looked and acted far more like Robert Blake."

Of course, what made Redford wrong for the title role in *The Great Gatsby* made him perfect for Hubbell. It was a busy time for the actor. He'd also signed to do *The Sting*, which would start shooting at the end of January.

Unfortunately for Pollack, the gift of the gold watch from Streisand did not bring an end to the eleven o'clock phone calls. They resumed in early January, when additional scenes needed to be filmed. And it didn't stop there. As late as spring 1973, that a new scene was written and filmed, and only then could *The Way We Were* be considered a complete wrap.

Meanwhile, the editors Margaret Booth and John Burnett continued to assemble rough cuts of *The Way We Were*. Their work did not inspire confidence in the film, and Ray Stark brought back the film's original screenwriter a second time. That December Arthur Laurents wrote a new scene and rewrote the Beekman Place terrace scenes between Katie and Hubbell and also Katie and Carol Ann. In addition, Laurents wrote voice-overs to provide a few needed segues. In his memoir, Laurents wrote that Stark was apologetic about his second rehire, telling him, "You win, pal!"

"They started shooting and got into trouble, and Ray called me," the writer explained. "By then I was over the pain, but I was also over the Walter Mitty dream. I asked for a lot of money." Laurents had only good things to say about Streisand. He called her a "pack rat" who remembered bits of dialogue that had been cut and who insisted they be reinstated.

"Some I got and some I didn't," said Streisand.

Before Laurents could turn in his new material that December, Stark put together some rushes to show him what was needed. The move infuriated Pollack. At that point, Booth and Burnett were assembling the movie with no input from him, with no knowledge of "my concept."

Stark ignored Pollack's concerns. He showed Laurents a nearly three-hour compilation of rushes assembled by his two handpicked editors. And to no one's surprise, Laurents hated it. How much he hated it, however, shook Stark's confidence in the film. Laurents called *The Way We Were* a "disaster," which no amount of judicious editing could possibly salvage.

His complaints were both general and nitpicking and

could have filled a few black holes. Among the latter small details, he wanted cut a seconds-long moment in the title sequence, when Hubbell, with the help of J.J., puts a fishing rod in the arms of a campus statue. Much more significant, he claimed that Redford came off "cold" and Streisand "too classy." Worse, the couple had no chemistry. Laurents considered the dynamic between Katie and Hubbell in the college scenes completely off-kilter: she should show interest in him, but he should show absolutely no interest in her. He wanted the dance at the prom cut and replaced with Katie's seduction of Frankie McVeigh, even though the latter scene had never been filmed. He also found nothing to like about the outdoor café scene in front of the Medbery Hotel in Ballston Spa. Laurents contended that Hubbell appeared to be "pursuing her" and she appeared suddenly "cool." He insisted that the dynamic should be the absolute opposite.

His criticism didn't stop with the college scenes. He expressed dismay that Streisand's big telephone scene after their breakup had been poorly lit. He couldn't see her tears, if there were any. And her too-long fingernails got in the way. And he wanted the scene reshot. He also wanted cuts in the following scene, when Hubbell brings Katie sleeping pills. He objected to Katie's references to Alice Faye ("I like Hollywood! I like Alice Faye! What's not to like?"), and Hubbell telling her, "You expect too much," and Katie swooning, "Oh, but look what I've got!"

Laurents continued to tear apart the World War II scenes. Only he understood the Katie-Hubbell dynamic, and he demanded that the second love scene in Katie's New York apartment be radically trimmed. Alvin Sargent had given Hubbell a speech in which the character recalls "drawing her face in the sand." Laurents insisted that only Katie had been fantasizing about Hubbell since college; Hubbell had not ever been thinking about Katie, much less entertaining romantic fantasies about her. Laurents could not repeat it often enough: Hubbell had completely forgotten about Katie—until they meet accidentally at El Morocco in 1945. Laurents stressed that Hubbell's romantic interest in Katie begins *after* their having sex, around the time he asks her, "What kind of pie?" on the street outside her New York apartment.

Also stuck in this second love scene was Hubbell talking about his being an "American eagle." Laurents called it atrocious writing and insisted it be axed. And where, he wanted to know, was Hubbell's crucial line "It'll be better this time"? Would they be filming *that* in January, along with his new and rewritten scenes?

Laurents reserved his harshest criticism for the film's third act, set in Hollywood. He found both Streisand and Redford "annoying" at the Marx Brothers party. He did not understand all the talk in the film about "freedom of speech." In his opinion, the blacklist had nothing to do with free speech and everything to do with the First Amendment and the Thought Control Conference. Minor but nonetheless paramount to him, he couldn't believe that every character in the movie calls her "Katie." Only Hubbell calls her "Katie" in both his original screenplay and his novel. Everyone else calls her "Kate." "Katie" is an endearment that only Hubbell uses. Laurents saw it as an easy problem to solve with a little sound editing, and he recommended that the long *e* sound at the end of every "Katie" not spoken by Redford be snipped.

And one more thing: The Union Station scene made no sense, in his opinion. Why would the cafeteria at a busy train station be empty, as if reserved for Katie and Hubbell to have their little private spat after the protesters attacked them? And besides, the scene should have been shot at an airline terminal, because John Huston, Humphrey Bogart, Lauren Bacall, and company flew back to Los Angeles on an airplane. A train took days! Movie stars didn't take days to travel from coast to coast.

And one more last thing: Absolutely no woman in 1947 would be wrapping her hair in that "ugly" snood that Streisand wore in the scene. Laurents laughed out loud when he saw that snood on the screen. Worried that his "It'll be better this time" would never be filmed, Laurents looked to Streisand to refer to the couple's lousy sex the first time around. For one of the Malibu cottage scenes, he took a line from his novel, the one where Katie tells Hubbell, "Months and months ago we went to bed and it wasn't good, not at all, and I was glad. For both of us. But it was only that once . . ." Despite his demands, neither Hubbell's "It'll be better this time" line nor Katie's "Months and months ago" speech was ever filmed.

In his written diatribe about the "disaster" that was *The Way We Were*, Laurents stepped on a few egos he should have avoided. Laurents didn't know that the Rayfiel line "Oh, but look what I've got!" was one of Streisand's favorites. He also didn't know that Stark had personally ordered all references to the Thought Control Conference be replaced with talk about the right to free speech.

Before any of the new material could be filmed, Streisand had to endure the Christmas 1972 release of *Up the Sandbox*, a failure with both the critics and the audiences.

"Barbra had been told that she was star insurance and she believed it," said Laurents. Then along came a very personal project that she also had produced. "*Sandbox* was her own little picture. Now her pride and joy was rejected."

Streisand turned defensive on the subject. "I liked *Up the Sandbox*," she insisted. "That was my statement about what it meant to be a woman. It's what I wanted to say, and I'm glad I said it, even if it didn't make a nickel." The film went on to gross ten million dollars, but the aura of

Streisand being box office candy had lost some of its sweet taste.

The commercial problems with *On a Clear Day You Can See Forever* and *Hello, Dolly!* could be blamed on the public's waning interest in outdated Broadway musicals being turned into even more outdated movies. Rather, audiences were eager to see movies like *Easy Rider* and *Five Easy Pieces*. In that same time frame, the movie musicals *Sweet Charity* and *Paint Your Wagon* fared even worse at the box office than Streisand's back-to-back tuners. Whatever explained her box office slump, Streisand needed a hit, and maybe she needed a costar that was as much star insurance as she used to be.

Laurents, for one, didn't think it would be either *The Way We Were* or Redford. That December the writer changed hats to fly off to London to begin work directing a new revival of *Gypsy*, starring Elaine Stritch, who would quickly be replaced by Angela Lansbury. The venture introduced Laurents to a Broadway stage manager, Fritz Holt, who was looking to expand his theater résumé to that of producer. Holt and Barry Brown, his new boyfriend, would produce the musical revival on the West End and then bring it to Broadway, again with Lansbury as star and Laurents as director. Much to Brown's quick disappointment, the handsome six-foot-four Holt too easily fit Laurents's fantasy WASP mold of Tyrone Power, Farley Granger, Erik Bruhn, Harold Lang, and Tom Hatcher.

Erik Bruhn?

"Arthur told me about an affair he had with the ballet dancer," Ashley Feinstein recalled. "He didn't tell me about Tyrone Power, but he did mention Bruhn. He talked about what an elegant dancer he was."

At the time, the Danish ballet dancer enjoyed a long-term relationship with fellow danseur Rudolf Nureyev, but that did not deter Laurents. Or Bruhn. Hatcher had made it clear to Laurents when they fell in love that theirs would have to be an open relationship. Nothing required them to imitate a heterosexual marriage.

With Hatcher back in New York, Laurents became entranced by one of his *Gypsy* producers in London. "Arthur loved being with Fritz," said Brown. "The world revolved around Fritz. He revered him. Fritz could do no wrong."

Laurents's unrequited lust made it a difficult working relationship for the three men bringing *Gypsy* to the West End. Despite its legendary status on Broadway, the musical had never been staged in London. Would British audiences go for a very American story about vaudeville, burlesque, and a stripper named Gypsy Rose Lee, or, more specifically, a musical about the ecdysiast's monster of a stage mother, Rose?

Laurents's deep attraction to Holt quickly isolated Brown. Despite having been a top executive in writer relationships at BMI, the country's largest music-rights organization, Brown never won Laurents's respect. "Arthur marginalized me in favor of Fritz in every way possible," Brown recalled. "Arthur could be beyond cruel. His MO was that he could say what he wanted if it was the truth, without any regard for how it might affect the person it was directed [at]. There was no sensitivity. That's why so many people ended up not speaking to him."

One of those people was the gay activist and author Larry Kramer, who said of his erstwhile friend, "It's only what Laurents thinks. And he doesn't say it to be truthful but to wound and to shock."

Laurents never stopped defending such behavior. As he put it, "What other people call mean, I call telling the truth unguardedly."

Directing *Gypsy* and pursuing Holt, Laurents ignored missives written by Stark in faraway Hollywood that December. It was good news for David Rayfiel, who, despite his contretemps with the producer, filled the writing gap created by the original screenwriter's sojourn in London.

Laurents could be selective that way: On one hand, he knew how to ignore Stark. He also knew how to keep in touch with spies at Columbia Pictures, who fed him rumors emanating from the editing rooms there. He hated the rough cut of *The Way We Were* shown him in early December. Later that month, he heard stories that four scenes he'd been shown were suddenly on the chopping block. No surprise, all of them had to do with the blacklist and the HUAC witch hunt, which, in his opinion, already "made no sense." Suddenly no longer incommunicado, Laurents wrote a letter on Christmas Eve to inform Stark that under no circumstances should the following four scenes be cut: Paula Reisner's revelation to Katie that she has been blacklisted as a screenwriter, Brooks Carpenter's speech against HUAC at the Beverly Hills Hotel, Carpenter's plea to Hubbell to be a "front" to sell his latest screenplay, and agent Rhea Edwards's defense for naming names before the committee. Katie, in turn, tells Edwards, in a line taken from the novel *The Way We Were*, "I think you're a shit." The line replicated what Laurents had told Jerome Robbins after the director-choreographer's testimony before HUAC in 1953.

The moment also exposed a character trait with which Streisand strongly identified. After the "shit" remark, Katie adds, in another line lifted from the novel, "And I never used that word before." When Streisand had first read that scene in Laurents's original treatment, she'd exclaimed, "That's me! You've got it!" Streisand also did not use four-letter words before she migrated west.

In the end, Laurents came out of this latest showdown one for four. Only the scene with Paula Reisner would stay in the finished film. Without it, as Laurents continued to argue, there would be no mention of screenwriters being blacklisted in a film about the blacklist. Of the four scenes, it was also his least favorite. He "loathed" Lindfors's performance and couldn't believe that Pollack had encouraged, much less tolerated, such blatant overacting. In an early draft of his memoir *Original Story By*, he savaged the actress, but that ultra-negative critique got cut prepublication.

Chapter 14

The Editors and the Rewriters

Ray Stark waited until January 8 to show a rough cut of *The Way We Were* to Barbra Streisand. He wanted to extend the same courtesy to Robert Redford but found it "difficult to get through" to him. Again, Stark blamed Sydney Pollack for being overly protective of his star friend.

Streisand watched the unfinished movie with her lyricist friends. "Redford's the best leading man she's ever had, and she knew it," said Marilyn Bergman, who attended with her husband and writing partner, Alan Bergman. "We sat with her when she first saw the movie. She kept nudging me and saying how great he was."

Despite reports from Arthur Laurents that Streisand expressed disappointment with the initial screening, Stark reported that the actress was basically "happy" with what she saw. She did voice concern to the producer that the romance between Katie and Hubbell could be stronger in act two, the World War II sequence.

As late as January 9, Stark reiterated the importance of Redford saying, "It'll be better this time." He believed the line would give Hubbell the same emotional connection with the audience that Katie evokes during the crying telephone scene. Otherwise, Stark feared that Hubbell was coming off as "a shit." Since shooting began, it was the only time in his dozens of memos and letters to Pollack that Stark expressed any qualms about the Hubbell character and Redford's performance. He had always leveled his criticism at the Katie character and Streisand's performance.

The reshoot of the Beekman Place terrace scenes between Hubbell and Katie, and Katie and Carol Ann, took place on January 10 and 11, with rehearsals reserved for the day before. Laurents had also written a new scene that features the couple riding in a car on the Malibu highway after the hidden microphone had been discovered at George Bissinger's screening party. In the car, Katie admits to having a Joan of Arc complex, and Hubbell tells her she looks "wildly sexy" when she gets angry. Only close-ups of Streisand and Redford taken that January were inserted into the terrace scene originally shot in New York City at the Beekman Tower. As for the new car ride, Hubbell getting turned on by a Jewish saint in men's armor was deemed a complete waste of time and money.

Late in January, Redford reported to the backlot at Universal Pictures to begin work on *The Sting* with Paul Newman. Streisand, for her part, contemplated doing a trifle called *For Pete's Sake*. The two stars were not close friends, but to everyone's surprise, they were not enemies, either. "Considering that they are both strong-willed people and very different kinds of people, it's amazing that they got along as well as they did," said Pollack.

With the new and rewritten scenes now in the can, John Burnett went to work editing the film in earnest. He needed to present Pollack and Stark with a far more polished version than the extremely rough cut of rushes he and Margaret Booth had hurriedly assembled in December and early January.

Burnett did with *The Way We Were* what he'd done on previous movies, like *The Heart Is a Lonely Hunter* and *The Owl and the Pussycat*. "I was pretty quick in putting movies together," he said. "With *The Way We Were*, [my editing] wasn't a whole new construction where you tear it all apart. I've never done that in my whole career." As with his previous movie projects, he scheduled a private screening of his cut for the director at ten o'clock in the morning. "And I went and had breakfast," he recalled. Then he scheduled another screening for Pollack at two in the afternoon that same day. "And then we talked about it. Sydney's wasn't a negative reaction," the editor recalled.

There had been a thousand compromises due to the schedule, the budget, and the limitations of the script. "You put the movie together and it's not exactly what the director for a year or two has had in his head," said Burnett. "What he had in his head is not shot. The first screening is a shock, even though [the director] may like it. After they've run the film two or three times, now they're ready to talk about the movie."

Pollack expressed no negativity about what he had just seen that morning in February and again that afternoon. Laurents told reporters a different story. "Sydney cried that it was so terrible," he said, and even went so far as to say that the director "apologized" to him for having mangled the original screenplay. The director's two daughters insisted that they had never witnessed such a reaction from their father. "My father didn't cry," said Rebecca Pollack. However, there was some agreement between Pollack's daughters and Laurents regarding the degree of control the director wielded over *The Way We Were*. Although Pollack had been given final cut, Rebecca Pollack remarked, "My father didn't have the control then that he would have on his later films."

"At that time, it was in Ray's hands," Laurents agreed. "Sydney Pollack didn't have the power then. Ray had the final control."

Pollack's tears were another matter.

"Crying over something was completely out of character for my father," said Rebecca Pollack. Burnett agreed. He remembered the director being very calm, sober, in control.

Pollack told the editor, "We'll tighten this up. We'll shorten this and mix it and put music to it. Yes, the movie is too long."

It was only then, after those first two private screenings for Pollack, that the two men removed whole chunks of the movie. "We took out most of the blacklist [material]," said Burnett, and that included the two Brooks Carpenter scenes and the one in which Katie tells the agent Rhea Edwards that she's a "shit."

"The blacklist didn't work. It didn't make any difference story-wise," said Burnett. "The important thing was that Katie had to have a cause, whether it was Franco or the blacklist or the bomb, her handing out flyers. When we got to the Hollywood section of the movie and the blacklist group, it started to become a story about that group, and [the movie] wasn't about that. It was about this couple, basically. That's what it was. The scenes of the blacklist were well-acted and shot, but something had to go. The film was two hours and twenty minutes. It had to be two hours."

One thing mystified Burnett about the movie: it lacked a wedding scene, to show that Katie and Hubbell had actually gotten married. Laurents never put such a scene in his original screenplay, although he did write one for his novel. He handled their wedding in the book as a flashback in the middle of the Hollywood section, having J.J. host the ceremony and party at his Beekman Place apartment. Katie wears a "champagne-colored chiffon" because "white is impractical." Her parents are present—"a Trotskyite mother and her anarchist father"—and it's revealed that her mother and father had never bothered to marry. Katie doesn't consider herself marriage material, either, and it's Hubbell who insists that they wed. She responds, "What for?" And there is no indication, judging from what Laurents wrote, that his character is being in any way ironic.

Regarding the wedding in the movie, Burnett remarked, "All we had was them on the sailboat and then a photograph of them in wedding clothes in their Malibu cottage." In a memo dated October 27, 1972, Stark ordered that a wedding photograph of Hubbell and Katie be placed in that cottage to indicate they were, in fact, married. In the finished film, it is not a photograph but tiny bride-and-groom figures from a wedding cake that Katie unpacks and places on a shelf in the Malibu cottage. A much more complicated "wedding montage" had been planned, written by Alvin Sargent and David Rayfiel. It featured a dialogue-less VE Day celebration that segued to the couple's wedding day, at which Katie's father is present (but not her mother) and Hubbell's parents. From there, the two screenwriters planned an ambitious sequence of shots where the couple bicycles through the major cities of the world, as well as an African jungle and a Mexican village, and they end their long excursion on wheels at the gates of the Hollywood studio where Hubbell's movie, A Country Made of Ice Cream, is being shot. Fearing the production costs, Stark canceled the wedding and "bicycle scenes" in a memo dated November 20, 1972.

Laurents's "disaster" assessment of The Way We Were

continued to concern Stark. Now that Pollack had seen Burnett's more polished cut and the two of them had removed several scenes, Stark asked his director to clarify what their movie was all about.

Pollack responded in a memo dated February 17, 1973. He basically repeated the synopsis he had given Laurents back in the Beverly Hills Hotel a year before: "I think it is the story of a girl who thinks she isn't pretty, and a guy who is afraid that he is only pretty." Having lived with the characters for months, he could now expand on that one-sentence analysis to include how Katie gives Hubbell an "identity" and he likes that identity. He is unsure of everything, and he likes her "certainty." The couple makes superficial changes to accommodate each other: She wears his varsity letter sweater on the beach; he indulges her fantasy about eventually moving to France. But the marriage ultimately fails "because they never really change at heart." She needs her politics, and he needs to go on "searching."

Pollack expressed extreme satisfaction with Redford's performance. He also called Streisand's performance "wonderful," but with caveats. He needed to go back and look over all the rushes. As he put it, he wanted to "crawl" over every frame of the film to improve her performance. He mentioned little adjustments here and there, some of which could be corrected with looping or finding a better reaction shot.

Stark and Pollack then launched into a great debate over the smile scene, which both men had dubbed "the Steps" scene, shot in front of the historic Medbery Hotel in Ballston Spa. Pollack agreed with Stark regarding Hubbell's long speech in which he tells Katie how his grade-school teachers had favored him because of his "fantastic smile." Both men wanted to cut it. Sargent also found it superfluous. However, the director revealed major support for the scene from the few people who had seen the more polished cut of the film that February. Many of them called it "one of my favorite" moments in the movie, and that included Pollack's wife, Claire; composer Marvin Hamlisch; and the lyricists Alan and Marilyn Bergman. Pollack knew that Redford harbored no special affection for the speech.

Much more sensitive was what they should do with the UCLA scene in which Katie is reminded of her political past. Very pregnant, she drives across the campus to see a young coed who is giving an impassioned speech to fellow students. "We must support the faculty in its determination to resist the loyalty oath!" the teenager yells. "The witch hunt has already blacklisted teachers, put informants in our classrooms and our laboratories!" Just as Katie was ridiculed at her alma mater years ago, the UCLA students now taunt this committed young woman in a similar fashion, with charges of "Mind your own business!" and "Who does she think she is?" and "Go back to Russia!" Pollack believed the movie already had one too many scenes of Streisand crying. Plus, he found the scene downright "corny."

The big problem: Streisand loved the scene.

Pollack wisely decided to leave both the UCLA protestor, played by actress Ellen Sherman, and Hubbell's smile dissertation in the movie and let the preview audiences decide. He harbored no such qualms about cutting another scene. After Hubbell and Carol Ann have made plans for a rendezvous, a brief scene had been shot that shows Katie driving onto the studio lot and surreptitiously witnessing their tête-à-tête on the staircase to the studio's projection rooms. Pollack found Katie's appearance here "unnecessary," because the character later asks Hubbell, "Are you still a nice Gentile boy?" Her question makes it clear she knows of the affair, however brief. Pollack found it a more sophisticated way to handle the situation. Again, he used the word *corny* to describe Katie's unexpected appearance on the studio lot.

Despite the movie running about two hours and fifteen minutes, Pollack decided they needed yet another scene. So many blacklist scenes had been cut that the characters George Bissinger, Paula Reisner, Rhea Edwards, and Brooks Carpenter appear to have wandered in from another movie. Regarding the new scene, "It just served to introduce the other characters," Streisand recalled.

In Laurents's original screenplay, the four Hollywood characters first appear together in the studio commissary, discussing the creation of the Thought Control Conference. Stark's banishment of any mention of that event meant scrapping the scene, although some of the dialogue did end up in the Marx Brothers party.

Stark approached Laurents about writing the new scene, but he refused the offer. He claimed that the Writers Guild of America had recently gone on strike and he would not be a "scab," especially on a film about the blacklist. Stark ignored the refusal, as well as the "scab" remark, because the WGA had not gone on strike, despite Laurents's claims to the contrary. The guild hadn't gone on strike since 1960 and wouldn't again until 1981. It was yet another example of the writer mixing up fact and fiction to enhance a story, especially one that embellished his victim status.

His decision not to cooperate placed Laurents in a difficult position with the WGA, or so he believed. Sargent and Rayfiel were clocking up rewrites after rewrites, of which the guild kept record to determine the final screenwriter credit on *The Way We Were*. Although Laurents thought he risked losing his sole credit on the film, his two competitors saw the situation differently. "Alvin and David never thought they would receive credit," said Lynne Rayfiel.

Nonetheless, Laurents felt threatened and begged Stark to give him the shared credit of "screenplay by Arthur Laurents and Alvin Sargent," rather than "screenplay by Arthur Laurents—additional dialogue by Alvin Sargent." He didn't want anyone to think that he had provided only the story and Sargent had written all the dialogue.

In the end, Laurents received sole credit from the guild, but Sargent and Rayfiel also got their revenge. They didn't so much write the new scene, set at a croquet match on the lawn of Bissinger's estate, as edit it, borrowing lines from other scenes that had been cut, such as Bissinger saying, "Can you believe this fearless band of Hollywood intellectuals is plotting to overthrow the government? They couldn't overthrow Louella Parsons." Sargent and Rayfiel then gave Katie's response, "Alice in Wonderland," to Hubbell but left out Paula Reisner's retort, "Malice in Wonderland—that's Nixon."

They did contribute a totally original exchange between Katie and Bissinger, one that especially infuriated Laurents. He had insisted that only Hubbell call her Katie. Sargent and Rayfiel took care of that problem, not by editing the final e in "Katie," as Laurents demanded. They wrote dialogue in which Bissinger introduces himself to the couple and asks, "It's Kate?" And she corrects him, saying, "It's Katie."

That exchange enraged Laurents. It also failed in any way to enliven the scene beyond the original writer's distress. Sargent and Rayfiel delivered the new scene on April 30, and it was filmed on May 3 at 283 Bel Air Road. And Stark hated it.

In a missive sent from the Cannes Film Festival, Stark called the scene "lifeless." Also upsetting to the producer was Streisand's appearance in white knit sports pants to play croquet on Bissinger's lawn. Stark was known to send his leading ladies diet regimens if he found any of them too zaftig to face the cameras. Ready to swing a mallet, Streisand had gained more than a few pounds before performing the new scene, which took only a day to film.

On May 9 Stark returned to Los Angeles and immediately ordered a screening of *The Way We Were* with the new croquet scene included. He was not happy. He found the so-called third act, the scenes set in Hollywood, a "damn bore." In addition to shooting the croquet scene, Pollack had reshot the moment in the Malibu cottage when Hubbell tells Katie that her old communist college chum, Frankie McVeigh, has informed on her. The director had expressed displeasure in Streisand's original performance here, shot back in November. In the interim, she had not only gained weight. She had changed her nails, lipstick, and hair. Her new look incensed Stark, who wanted to cut moments that he liked from the November footage into the May footage, which was now impossible.

Although its producer wasn't pleased, the fortunes of *The Way We Were* improved in 1973, when the investment bank Allen & Company bought Columbia Pictures. "Ray Stark was very close with Charles Allen," said Richard Roth. "Ray had a very powerful position there and was a kind of power behind the scenes."

The bad news for *The Way We Were* came when the new CEO of Columbia Pictures looked over the studio's upcoming slate of movies and did not see much to admire. Alan Hirschfield specifically remarked on one potential dud, saying, "And there's this movie on the docket in which Barbra Streisand plays a communist. Does that sound like good box office to you?"

Columbia Pictures did not stand alone among institutions experiencing convulsions in 1973. The country's political landscape also saw a major shake-up when President Richard Nixon quickly went from a landslide victory the year before to being embroiled in a scandal that bore the scope and impact of the political story in *The Way We Were*. It's debatable which debacle in Washington, D.C., more adversely affected the country—HUAC or Watergate. Richard Nixon's White House counsel John Dean picked the latter, calling what happened on his watch in the White House "the opening scene of the worst political scandal of the twentieth century and the beginning of the end of the Nixon presidency."

Chapter 15

The Enemy and the Activist

In June 1972 the Democratic National Committee head-quarters at the Watergate complex in Washington, D.C., found its offices burglarized. The Republican Party at its highest level had bugged phones and photographed campaign documents there. A grand jury soon indicted the five burglars, as well as Howard Hunt and G. Gordon Liddy, who served on Richard Nixon's reelection campaign. Senator George McGovern, running for president on the Democratic ticket, tried to use the Watergate scandal against Nixon, but without success. Only later, after McGovern's landslide loss, did the Committee for the Re-Election of the President become known as CREEP.

The Watergate scandal taught Streisand the lessons of going against conservative political forces in ways eerily similar to what her character witnesses in *The Way We Were*. Nixon put Streisand on his infamous "enemies list," and in the entertainment business, she ranked second after only Jane Fonda, better known as "Hanoi Jane" by the conservative Right. "That Barbra Streisand is so obnoxious," President Nixon declared from the Oval Office. "Who can stand her? Her singing is so nasal, so whiny. And that nose—a real Jimmy Durante schnoz. But I guess she appeals to that whole New York crowd."

The enemies list went public on June 27, 1973, when Dean provided the "master list" of the president's political opponents to the Senate Watergate Committee. Nixon had begun compiling his roll call of adversaries in 1971, and with Streisand's name on that list now made public, the president's erstwhile involvement in HUAC and its Hollywood blacklist came home to haunt the star just as Columbia Pictures readied *The Way We Were* for release.

"I was on Nixon's enemies list," Streisand said. "I was very proud to be, and I still am very proud to be." She said those words in 2018, but in 1973 she felt as much fear as pride. Blacklist or enemies list, Streisand could not know if she would soon be in an ostracized position similar to what Dalton Trumbo and others working in the film industry experienced during the Red Scare of the 1940s and 1950s. Playing a political activist in *The Way We Were* stirred her political consciousness.

While Warren Beatty felt he needed to dangle the possibility of his accepting the Hubbell role to get her to perform at a McGovern fundraiser, Streisand required no such lure for putting on her calendar a second, far more politically fraught political function. On the evening of April 7, 1973, Hollywood held a very exclusive benefit for the man who had recently leaked the Pentagon Papers to the *Washington Post*. That act of patriotism incurred the wrath of the Justice Department, which charged Daniel Ellsberg with espionage and conspiracy. Although the charges were later dropped, the whistleblower ran up some spectacular legal bills. Streisand quickly joined ranks to raise fifty thousand dollars at the benefit, held at an elite

Beverly Hills estate. Despite John Lennon, Yoko Ono, George Harrison, Ringo Starr, and Joni Mitchell being present that evening, only Streisand took to the stage to sing.

In her vigorous fundraising for Ellsberg, she renewed her friendship friendly with a US representative from New York State whose campaign slogan boasted, "A woman's place is in the House—the House of Representatives." Bella Abzug also enjoyed a connection to the Hollywood blacklist of the 1950s: she was one of the few attorneys in the country who dared to take the House Un-American Activities Committee to court. Since she also made Nixon's enemies list, the attorney-turned-politician identified with the Oscar-winning singer-actress and vice versa.

"I think it came as a complete and total shock to [Streisand] that she had been targeted by the White House," said Abzug. "She wanted to know what it meant—if she was in danger, if Jason was in danger . . . It was a scary time, and I told her she had every right to be frightened."

Watergate and the Pentagon Papers scandal only reinforced Streisand's commitment to *The Way We Were*. "I always fight hard for things I believe in, and so does Katie," said Streisand. "She was a political person just like I am."

Together with Laurents, she worried about all the blacklist scenes being cut from *The Way We Were* as it headed to preview audiences that summer. She wasn't the only one getting an education in right-wing politics in 1973.

That spring, while Laurents was busy directing Angela Lansbury in *Gypsy* on the West End, his longtime partner entered the political foray for the first time in his life. Tom Hatcher became a gay activist, and with Laurents off in London, he almost took up residence at the Firehouse, at 99 Wooster Street, in the SoHo neighborhood of Manhattan. The converted fire station had become the focal point for political activism in the gay and lesbian community in

New York City. Before it burnt down under suspicious circumstances in 1974, the Firehouse was home to the Gay Activists Alliance, and high on the group's agenda continued to be passing Intro 475, a long-gestating bill that sought to outlaw discrimination against gays and lesbians in housing and employment in the State of New York.

Hatcher worked to get Laurents's writer friends Edward Albee and Stephen Sondheim involved. At the time, Sondheim and Laurents were not speaking to each other, again. Over the years, the two men fought and then made up, and later, they went on to fight another fight. Hatcher shared with his partner the good news that "Steve" appeared anxious to be friendly again. Although the Broadway composer remained politically uninvolved, Hatcher reported that Albee would be traveling with him to the state capitol in Albany to lobby for the passage of Intro 475. One Republican official had referred to it as that "fag bill," and Hatcher looked to make public that slur in order to help publicize the cause.

One incident at the state capitol in Albany stood out for him: A congressman who supported Intro 475 asked Hatcher who Arthur was. Tom paused, then answered, "My lover." It was the first time he'd ever mentioned the true nature of their relationship to a total stranger, and it sent "shivers" through him—and in a wonderful way. He also wrote about the ongoing problems he had with his parents: his mother objected to his involvement in GAA, and his father kept asking his other son, David, if Tom was really gay. Laurents could have been describing Hatcher's parents when, in the novel *The Way We Were*, he wrote about Hubbell's mother and father: "They behaved as though they didn't know him very well, as though he were a distant nephew and they were filling in for his absent parents."

Hatcher hoped *Gypsy*, to open that May, was going

well in London, and he looked forward to the upcoming Off-Broadway production of Laurents's new play, *The Enclave*, whose same-sex couple Bruno and Wyman was based on their relationship.

Otherwise, he spent his days passing out leaflets in Sheridan Square and organizing vigils in front of City Hall and having sex with other gay activists, whom he brought back to 9 St. Luke's Place on a regular basis. Hatcher sprinkled his letters to Laurents with revelations of these fleeting but frequent sexual encounters. In one letter Hatcher asked his lover if other civil rights activists had sex with each other the way gay activists did.

Laurents's letters from London to Hatcher never mention sex outside their relationship, but he often used those missives to express his deep love for the former men's store manager whom he had met all those years ago in Hollywood. Referring to his relationship with Hatcher, Laurents explained, "He was my reason for living. My reason for writing."

"Arthur believed in love, and he wanted a love story, and *The Way We Were* is a story of mismatches," said Mary Corliss. "How could it not be about them?"

Corliss met the two men in 1973, when she and her husband, Richard Corliss, spent summer weekends at a house near Laurents's cottage on Quogue, Long Island. The couple was part of a close network of movie aficionados from the Museum of Modern Art, where she and others worked as curators in the film department. Her husband edited *Film Comment* and later became the chief film critic at *Time* magazine. Fellow critics Andrew Sarris and Molly Haskell often joined the group. At the time, whenever any of these movie mavens asked about his upcoming movie, Laurents simply referred to *The Way We Were* as "trouble in paradise." It was one of the few times he refused to say more.

"Arthur was very loquacious," Corliss recalled. "He

had a history and he had the stories. He didn't care about you. He didn't ask questions about you. But it didn't matter. You never wanted him to stop talking." Hatcher may have been the activist, but Laurents did all the talking whatever the topic, including politics. "With Tom always being supportive of what he said," Corliss noted.

The MoMA movie crowd's hosts that summer were the leftist attorney Monty Shapiro and his wife, Barbara, a casting director who worked on some of John Sayles's movies. The Shapiros were also friendly with Budd Schulberg, and the couple made sure never to invite the *On the Waterfront* screenwriter to any gathering where Laurents and Hatcher might be present. Schulberg's testimony before HUAC in 1951 continued to loom large among the dunes of Long Island even two decades after that rightwing dustup.

"Arthur and Tom always came together," said Corliss. "They were very modern, very open." On the subject of how much Laurents borrowed from their relationship to write about Katie and Hubbell, Corliss believed the film romance to be "a very idealized" version of the two men's life together. "Hubbell is patrician. He is an idealized Tom. Tom was an Oklahoma boy. He was a fun kid."

Beyond the blond hair and the incredible great looks, both Redford and Hatcher sported amazing smiles that could not have been more dazzlingly unique. They exemplified the difference between being patrician and being fun. Redford's smile communicated that he could be admired, but not to touch. Hatcher's was an invitation for full engagement. Barbara and Monty Shapiro's guests that summer on Quogue came to know Laurents's lover as a very bisexual man.

Ashley Feinstein also noted similarities and differences between Hatcher and Hubbell. "Robert Redford is more like Tom, and Arthur is more like Barbra, Tom being Gentile and Arthur being Jewish," he recalled. When Feinstein's boss was working on *The Way We Were*, he told him, "I'm writing something for Barbra, but it is really a lot of me from my college days." The character of Katie most specifically resembles her real-life doppelgänger, because "Arthur was always doing more to keep the relationship with Tom going," said Feinstein. "Arthur was afraid Tom was going to leave him, because he did leave him a few times."

That summer, Laurents divided his time on Quogue by fretting about *The Way We Were* and preparing his *Gypsy* revival for Broadway after its spectacular West End bow. The revival gave the writer-director more opportunity to pursue his unfulfilled quest to have an affair with one of his producers, Fritz Holt, and to snub his other producer. "It was the bile that kept Arthur going," said Barry Brown. Never was that verbal poison, however, directed at Hatcher. Brown and Holt's few pleasant moments with Laurents came when Hatcher joined them in the days leading up to the Broadway opening of the *Gypsy* revival. "I only saw Tom if we were all going out to dinner. I thought he was delightful," said Brown. "He was very outgoing, great personality, quick to laugh. Arthur was a good talker. He was prolific verbally, like the way he wrote. I never felt Tom was pushed aside by Arthur. By that time, Tom had a wonderful [real estate] business on Quoque, and he was good at it."

Regardless of his own late-in-life success, insecurities loomed as Hatcher continued to live in the shadow of a far more famous partner. As an introduction, Hatcher often made a point to tell strangers, "I renovate houses, that's what I do."

Back in Hatcher's actor days, Feinstein remembered him being sober during the rehearsals and the run of *Invitation to a March*. Later, when Hatcher returned to New York to become his lover's manager, he took solace in alcohol.

"They were both terrible drunks," Zvi Howard Rosenman said of the couple.

"Tom became especially belligerent when he drank," Feinstein agreed. One evening at 9 St. Luke's Place the conversation turned especially ugly after Hatcher had consumed too much alcohol. He looked at his lover sitting across the living room and cracked, "Well, what would you know about it, Mr. Arthur Milton Levine?"

Feinstein felt the temperature in the room drop several degrees. Laurents bristled then immediately changed the subject. "I thought it was some joke they had between them," noted the assistant.

Chapter 16

The Fans and the No-Show

Ray Stark originally wanted the first preview of *The Way We Were* to take place in early July, but too much postproduction work remained, and midsummer turned into late summer. About ten minutes still needed to be cut to get *The Way We Were* down to that optimal two-hour running time. Finally, Stark felt confident enough with his film to book two weekend previews in San Francisco for the middle of September. The editors John Burnett and Margaret Booth attended the first screening with Stark, Sydney Pollack, and Francis Ford Coppola, who had driven into town that day from his vineyard residence in Sonoma County. Earlier in the week, Burnett had used Coppola's Zoetrope Studios in San Francisco to make some editing changes in the film, and Stark had told him to extend an invitation to the screening to the maker of *The Godfather*, which had won the Oscar for Best Picture that spring.

"Ray didn't tell Pollack where the screening would be held," Burnett recalled. "It was his way of controlling things. He didn't want Sydney surrounded by his friends."

When Stark picked up his director in the limousine, Pollack kept asking, "Where are we going?"

"We'll know when we get there," the producer replied more than once. The tension in the limousine only intensified as they approached the Northpoint Theatre. "This is it!" Stark announced. A long line of theatergoers already circled around the corner of Bay and Powell Streets on that uncommonly hot Friday night.

Until now, Pollack had been able to immunize himself from the gleeful poison-pen reports emanating from *Variety* and the *Hollywood Reporter*. His inoculation technique was simple: he stopped reading the trades, which luxuriated in the constant updates on the new script doctor du jour, from Coppola to Dalton Trumbo. With half a dozen films already to his credit, Pollack knew that regular moviegoers did not dirty their fingers with the cheap newsprint of the entertainment trade papers. All they cared about was seeing Barbra Streisand and Robert Redford make out together for the first time in something called *The Way We Were*. Columbia Records had recently released the title song, but many radio stations were refusing to play it, much to the disappointment of Streisand, Marvin Hamlisch, Alan and Marilyn Bergman, and everyone else working on the movie. DJs across the country considered the singer's recording career to be in serious decline, if not finished. Streisand hadn't recorded a hit song since she did a cover of Laura Nyro's "Stoney End," and that was over two years ago.

Her most loyal fans felt differently, of course. Sitting in the Northpoint Theatre, they were thrilled to see another of the star's movies, musical or not. And those unimpressed by *Funny Girl* or *The Owl and the Pussycat* were there to see the Sundance Kid. And everyone else looked forward to phoning their friends the next morning to tell them how wonderful or dreadful or somewhere in between Streisand, Redford, and *The Way We Were* had been to sit through a month before the rest of the world got to see the movie in October. In other words, these moviegoers were buzzed for a variety of reasons.

But something happened about one hour into the story of the Jewish campus communist who pursues a gorgeous Gentile jock through much of World War II before the two of them crash-land in Hollywood amid a right-wing-inspired witch hunt. Streisand and Redford were clearly too old to be absolutely convincing as college students, but that slight suspension of belief didn't matter. They had chemistry, despite Arthur Laurents's claim to the contrary. (He would later change his assessment on that subject to say that the film "works" because of their chemistry.) On-screen it was not so much the young Katie and the young Hubbell falling in love as it was two major movie stars sharing the hot fudge sundae of their twin mega-celebrity with each other. It helped, too, that the film's first hour of 1930s college scenes, with Streisand's hair permed into a frizzy mop, was preceded and followed with scenes set during World War II, where her hair is more attractively straightened and he takes off his white navy uniform to expose chest hair that glistens every bit as blond as the errant locks that her long red-hot fingernails keep having to wipe off his cool WASP forehead. The ridiculous length of those fingernails let everyone know her Katie is not really a coffee-shop radical but their beloved Fanny Brice imitating a communist. And the luxurious crop of hair on his chest! Gone were the days when William Holden had to wax his body to take off his shirt in *Picnic* or when only non-hirsute stars, like Paul Newman, could run around bare-chested in the movies.

Alan Hirschfield's fear about Streisand playing a Red never caught on among the theatergoers watching *The Way We Were* for the first time. The opposites-attract love story made bearable the politically charged arguments about Franco and the USSR and whether or not FDR was a great president, because most of the baby boomers sitting in the Northpoint Theatre were born long after World War II, anyway.

That Friday night in a rather ordinary movie theater on the corner of Bay and Powell Streets in San Francisco at around 9:00 p.m.—or about one hour into the film— Pollack and Stark thought they had a big hit with *The Way We Were*.

Especially effective was the instrumental reprise of the haunting theme song that accompanies Hubbell as he now extends his physical prowess as a college jock to single-handedly maneuver a large schooner along the Malibu coast while Katie lounges leisurely on deck and cinematographer Harry Stradling Jr.'s camera captures them from a helicopter that does what her fingernails never can: keeps his immaculate blondness off that magnificent Panavision-worthy face.

Then it happened, just after 9:00 p.m. that Friday night in San Francisco, and a little more than one hour into the movie: Streisand and Redford, ensconced on terra firma on a movie director's lawn, playing croquet in Beverly Hills, start to talk 1947 politics with the actors Patrick O'Neal, Viveca Lindfors, Allyn Ann McLerie, and Murray Hamilton, all of whom are playing fellow leftists in *The Way We Were*. With his two big scenes already cut, about all that remained of Hamilton's performance was his line, "But we can't even write our congressman. He's on the committee. C'mon, George, your [croquet] shot."

Stark hated the scene, and sitting there with a preview audience, he believed more than ever that it was "lifeless." Streisand looked even heavier than in the rushes. Lindfors's foreign accent sounded even phonier. And no one in the audience noticed that O'Neal was channeling John

Huston, since few of them knew anything about the legendary director. Burnett, however, did notice an increase in the popcorn chewing. At least no one got up to use the bathroom.

The audience revived in a following scene, where the two stars attend a Marx Brothers–themed party and Streisand's Harpo costume and blond fright wig mean she must remain mute for the night, or at least for a few seconds, while everyone around the couple talks about HUAC and wonders how many Reds there really are in the film world. It was basically Laurents's dialogue, except the stuff about the Marx Brothers, which Alvin Sargent and David Rayfiel concocted to give the film "production value" and, more important, to distract from that political talk written by Laurents. Was anyone in the Northpoint Theatre listening to any of the blacklist chatter? Or were they thinking how much Streisand really looked like Harpo and how Redford, even wearing a fake Groucho mustache and chomping on a Groucho cigar, looked gorgeous? Did anyone in that preview audience remember seeing the photos of Groucho with Streisand (but not Redford) in gossip columns from coast to coast nearly a year ago?

The preview audience stayed with *The Way We Were* through scenes where a Picasso painting is ripped by an errant "bug" microphone ("We've got to take action," says Katie) and Hubbell's movie gets panned ("So true to life," says Paula) and he plans an extramarital rendezvous on the staircase to projection rooms ("I'm going back to New York," says Carol Ann).

Then the unspeakable happened in the movie world of preview screenings. No sooner does Hubbell tell Katie that Frankie McVeigh had informed on her than people started to get up to leave the auditorium. It didn't make any difference if they were getting up to make a telephone call or use the restroom or buy more Jujubes. They were walking out and maybe not returning. Suddenly, many moviegoers didn't care about Hubbell's fears regarding his ex-communist wife and how her political radicalism might translate into his getting fired from the studio. Nor did they care that Katie has a solution, which is to divorce him.

"I don't know. I don't know anymore," Katie tells Hubbell in a scene written by Laurents and replicated in his novel. "All I know is, if I don't name names, you can't get a job. If we got a divorce, you wouldn't have a subversive wife. That would solve everything."

She has only one request: "Stay with me until the baby is born."

Having read the original screenplay, Stark called the scene where Katie learns of McVeigh informing on her "tear-jerking," because it was "the last nail" to be struck into their already fragile marriage. He did not find it either of those things when he saw the rushes—nor did he find it emotionally moving now that he sat among a few hundred other moviegoers, who were getting up to do what comes naturally when an audience finds a movie boring.

Pollack always worried that the movie had too many endings. There was the couple's parting in Malibu, followed by their parting in the hospital room after the delivery of the baby, and then there was Katie and Hubbell's final-final parting in front of the Plaza Hotel. Pollack now realized his movie romance ran as long as a David Lean epic. At least it felt that long, suddenly.

After the screening, Coppola congratulated Pollack and Stark on their movie but without much enthusiasm. Before he went back to his Sonoma winery, he added, "But it's too long. Cut it."

Stark and Pollack agreed, especially Stark.

Not that the producer gave his editors any specifics on

what to cut. On *The Owl and the Pussycat,* he had tended to keep it very simple, telling Burnett, "You have to go back and rework it. Figure out another approach."

"You never knew why he thought the way he did," said the editor. "You went back, worked on it. Hopefully, Ray would say, 'Oh, it works better now.'"

Likewise, Stark gave no instructions on what to cut from *The Way We Were.* He just wanted it shorter. Two hours long, to be precise.

Pollack spent the following Saturday cutting five scenes from the movie. Gone was the college scene where Hubbell tells Katie his "fantastic smile" story. Also dropped were two moments in Katie's Manhattan apartment that showcase their second lovemaking scene: Pollack trimmed the cliché of Katie feeding Hubbell grapes in front of the fireplace (after which he was supposed to say, "It'll be better this time," but never did), and much to Laurents's subsequent delight, he axed Hubbell talking about being an American eagle and drawing Katie's face in the sand at the beach.

Pollack then turned ruthless with his cuts. He even snipped a subsequent scene, one that finds Hubbell suffering from writer's block regarding his second novel. "I can't! I'm stuck!" he whines. "We've been cooped up here for two whole days!"

Katie, in a major switch from her college activist days, now finds herself playing cheerleader to the man she loves. "You only have a few more pages. You've got to stay with it . . . Besides, I like being cooped up with you," she tells him.

When Sargent and Rayfiel reworked the original screenplay, Redford explained how those changes helped to clarify the couple's opposites-attract relationship. "[Hubbell] looked like things came easily. He worried he would put too much pressure for expectations on himself. And she came and put a lot of pressure of expectation. And that eventually was the clash," he said.

Perhaps there was now too much clash in *The Way We Were*. Pollack cut the writer's block scene. More crucial to the film's extended denouement in Hollywood was his decision to cut Streisand's much-admired UCLA scene.

"I didn't even have the negative with me. I just made the cut with a razor blade on the positive print before previewing it the next night," said the director, who didn't stop there with his Gillette blade. He made two more cuts—one little and one humongous, in the opinion of Streisand and Laurents.

Pollack dropped a short scene that explained Katie's decision, over Hubbell's strong objections, to go to Washington, D.C., to support the Hollywood Ten.

It begins with Katie musing, "In college, I stood under a maple tree selling loyalist Spain, and you wouldn't let Jews into your fraternity house. Now you've married one and she's going to have your baby. We live on the beach in Malibu, California, and that's not where we started."

Hubbell hits back, saying, "Why? Are you such a rare blood type that they need you?"

And she argues, "Hubbell, I'm going to Washington because it isn't fair to let our friends, Brooks and the Hollywood Ten take a beating for us and not do something."

In the movies, it's typically the male character that starts a crusade, to prove himself and flex his muscles, and it's the female character that worries about security and staying safe. Typically, male characters think big; female characters think of the kids. By reversing those roles, Laurents achieved something very different with *The Way We Were*. Here it's the guy who calls his wife's risk-taking a "futile, pointless gesture that can cause a helluva lot of trouble." Here it's the woman who stands strong against all odds.

"I'm not afraid of trouble," Katie says.

"Not even for us?" Hubbell asks.

Streisand and Laurents liked the scene but would not go on to fight for it. Or at least, they didn't fight for it as much as they fought for "the subversive wife scene," as Laurents dubbed the scene in which Katie learns that Frankie McVeigh has informed on her. It is Hubbell who breaks the news to Katie of her college comrade's betrayal. Dumbfounded, she calls McVeigh a "little rat," but then she goes on to wonder, "He was my date at senior prom and you cut in for ten seconds. What could he tell them?"

Hubbell says it doesn't make any difference what McVeigh tells HUAC. Then it dawns on her. "All I know is, if I don't name names, you can't get a job. If we got a divorce, you wouldn't have a subversive wife. That would solve everything," Katie says.

"No, it wouldn't," says Hubbell. But off camera, he accepts her decision, and they divorce.

Laurents explained the significance of the scene. "You have a subversive wife, and if you continue to have a subversive wife, you're fired. What's the choice?" he said.

By deleting the scene, Pollack took out even more of the film's politics but managed to keep most of the romance. He kept the rendezvous scene between Hubbell and Carol Ann and immediately followed it with Katie saying, "Stay with me until the baby is born." He believed it created "a clearer through line" to the end.

Pollack and his razor blade worked overtime to make the eight o'clock screening on Saturday night at the North-point Theatre. Eleven minutes shorter, the freshly edited version of *The Way We Were* proceeded without the coughing, the restlessness, the trips for popcorn and candy, and the bathroom breaks. "Never in my career have I seen such a reversal of fortunes, from having a near-disaster one night to a big success the following night with those cuts," said Pollack.

The audiences may not have fallen in love with Hubbell, but at least now they could continue to love the actor playing him. Pollack braced himself for Streisand's reaction to another cut. He had also snipped the UCLA scene. Sometimes the actress wanted it both ways. She thought the UCLA scene was one of her best in the movie. Then again, Streisand also thought Katie cried too much in the film. "You're making Katie look like a sap," she complained to Pollack. "She's a strong woman. She's not going to be destroyed by a guy. Any guy." She even went so far as to speak to Margaret Booth about editing out some of her tears in certain scenes. With the UCLA scene now cut, one thing was for sure: Katie would be crying a lot less in *The Way We Were*.

Not everyone was happy. "[T]he scene where the love story and the political story came together . . . That was precisely what that unholy trio cut," Laurents groused, referring to the director, producer, and editor.

Streisand explained her disillusionment with the cuts in somewhat less dramatic terms. "If you lose the Frankie McVeigh scene, the audience has no idea why they broke up and is left thinking it's because Hubbell schtupped this other girl one time," she believed. "With that cut, you've lost the reason why Katie makes the selfless decision to let Hubbell go, which means you've also lost the climax of the story and the essence of her character. And dramatically, you've lost the moment when the politics and the love story come together."

She remained only marginally less upset about the other major cut. "My fight to reinstate two crucial scenes was never about me; it was always about the character,"

Streisand said. "The scene where Katie sees a girl making a speech on the UCLA campus is a watershed moment for her. It makes her stop and think about the way she was, as opposed to her life in Hollywood, and it shakes her to her core."

Laurents agreed, and added, "Barbra was very good in it."

Streisand fretted, "I fought and fought with Sydney to keep that."

In one sense, Pollack agreed with his star regarding the UCLA scene. "It's very fantastically right and it's very 'the way we were' and 'God, I was there once' and everything about it is wonderful," he said. At least that was the way he spoke when he knew Streisand was listening or his opinion would get back to her. What he never said to her face was what he had told Stark: he found the scene "corny."

Ultimately, the director always thought he made the right choice by bringing in *The Way We Were* at two hours. He admitted to cutting almost sixty minutes, most of it having to do with politics. The movie was a romance. Pollack explained, "The danger was that the background [had] become so interesting to those of us making the film that people watching it would say, 'Oh, yes, this is all very interesting. But let's get back to 'Is he going to kiss her?' or 'Are they going to fall in love?' or 'Are they going to get back together?'"

Pollack ignored his gut reaction. He followed what those two previews in San Francisco were telling him: "The audiences were just plain bored when we got into politics. They wanted to know what was happening with Bob and Barbra." The film was never intended to be the "definitive film about McCarthyism," he added, again making the mistake that put the Wisconsin senator in the middle of this 1947 story.

In the end, Pollack emerged a good company man. "I was signed by Ray Stark to deliver a vehicle for Streisand, and that was the first principle I served," he said.

As always, Redford remained firmly in the Pollack camp. "The rough cut was too long and too often overly dramatic," he noted. "I felt it was a bit overbaked. I told Sydney, he agreed, and he cut it way back, and he did a good job doing that." *The Way We Were* was never going to be a film the actor deeply cared about, at least not the way he cared about *The Candidate* or *All the President's Men* or any film he would go on to direct. "I took myself out of the decision making and turned it over to Sydney," he said.

The shorter Saturday night version of *The Way We Were* did not bring an end to the changes for the film. Suddenly, Marvin Hamlisch expressed dissatisfaction, but for different reasons. Before the screenings in San Francisco, he believed he had overplayed his hand with the original theme music. "I've hit it too many times," he thought. So he composed a second theme, one that he introduced in the film's finale in front of the Plaza Hotel.

"Big mistake!" he announced. At preview screenings, he didn't see people being emotionally taken by the film's conclusion. He told Stark, "You've got to let me go back and rerecord the ending." The producer told him no. The picture was already over budget. In the end, "I went into my pocket and put in the [original] melody at the end. And then there was the thing I wanted—the sobbing," said Hamlisch.

An October 4 preview at the Avco Theatre in Westwood featured the new score, and Stark expressed relief that the audience now responded to the film. He could hear people sobbing in the theater. However, the sound in some of the scenes did not sync with the images, and it troubled him, because important critics were present, including Charles Champlin from the *Los Angeles Times.*

Finally, the film had its world premiere on October 16, 1973, at the Loew's State Theatre in Times Square, and for the after-party at the Plaza Hotel, the publicity department at Columbia Pictures got Bergdorf Goodman to decorate its store windows facing the Pulitzer Fountain and the hotel with vintage fashion from the 1940s. Even prominent Republicans like Governor Nelson Rockefeller and Mayor John Lindsay attended. On the red carpet, Pollack downplayed the film's politics, but not its love story. He stressed the movie's poster, which advertised "Streisand and Redford Together."

"It's a star vehicle for our two reigning superstars," he told reporters more than once. He had carefully memorized the line to answer almost all questions, negative or positive.

The gala screening didn't start on time, and again, Redford could claim credit for that lateness. Earl Wilson was working the red carpet on premiere night for his syndicated column, and when he spotted Stark through all the flashing cameras, he felt compelled to ask, "So where's Redford?"

The producer didn't hide his pique. "I heard he went to the World Series . . . or his own private Valhalla," said Stark, referring to the actor's home in Provo Canyon, Utah.

But neither his ranch nor a baseball game was Redford's hideout that evening. "I remember bypassing the premiere," Redford recalled. He drove himself to Times Square, but when he saw all the lights, the crowds of people, and the reporters asking questions, he kept on going. "And I just drove right past it and kept going, and it felt so great," he said.

The actor also skipped the Los Angeles premiere of *The*

Way We Were on October 30. Streisand made fashion news by showing up in a turban.

Between the two premieres, the initial reviews for the film were all over the place.

Roger Ebert in the *Chicago Sun-Times* dismissed it as "essentially just a love story, and not sturdy enough to carry the burden of both radical politics and a bittersweet ending." But he loved Streisand, calling her "fantastic. She's the brightest, quickest female in movies today. . . ."

Gene Siskel in the *Chicago Tribune* also lambasted the film's politics, as Laurents had predicted the press would. For his part, Siskel linked that weakness to its female star. "[W]ith Streisand as the film's intellectual mouthpiece— and listen, as a singer, God bless her—there is no way that the film's ideas are going to come off as anything but patronizing and tinged with comedy," he wrote.

Among the most-read critics on the East Coast, Vincent Canby in the *New York Times* found the first half of the movie "not at all bad." He went on to ignore Redford's performance completely but called Streisand's talent "huge, eccentric and intractable. When she goes one way and the movie goes another, it's no contest. The movie is turned into junk."

At the *New Yorker*, Pauline Kael had long been a Streisand loyalist—until she jumped overboard around the time of *Funny Lady*, when the critic famously turned on the star. With *The Way We Were*, Kael remained firmly in Streisand's corner, writing that the actress possessed "miraculous audience empathy" and that her charisma "puts the audience on Katie's side." Regarding the movie itself, Kael paid what Pollack would go on to call the ultimate "backhanded compliment." She called the movie "a fluke—a torpedoed ship full of gaping holes which comes snuggling into port. There is just about every reason for this film to be a disaster. . . ." The critic lambasted everything from the screenplay ("hardly makes sense") to the theme song ("whining"). "Yet the damned thing is enjoyable," she wrote. "It stays afloat because of the chemistry of Barbra Streisand and Robert Redford."

Judith Crist at *New York* magazine agreed, calling *The Way We Were* "a thoroughly enjoyable movie." She found "the lack of secondary character to provide more than atmosphere" to be a problem. Evidently, the critic did not read *Variety* or the *Hollywood Reporter* to learn of all the cuts made pre- and post-previews. She praised a movie that was "so richly produced by Ray Stark, so intelligently directed by Sydney Pollack, and so amazingly performed by superstars Robert Redford and Barbra Streisand that movie lovers of a certain age needn't feel totally ashamed of walking out with a trace of a tear and a sigh." Crist went on to gush that Streisand and Redford, respectively, embodied for her every Jewish radical and Gentile jock she ever knew in college.

Moviegoers often call a movie "enjoyable," but it's a word not much used among critics when they sit down to write a review. That both Kael and Crist called *The Way We Were* "enjoyable" speaks to a larger issue, since they were the two most influential female film critics in the country. Both women had spent decades in movie theaters watching such ordinary-looking average Joes as Humphrey Bogart and Spencer Tracy and James Stewart win the affections of such extraordinarily uncommon-looking beauties as Ingrid Bergman and Katharine Hepburn and Kim Novak. How "enjoyable" it must have been for Kael and Crist to see the reverse fantasy materialize on-screen, finally.

The day after the film's premiere, *Variety* took a swipe at its motion picture company with the headline OOPS, SORRY! ON COLUMBIA "UNLOADS." In deep financial distress, Columbia Pictures had run into trouble selling some of its flagship properties as well as several unprofitable subsidiaries.

The following week *Variety* posted better news for the studio. "The movie biz hasn't seen grosses like this for a long time," its analyst wrote. Playing in only five theaters, *The Way We Were* took in over $225,000, placing it in the top five grossing pictures of the week. If Ryan O'Neal continued to lick his wounds over losing the Hubbell role to Redford, he took solace in his latest movie, *Paper Moon*, which easily topped that same box office chart, earning over $465,000 in 159 theaters.

Audiences appeared to be equally split—and along the same gender lines as the critics. The man who edited *The Way We Were* noticed it immediately. Men told John Burnett that they didn't care for the film, but invariably added, "It's my wife's favorite movie."

Pollack would look back to surmise, "We got sixty-five to seventy percent lousy reviews," he noted.

Actually, the week of the film's release, *Variety*'s N.Y. Critics' Opinion column counted twelve positive reviews and seven negative. The week before, the newspaper greeted Martin Scorsese's soon-to-be-a-classic *Mean Streets* with the same tally: twelve positive, seven negative.

On November 8, 1973, Stark issued Pollack a check for twenty-five thousand dollars; it was the same amount that the director had been charged for overages on the film. Since the film had quickly become a big hit, Stark saw no reason to "penalize."

The Way We Were went on to become the year's fifth most popular film, earning nearly fifty million dollars. Redford did better with *The Sting*, which became 1973's second most popular film, after *The Exorcist*. And Streisand's manager was right about the song. Not only did "The Way We Were" become the number one song in America in January—the exact month of Marty Erlichman's prediction—but the song also stayed there for several weeks, to become the best-selling single of the year.

It was expected that Streisand would sing "The Way We Were" at the Academy Awards on April 2, 1974. She had been nominated for her performance in the film; Robert Redford was also nominated, but for his performance as a grifter in *The Sting*. Jack Haley asked Streisand to perform. When she refused, the producer of the awards show turned to Peggy Lee, who agreed to sing the hit song. She even changed her tour schedule to be in Los Angeles the night of the telecast. A few weeks later, within days of the awards show, Streisand decided she should sing. Now it was Haley's turn to be the bearer of bad news.

"That boggles the mind. I'm gonna fire Peggy Lee off the show?" he complained. "She canceled a club date in Canada to do it." Haley declined to replace Lee at the last minute, which meant that Streisand would not be singing "The Way We Were" at the Oscars.

She had been nominated along with Joanne Woodward for *Summer Wishes, Winter Dreams*, Marsha Mason for *Cinderella Liberty*, Ellen Burstyn for *The Exorcist*, and Glenda Jackson for *A Touch of Class*. Regarding her performance, Streisand didn't hold back. She opined, "I felt it was the best of those five for the year." It probably would have helped her chances if she had sung the title song from her film. The voters expected it, and the Oscars themselves were undergoing something of a rehabilitation campaign in the early 1970s. In the previous decade, nominated actors made a habit of skipping the ceremony. Winners who failed to show up included Sophia Loren (*Two Women*), Anne Bancroft (*The Miracle Worker*), Patricia Neal (*Hud*), Elizabeth Taylor (*Who's Afraid of Virginia Woolf?*), Paul Scofield (*A Man for All Seasons*) and, of course, Katharine Hepburn (*Guess Who's Coming to Dinner* and *The Lion in Winter*).

Haley made a special push to convince the nominated actors to appear. Streisand complied but did not sit in the auditorium of the Dorothy Chandler Pavilion with all the other nominees in attendance. She sat backstage in the greenroom with her new boyfriend, Jon Peters, and there she watched and listened as Peggy Lee sang a less than inspired rendition of "The Way We Were."

The writers of the song had been nominated and were thoroughly unimpressed with the singer's performance. "Peggy Lee mixed up the lyrics," said Alan Bergman, the man who had written them with his wife, Marilyn. The singer's flub didn't matter. The Academy members had already voted, and the song won the Oscar for the Bergmans and Marvin Hamlisch, who also won the Oscar for the film's original dramatic score. Nominated but not winning the Oscar were cinematographer Harry Stradling Jr., costume designers Dorothy Jeakins and Moss Mabry, Streisand, and Redford, who lost to Jack Lemmon for his performance in *Save the Tiger*. When she heard the name Glenda Jackson announced as the winner in the Best Actress category, Streisand and Peters promptly left the greenroom at the Dorothy Chandler Pavilion. Jackson, for her part, had stayed home in England, just as she had done two years earlier, when she won for her performance in *Women in Love*. The actress said of her second win, "Watching it on television . . . I kept telling myself that I ought to turn it off and go to bed. I felt disgusted with myself, as though I were attending a public hanging."

Chapter 17

Katie and Hubbell at Fifty

It wasn't long before talk of a sequel to *The Way We Were* began to circulate. No one, however, seemed to be in a hurry.

In 1980, gossip columnist Jack Martin reported that Barbra Streisand and Robert Redford would be receiving eight million dollars each for the sequel. At the time, Sydney Pollack told another gossip columnist, Marilyn Beck, that Katie and Hubbell would reunite in the sequel "when she phones for help with their daughter, who's grown up to be a Berkeley hippie with a drug problem. They'll get back together permanently. And happily."

And six years later, Pollack continued to hold out hope for such a sequel. He told the reporter Stephen M. Silverman, "You could literally see them as they were, because there's an hour of the original film we shot but that nobody ever saw, and it's the idea of using flashbacks that's intriguing to me. . . . A lot of things that worked the first time, such as Katie being the ugly duckling, couldn't be used again."

The man who first brought Katie to life on the page never referred to her as the ugly duckling. In Arthur Laurents's novel, the character is referred to alternately as Sleeping Beauty and Little Red Riding Hood with regard to the handsome prince Hubbell. But never the ugly duckling.

Pollack had a lot of other ideas for the sequel. At a seminar held by film critic Judith Crist in 1982, he told the audience that Hubbell would have an affair with his daughter's roommate at Berkeley, Bradford Dillman's J.J. would commit suicide, and Lois Chiles's Carol Ann would write a feminist bestseller, having "become a Gloria Steinem kind of lady." He went on to reveal a big obstacle, adding, "I know that Redford and Barbra should end up together somehow. I don't know how."

Despite all the sequel talk, Redford emerged as more roadblock than simple obstacle. But as Ray Stark put it to Laurents, "The sequel can begin with a funeral."

Laurents didn't see it that way. He took Tom Hatcher's conversion to political activism in the early 1970s and put it into his sequel plotline—not that he made Hubbell a gay activist. As the writer envisioned it, Hubbell goes on to be a TV newscaster at the 1968 Democratic Convention in Chicago, and the character gets swept up in the liberal politics of the moment. His daughter, Rachel, is now a demonstrator protesting the Vietnam War. In one version, Laurents wrote that father and daughter meet when he bails her out of jail. In another account, she doesn't know Hubbell Gardiner is her father and makes sexual advances toward him. Apparently, Rachel has not watched much TV lately and remains totally ignorant of her biological father's current occupation, which has continued in its rapid downward trajectory from novelist to screenwriter to TV writer to newscaster.

Beyond the implications of impending incest, Laurents's screenplay for the sequel, titled *The Way We Changed*, detonates another bombshell: Katie merely floats around the edges of this father-daughter drama.

Laurents did manage to give Katie one night of lovemaking with Hubbell before she returns sadder but wiser to husband number two, David X. Cohen, who shows up occasionally in the sequel. The screenplay is replete with flashbacks, but none use any footage cut from the movie, as Pollack suggested. All the flashbacks are famous scenes from *The Way We Were* as released in October 1973.

Redford insisted he never had any interest in making a sequel. "I didn't, but Barbra did," he added.

Streisand very much did. "It's a powerful love story, and the sequel was important to me because these characters were so compelling," she said. "I wanted to know how their lives unfolded and I envisioned a story in which their daughter, now in college and politically active herself, inadvertently brings them back together. Both have changed in ways that make them more aligned politically, while their feelings for each other remain the same, so it's inevitable that they reconnect. I still regret that we didn't make it."

In one of his memoirs, Laurents tells another story. He reveals that Redford asked him to bypass Stark and send the sequel screenplay directly to the actor. Throughout *Original Story By*, Laurents categorizes the star's behavior toward him as condescending and dismissive in their few brief encounters. Suddenly, a couple dozen pages later, with the telling of this sequel anecdote, the two men appear to be on speaking terms, friendly if not exactly buddies, and Redford instructs Laurents to leave Stark out of the process. Laurents goes on to complain that Redford never acknowledged receipt of his screenplay.

Redford, who eschewed making any sequel in his long film career, refuted Laurents's story.

"No, because I never believed in or supported a sequel," he insisted. "Stark and Laurents were willing to do anything to keep the project alive. To me, it was a one-off, left to the assumptions and imagination of the audience."

Streisand, for her part, did the next best thing. Thwarted in making a sequel, she secured the "lost" scenes from *The Way We Were*.

"Back in 1973, I asked for the deleted scenes from the film," she said. "I always thought certain scenes should be restored and I wanted to make sure they were preserved." Streisand put that footage in a temperature-controlled vault that was also home to outtakes from her recordings, TV shows, and other films. "And I've been trying since 1973 to restore some of the most crucial scenes back into the film," she added. "Maybe it will happen someday. Who knows?"

Pollack never agreed with his star. "Barbra Streisand and I have had this ongoing conversation for thirty years," the director said in 1995, which was only twenty-two years after the release of the movie. Maybe it only felt like thirty years. Streisand was known in Hollywood circles for strongly voicing her dream regarding a new, expanded version of *The Way We Were*. At one soiree at her agent's home, she held court on the subject for an extended period of time, until Sue Mengers finally interjected, "When do we get to *The Owl and the Pussycat*?"

None of which ever persuaded Pollack. He adamantly refused to grant Streisand her wish. "There will not be an extended director's cut of *The Way We Were*," Pollack said in a 1995 interview. "The blacklist scenes don't work." At the time, James Spada's recently published biography of Streisand editorialized that she would have won the Oscar if the UCLA scene had not been cut. "That's bullshit!" said Pollack.

Streisand's resentment regarding the crucial but cut scenes is understandable. She got the film made. Stark could have replaced either Pollack or Redford, but *The Way We Were* without Streisand is inconceivable.

Despite their twenty-two- or thirty-year ongoing conversation, she and Pollack remained on friendly terms and decided to disagree respectfully about what got cut from the film. Diagnosed with cancer, Pollack passed away in 2008, at the age of seventy-three. His had been a most successful, prolific career. In film and television, he boasted forty-one credits as director, forty-eight as producer, and he delivered memorable featured performances in films like *The Player*, *Eyes Wide Shut*, and *Tootsie*, working under such great directors as Robert Altman, Stanley Kubrick, and himself.

To celebrate the fiftieth anniversary of *The Way We Were* in 2023, Streisand encouraged Columbia Pictures to rerelease the film with two cut scenes reinstated. She wanted to put back her beloved UCLA scene in which Katie is reminded of her political activist past. The young woman she sees in 1947 on the university campus rails against HUAC and the emerging blacklist. She is also atrociously dressed. As if the plaid skirt and lumpy cardigan aren't fashion challenged enough, the actress Ellen Sherman wears long pigtails out of an Andy Hardy movie from another era. She looks pathetic. Katie in her college days in 1937 doesn't dress like the other coeds, i.e., the Carol Anns and the Judiannes, in their frilly dresses and cashmere sweaters. Katie sports a much more tailored look. She's different, but not different to the point of being a fashion victim. The UCLA coed sports a clunky look, and hardly the one a political liberal in 1947 would feel comfortable sporting. Curiously, in his first memoir, Laurents complains about the scene being cut, and he goes on to describe the coed as protesting the war in Vietnam!

Pollack never liked the UCLA scene. Perhaps the film's costume designers, Moss Mabry and Dorothy Jeakins, were also unimpressed enough to let a glaring cliché adversely color the moment. Regardless, the scene does add a significant moment of judgment to *The Way We Were*. It tells the audience that Katie knows she has made a mistake. By falling in love with the shegetz, she went too far. She gave up too much. Her sacrifice meant losing what is most important to her: a social conscience.

The Way We Were came at an important moment in the development of the Jewish character in the American cinema. In 1969 Philip Roth's *Goodbye, Columbus* finally arrived on the screen, starring Richard Benjamin and Ali MacGraw. Roth had written the novella a decade earlier, but its story of a young Jewish man, Neil Klugman, who falls in love with a rich, spoiled Jewish girl, Brenda Patimkin, did not sell many copies. (Widespread popular success eluded Roth until he published the controversial *Portnoy's Complaint*, his fourth novel, in 1969. It became an instant bestseller.)

Back in the 1950s, Jewish performers, like Jack Benny, Dinah Shore, and George Burns, were still celebrating Christmas on their TV series. At the movies, a romance like *Marjorie Morningstar* featured Natalie Wood and Gene Kelly in Jewish roles. Even the film version of *The Diary of Anne Frank* cast the Irish American actress Millie Perkins as the lead, with her love interest being the perennial male ingénue Richard Beymer.

The film version of *Goodbye, Columbus* broke ground by casting Jewish actors in its leading roles. The shiksa topic, however, hadn't been covered extensively in a mainstream Hollywood movie until Elaine May directed Neil Simon's original screenplay *The Heartbreak Kid*. The

1972 comedy stars Charles Grodin and Cybill Shepherd. On his honeymoon, the Jewish groom, Lenny Cantrow, dumps his Jewish bride, Lila Kolodny, as soon as he spots the beautiful shiksa Kelly Corcoran on the beaches of Miami. In the role of Lila, Jeannie Berlin set the mold for the frazzled Jewish slob-slash-shrew to come in future American films and TV series. Lenny knows he has made a mistake when, surrounded by tastefully dressed and utterly boring Gentiles at his second wedding, to Kelly, he finds himself relegated to chatting with children, who are almost as dismissive of him as their parents. At the end of *The Heartbreak Kid*, Lenny is alone and aware of his mistake.

In *The Way We Were*, the very pregnant Katie is alone and aware of her mistake, finally, when she watches a lone protestor on the UCLA campus. Katie is also alone and singular among protagonists in the American cinema. Despite its success at the box office, *The Way We Were* did not spawn a crowd of young Jewish heroines standing up for what's right but nonetheless falling in love with their fantasy WASP. How different American cinema history is for the Jewish male. Presaged by *Goodbye, Columbus*, *The Heartbreak Kid* came to the screen within months of the release of Woody Allen's *Play It Again, Sam*. In the 1972 comedy, Allen plays the Jewish film critic Allan Felix, who falls in love with his good friend's wife, Linda, played by Diane Keaton, who became the most famous shiksa in movie history five years later, with Allen's most iconic film, *Annie Hall*, the only one of his many efforts to win an Academy Award for Best Picture. Soon, Jewish male characters in the person of Allen would turn romancing Gentile female characters (Keaton, Margaux Hemingway, Charlotte Rampling, Keaton, Mia Farrow, Helena Bonham Carter, Dianne Wiest, Helen Hunt, and Keaton yet again) into a virtual cottage industry.

As the hard defining lines between Jews and Gentiles softened in the late twentieth century, Allen came to represent a character that did not have to repent his love for the shiksa in the way Neil Klugman and Lenny Cantrow do. His playing the romantic lead opposite various actresses became more noteworthy for the difference in age than for anything having to do with heritage or ethnicity. When Allen started to romance actresses young enough to be his granddaughter, Ben Stiller essentially replaced him on the screen, and Allen gradually reduced his cinematic duties to behind-the-scenes work. Amid his *Meet the Parents*, *Meet the Fockers*, and *Little Fockers* films costarring Teri Polo, Stiller starred in a remake of *The Heartbreak Kid*, with Malin Akerman in the Shepherd role. Jerry Seinfeld and Larry David continued the franchise on TV, with Cheryl Hines playing the shiksa and Susie Essman and Tracey Ullman in competition for the medium's most abrasive Jewish female character, in *Curb Your Enthusiasm*.

Post–*The Way We Were*, the Jewish heroine falling in love with a shegetz lived on with Jennifer Grey's "Baby" in 1987's *Dirty Dancing*, opposite Patrick Swayze's Johnny Castle, and with a few other female characters played by Streisand in films from *A Star Is Born*, opposite Kris Kristofferson, to *The Mirror Has Two Faces*, opposite Jeff Bridges. As Streisand's movie output has decreased in the twenty-first century, so have the stories of a Jewish woman in love with a shegetz. On the HBO series *Girls*, Lena Dunham's character, Hannah Horvath, enjoys a Hubbell moment when she spends a couple of days in the stunningly renovated brownstone of a Gentile doctor, played by the handsome Patrick Wilson. That is season two; in season six and a few mazel tovs later, Horvath reveals that she's "half Jewish."

Fifty years after the release of *The Way We Were*, Katie stands singular. Basically, her status is unchanged, while

Hubbell can now be seen as an early critique of white male privilege. It's no surprise that the character came from the pen of a Jewish homosexual. It's also likely that Laurents, being deeply in love with Tom Hatcher, gave Hubbell more credit than he's due. The novel provides a closer look into the character's short story read aloud in class by Dr. Short. In the film, the professor's recitation cuts off after a couple of sentences. In the novel, it reads, "In a way, he was like the country he lived in: everything came too easily to him. But at least, he knew it. And if, more often than not, he took advantage of everything and everybody, at least he knew that too. About once a month, he felt he was a fraud, but since most everyone he knew was more fraudulent . . ."

That self-deprecating sentiment is something an outsider like Laurents would write about an insider like Hubbell. It's not something a straight white man like Hubbell would have written about himself in 1937 or, perhaps, in any other year since then. No man, regardless of his ethnicity or sexual orientation or social standing, feels everything comes too easily.

Laurents wrote at a time when the theater, especially Broadway, was a refuge for two groups that much of America hated and had excluded: homosexuals and Jews. That refuge of two began to expand before the Covid-19 pandemic of 2020, and it accelerated when New York theaters reopened the following year. Nine of the twenty-one plays opening on Broadway in the 2021–22 seasons were written by people of color. Off Broadway, in the nonprofit theater, the percentage was even greater. In his review of one of those shows, *Black No More*, the African American critic and journalist Touré praised the musical based on George S. Schuyler's 1931 novel of the same name. In that satiric classic, "black no more" refers to a process by which African Americans are made to look like Caucasians and pass for them. Touré condemned the nonexistent "black no more," but he went on to wonder aloud in print: "Imagine getting jobs and promotions and bank loans with ease— even if you're mediocre." That is, white.

Touré's "with ease" makes a pair with Laurents's "too easily." They are comments made by outsiders about the privileged. They are not the comments the privileged ever make about themselves. Today Laurents being Jewish and homosexual would make him part of the establishment in the eyes of writers like Touré or the advocacy group Black Theatre United. Laurents's refuge, the theater, had changed, and so has his *The Way We Were*, the story as autobiographical as anything this artist ever wrote for the screen.

"Jewish!" and "Gentile!" Laurents wrote in the margins of Pollack's memo that criticized the lack of definition between the film's lead characters. Those two words, complete with exclamation points, explained everything for him. Fifty years later, Jews and Gentiles occupy the same category of white privilege, which is on the verge of losing its majority status in the United States. Fifty years later, *The Way We Were* tells a more universal story, and it's one that permeates the tragic view that Pollack held regarding the love affair, as opposed to Laurents's more melodramatic gaze. In most relationships, there's one person who's more passionate, more committed, who loves a little more and makes it all happen. *The Way We Were* is the story of a lover who ultimately resents giving too much. It's also the story of the beloved, and the inadequacy that comes when he, Hubbell, wishes he could love as intensely as his partner, Katie. For her, it can often appear to be a one-sided desire, and those are the relationships that hurt and linger the longest. The beloved may feel inadequate. But Hubbell has the luxury of being able to forget, the reunion in front of the Plaza Hotel a mere brief encounter for him.

Upon the film's release, the critics Pauline Kael and Judith Crist broke from the majority male opinion of *The Way We Were*. They found the film "enjoyable." Almost fifty years later, in Crist's editorial alma mater, *Vulture/ New York*, critic Christina Newland made no apologies for enjoying the film. She wrote, "It's wonderful because it addresses what so many women know to be true: some men want you to be less of yourself, and that simply will not do. Even if they are Robert Redford."

Laurents always denied that he based Hubbell on Hatcher in *The Way We Were*. "I was writing about my-self, my own life in college and Hollywood," he said. Cer-tainly by the time David Rayfiel and Alvin Sargent finished with their rewrites, Hubbell bore no resemblance to Hatcher, other than the blondness, the extraordinary good looks, and the aspect of fantasy that they both em-body in the all-enveloping light of a Jewish person's love. Redford's criticism of the character as a "Ken doll" accu-rately sums up the way Laurents wrote about Hatcher in his memoirs, as well as the characters he did admit were based on his partner: Wyman in *The Enclave* and Howard in *Two Lives*.

Written in 2002, *Two Lives* tells the story of an old gay couple who become a refuge of two, as they are living in a beach house on Quogue and are separated from many of their oldest friends in the New York theater world. What takes place in the play transpired offstage for its author and his lover. Laurents and Hatcher continued to weather the problem that had plagued them from the beginning: famous friends did not accept the one as the equal of the other. It was the reverse of what happens in *The Way We Were*, where it's Hubbell and J.J.'s friends who don't ac-cept the Jewish Katie. At least that's the way Katie sees it. It's definitely the way Hatcher saw it.

As late as 2002, Laurents's partner angrily unloaded to the Broadway producer-director Hal Prince about his extreme displeasure with Stephen Sondheim. Apparently, Hatcher and Sondheim's rapprochement thirty years before at the Firehouse, where they attended GAA meetings together, had long ended, to transmogrify into an intense animosity. Hatcher complained to Prince that Sondheim had invited Laurents and a couple of their friends to a cocktail party—without extending an invitation to him! Hatcher believed that Sondheim deliberately created such situations to drive a wedge between the couple. Old wounds incurred in one's youth don't always heal. Hatcher was seventy-three years old when he wrote the letter of complaint to Prince.

Laurents's love for Hatcher achieved its deepest and clearest expression with *Two Lives*. Lincoln Center Theater had tentatively planned the play's world premiere, but budget concerns upended some of the company's productions, including *Two Lives*. Laurents went so far as to offer money to stage his new play there, but such a donation by an artist violated the nonprofit theater's policy. As he put it in letters to André Bishop, the theater's artistic director, Laurents desperately wanted Hatcher, who had been diagnosed with lung cancer, to see the play before he passed away. That dream had to wait until 2005, when George Street Playhouse finally gave *Two Lives* its world premiere. That theater, in New Brunswick, New Jersey, did not object to receiving large monetary donations from Laurents.

Perhaps the author of *Two Lives* was not always the best judge of what his longtime partner wanted to see, especially with regard to a barely fictionalized version of himself. On opening night October 21, 2005, outside George Street Playhouse, Hatcher appeared shaken by what he had just seen onstage. He told the theater's artistic director, David Saint, "He's written me dead."

In *Two Lives*, the younger man in the relationship, the

architect Howard, dies from a heart attack at the end of act one, and the older and more famous of the two, the playwright Matt, lives to cope with that loss in act two. If it's true that people kill the thing they love most, there's no doubt that Laurents loved Hatcher, who died from lung cancer at the age of seventy-seven in 2006. Two years later, Laurents directed his third Broadway revival of *Gypsy*. "We did it in Tom's memory," said Patti LuPone, who won the Tony for playing Rose. "It came out of such love. Arthur honored his legacy by leading with love."

Hatcher remained the golden boy even in death. The only flaw in his character ever mentioned by Laurents was his partner's chronic alcoholism. It is mentioned in *Two Lives*, as well as the memoirs *Original Story By* and *The Rest of the Story*. According to friends, Hatcher tamed his addiction in 1982, when he began to attend Alcoholics Anonymous meetings. Laurents wrote about his partner's alcoholism as a flaw that is a thing apart, something mysterious and left unexplained. Otherwise, the Hatcher whom Laurents writes about in memoirs, plays, and in dozens of letters (now archived in the Library of Congress) was an accomplished architect who went through life as morally perfect as he was once physically beautiful.

In *Two Lives*, the playwright Matt is disappointed when the theater producer Leo decides against bringing his latest opus to the stage. "I don't count on Howard enough, Leo," Matt tells the producer. "He's always been more perceptive about people than I. I tend to endow them with shining traits they don't have. Then I overact when they disappoint me. Howard was leery of you from the beginning."

Laurents based the Leo character on the producer Scott Rudin, who remained a friend, despite not bringing the writer's 1992 play, *Jolson Sings Again*, to the Broadway stage, a contretemps that helped inspire the writing of *Two*

THE WAY THEY WERE   227

Lives. "Arthur was never judgmental with Tom the way the movie is with Hubbell," said Rudin.

Others in the Broadway community believed *The Way We Were* was inspired by a true love story. David Stone worked with Laurents on the 1989 Broadway revival of *Gypsy*, and the two men became friends. "I saw Arthur as Katie and Hubbell as Tom. Most people did," said the theater producer, who went on to bring *Wicked*, *The Vagina Monologues*, and the musical *Kimberly Akimbo* to the stage. Laurents sometimes offered advice about one of Stone's shows, not that the producer always took it.

Rudin's "judgmental" remark is one that many people used to describe Laurents. "Have you been cigar boxed?" became a leitmotif among former friends. After a fight or disagreement, Laurents made a habit of removing the offending person's photograph in his home and putting it in a cigar box. Legend had it that the collection of photos grew so large that several cigar boxes were used to store them all.

Laurents explained the importance of Hubbell having a "flaw." He believed that the flaw of Hubbell's "fantastic smile" gave Katie a reason to help him. Was Hatcher's alcoholism, mentioned occasionally but never explained, the flaw that gave Laurents a reason to help him? There's a total absence of critical judgment whenever Laurents wrote about his longtime partner. It's what Redford said about Hubbell and why, before rewrites were made, he didn't want to play the character. He's "more a figment of someone's imagination of what Prince Charming should be like," said the actor.

The chief theater critic at the *New York Times* agreed. "Arthur's writing about Tom is so fulsome," said Jesse Green.

In his days as a reporter and critic for *New York* magazine, Green interviewed Laurents. The assignment came about when, three years after Hatcher's death, Laurents directed a Broadway revival of *West Side Story*, a production he claimed was inspired by a trip his partner had made to South America. There in Colombia, Hatcher saw a production of the musical in Spanish, and Hatcher found himself for the first time identifying with the Sharks, the Puerto Rican gang, and not the Jets. Laurents took Hatcher's suggestion, and for the new revival under his direction, Lin-Manuel Miranda was engaged to translate some of the dialogue and lyrics into Spanish. It was a novel rethinking of the classic; and timed to the show's Broadway opening, the editors at *New York* magazine assigned Green to profile Laurents. It promised to be quite the portrait.

Out of town, in Washington, D.C., the *West Side Story* revival ran into trouble when audiences were bewildered by the Spanish, and some of the show's producers believed that the leading man was delivering a weak performance in the role of Tony. Decidedly more positively received was the performance of Karen Olivo in the role of Anita. She would go on to win the Tony. Laurents was often adored by actresses under his direction, but not so much by actors, especially if they were young and handsome. Olivo commented about working with Laurents, saying, "He's an extremely truthful person, and most people who have a problem with him have a problem with him being honest with them." He could be tough. "Absolutely, but not to hurt me. Mainly, he's trying to be as time efficient as possible."

Actresses tended to have better experiences under the direction of Laurents than actors. "I don't know if he was an innate director," said Patti LuPone. "He was a bit dictatorial at the beginning [on *Gypsy*], but that faded away when he trusted us."

He loved actresses. He also loved actors, but it was dif-

ferent with male performers. On the *West Side Story* revival in 2009, Laurents remained steadfast about not getting rid of the new Spanish lyrics and dialogue—or his
leading man. "Matt Cavenaugh is absolutely straight. And
I love him," Laurents confessed to the journalist Charles
Kaiser. "I had to unlock him. You know he comes from
Arkansas and he's really basically very conventional." In
the interview, Laurents kept repeating how much he "loved"
Cavenaugh.

Until he did not love him. When the actor married his
girlfriend shortly after the show opened on Broadway,
Laurents reevaluated Cavenaugh's performance, called it
"too preppy," and the actor never saw his one-year contract with the production renewed.

A lead producer on the show defended Laurents. "Sometimes what happens between a director and an actor can
seem strange to an outsider," said Kevin McCollum.
"Arthur came from a different time in terms of how we
put shows together. He was a genius."

"Arthur was human," said Hal Luftig, another producer on the revival. "He had a crush on Matt."

When Jeremy Jordan replaced Cavenaugh in *West Side
Story*, the fantasy WASP cycle started all over again for
Laurents. He lavished praise on the young actor, calling
him "the best Tony ever," as Jordan remembered it, then
turned on him the night he departed the production.
"That was the worst performance that you have ever
given. You've already left the show," Laurents chastised.

Reporting for *New York* magazine in 2009, Green had
more serious topics in mind to discuss with his profile subject than unrequited lust. He got right to it. Green asked
Laurents if it was true that his real name was Levine.
Green recalled that Laurents "bristled" at the question,
then answered, "Yes, but we don't talk about that."

New York magazine titled Green's profile "When You're a Shark You're a Shark All the Way," a clever spin on the opening lyrics of "Jet Song" from *West Side Story*.

"I was shocked when I read the profile of Arthur," said Ashley Feinstein. Laurents's former assistant recalled that night in the mid-1960s when a drunken Hatcher had taunted his partner by calling him Mr. Arthur Milton Levine. "I thought Tom was joking then. Arthur had always prided himself in being so honest. Lots of Jews changed their name. It was commonplace and they owned up to it. That Arthur didn't, even though he had always been so outspoken about the anti-Semitism and the homophobia he had suffered. It was shocking."

In his first memoir, Laurents wrote about sergeants in the army using the word *kike* and his being called "Sheeny!" when he was a kid. He told reporters, "I am a Jewish boy from Brooklyn who came up against anti-Semitism. That has an enormous effect on your life. That makes you very aware and . . . overly sensitive."

The name change was off-limits, however. The revelation being exposed in *New York* magazine so incensed Laurents that he called Green "a souped-up Rottweiler" and went on to mock the journalist's receding hairline in a subsequent memoir, *The Rest of the Story*.

Green didn't mind. "Arthur wanted me to be his publicist, and I wasn't there for that," he said. Regarding the Levine disclosure, "I was given a tip," revealed Green, who went on to cowrite the autobiography *Shy: The Alarmingly Outspoken Memoirs of Mary Rodgers*. "Arthur created a self-image which many people bought, as a truth teller. He did everything he could to suppress the name change. It's kind of funny the name he chose, Laurents being kind of poufy."

The name change came early in his life.

At Cornell University, the young Arthur Levine played it somewhere between being outspoken and pragmatic. He wrote his plays under the pseudonym G. G. Laurents, but at the school newspaper, where he held the position of associate editor during his senior year, he used his real name: A. M. Levine. He later claimed being denied the editorship of the *Cornell Daily Sun* due to his Jewish name. The episode so scarred him that as late as 1996, when he wrote the play *My Good Name*, set in the 1980s, his lead female character, Rachel Rose, claims, "I couldn't even get an interview with [the name] Rosen."

Shortly after graduating from Cornell, Levine became Laurents when he applied for his first job, submitting the script *Now Playing Tomorrow* under that new name. It worked. CBS Radio accepted and aired his innocuous comedy about a clairvoyant, by Arthur Laurents.

The Laurents disguise continued for decades and took its most extreme form of obfuscation in his first memoir, *Original Story By*, published in 2000. Laurents writes openly of being the victim of homophobia and anti-Semitism, yet he never reveals his real last name or even the real names of his parents, Ada Rabinowitz and Irving Levine. Although referred to often in the book, they are simply called "mother" and "father."

Regarding the name change, his Knopf editor did not considerate it relevant. "He may have told me the story," said Victoria Wilson. "I don't remember the details. Arthur was not somebody to hide."

Green took aim at another important facet of the Laurents legend. Having coauthored the book *Shy: The Alarmingly Outspoken Memoirs of Mary Rodgers*, Green revealed that both Rodgers and Stephen Sondheim had expressed doubts that Laurents ever ran into trouble from HUAC. "The whole thing about Arthur's being blacklisted

I never really believed," wrote Rodgers. "[T]here are a million reasons why people don't get work in Hollywood and only some of them involve communism."

Laurents told the story that in the late 1940s he had his US passport revoked after his name appeared in the anti-communist pamphlet *Red Channels*. To get his passport back, he wrote a four-page defense to the State Department in which he explained that his name appeared in the archconservative publication because his play *Home of the Brave* had been reviewed in the *Daily Worker*—and for no other reason. He claimed never to have joined the Communist Party, and went on to detail the various liberal charities to which he'd given donations. He wrote a detailed defense, and Laurents liked to brag that it was so "idiosyncratic" that no one at the State Department could believe he ever had been a member of any political party, much less a communist. In his memoir *Original Story By*, Laurents reveals that the State Department reissued his passport within a week of receiving his written defense, and a few days later the executives at MGM made him an offer to write the screenplay for Max Ophuls's 1949 film, *Caught*.

There's one big problem with Laurents's story. He got the dates wrong. Only the Hollywood Ten lost work in the film industry in the first three years of the blacklist, from 1947 to 1950. With his story, Laurents attempted to put himself in the august company of Dalton Trumbo, Ring Lardner, and eight other blacklisted writers who ended up being imprisoned. The letter that Laurents wrote to the State Department is dated January 6, 1952, not 1948. Also left out of the Laurents version of events is a second document he wrote to the State Department, in which he repeats never having been a communist. However, he goes even further to pledge his allegiance to the United States and to denounce the Communist Party and any of its subversive activities. He did not name names. He had never been a member of the Communist Party. However, he did submit the kind of loyalty oath that he had criticized others for signing.

"While Arthur was absolutely unrelenting in calling out what he believed were lies told by other people, he actually had an intermittent relationship with the truth himself," said one colleague. "He had a very ornate imagination."

The sympathetic view of Laurents's early career in Hollywood was that he ended up being "graylisted." In the 1950s he continued to write screenplays (*Anastasia* and *Bonjour Tristesse*) and be paid by the studios for others that never went into production. His play *The Time of the Cuckoo* was adapted to the screen and retitled *Summertime*. Most, but not all those projects, were foreign-based films that relied on American film companies for distribution in the United States. "I never went near Los Angeles," said Laurents, who was essentially working for the studios when he met Hatcher there in 1955. He explained, "*Anastasia* . . . was made in London and in Paris. You have to realize the studios only wanted what was expedient. They had no politics."

Fiction making is what Laurents knew best, and he was often a truly great fabulist. He knew how to make a good story even better by mixing up the facts and the fiction to the point where they became indistinguishable.

The second scene Streisand wanted restored to *The Way We Were* for a 2023 rerelease is one of Laurents's very best. He described it as "where the political and romantic story come together." It is also where the political story on-screen diverges from the romantic backstory in which Laurents had exquisitely wrapped it.

In the scene, Hubbell tells the very pregnant Katie that Frankie McVeigh has exposed her communist past to HUAC, and she offers to divorce him so he can continue working in Hollywood. Pollack cut the scene to create a "clearer through line" from Hubbell's fling with Carol Ann to his parting with Katie after the delivery of their baby, Rachel. Pollack was a director in the mold of an Alfred Hitchcock or an Otto Preminger, creative men who worked very much in the studio system. They saw the urgent need to score one commercial hit after another so that they could keep working if ever the inevitable happened and one of their efforts turned into a flop. Pollack was not a director in the mold of Orson Welles or Erich von Stroheim, who gambled on each film as if it were his last. (Talent aside, Streisand as a film director fell into the latter category, her need to control every aspect of the production limiting her directorial output to only three films: *Yentl*, *The Prince of Tides*, and *The Mirror Has Two Faces*.) As Pollack envisioned *The Way We Were*, Katie and Hubbell are destined to part—the title song tells us as much— and shorter, in this case, worked better with audiences in 1973. And Pollack had the preview audiences' reactions to prove it.

Laurents was also right: *The Way We Were* needed the "ex-communist wife" scene to bring the film to a climax, where the romance and the politics finally collided. With the scene included, the film escapes the "yenta-ism" that concerned Pollack.

Laurents knew how to promote his work where it counted most—not with audiences but with the actors and the production team. It's unfortunate that his flair for mixing up fact and fiction failed with Stark and Pollack at a critical moment. He knew how much Pollack enjoyed solving the roman à clef of *The Way We Were* by matching up real people with their fictional doppelgängers in the screenplay. Pollack may have underestimated how much those characters were based on Laurents himself. At one point in *The Way We Were*, Laurents can be seen as Katie passing out communist literature on campus and falling in love with the fantasy WASP. Elsewhere in the movie, Laurents can be seen as Hubbell having his short story read in class and later struggling with writer's block while his girl-friend, Katie, who can be seen as Hatcher, encourages him to continue writing. Laurents always said Hatcher was his best editor.

Regarding the "ex-communist for a wife" scene, Laurents liked to tell the story about his friends Jigee and Peter Vier-tel, whom he knew from his Hollywood days in the late 1940s. Peter was the son of Salka Viertel, and he wrote screenplays, beginning with Alfred Hitchcock's 1942 World War II espionage thriller, *Saboteur*. He married the actress Virginia "Jigee" Lee Ray in 1943, shortly after she gave birth to a daughter, Vicky, and she divorced her first hus-band, Budd Schulberg, who had been a member of the Communist Party USA. Jigee also joined, and that party affiliation brought her into social and political contact with Ring Lardner, one of the Hollywood Ten.

Laurents met Jigee and Peter Viertel in the first years of their marriage, when he and Farley Granger would hang out with them on Hollywood's more illustrious tennis courts. Later, when Laurents moved to New York, the Viertels split up but did not divorce. For much of the 1950s, Peter lived with the French fashion model Bettina Graziani, and when they parted ways, he began an affair with the movie star Deborah Kerr. She divorced her hus-band, the British film and television executive Anthony Bartley, in 1959, and that same year Jigee granted Viertel a divorce. On July 23, 1960, in Marbella, Spain, Kerr and Viertel married. It was also the year that Jigee died, on Jan-uary 31, and under rather ghastly circumstances. A ciga-rette she was smoking set her clothes on fire, and she perished.

Laurents claimed that Jigee had divorced Viertel to remove the wrath of HUAC and save his screenwriter career in Hollywood. He spun that story into the scene where Katie leaves Hubbell due to the Frankie McVeigh controversy—or, as he put it in his first memoir, "Katie and Hubbell facing what Jigee and Peter had faced." Left out of this story is that 1959 was late in the HUAC blacklist saga. A screenwriter like Peter Viertel wasn't so much low-hanging fruit as he was a forgotten lemon. By the late 1950s, his major calling card in town was being Deborah Kerr's boyfriend, and the fan magazines rejoiced over the illicitness of their love; in the pantheon of good girls, the prim British actress stood on a pedestal just to the left of Doris Day. Neither Jigee Viertel nor Anthony Bartley was a vindictive person, and each gave a respective spouse the divorce he and she wanted.

Facts can be pesky things, and being a good storyteller does not always mean being an accurate storyteller. In the movies and the theater, where Laurents lived and worked, it didn't matter. Outside that world of fantasy, however, people sometimes got upset or angry or even hurt when the lines between fiction and fact were purposefully blurred for someone to be an entertaining raconteur.

When *Original Story By* was published in 2000, Vicky Kingsland was not one of the book's first readers. She waited a couple of years before getting a copy, then sat down to write Laurents an angry letter. As the daughter of Jigee and Budd Schulberg, she disliked the way in which her mother's death had been described in the book. Kingsland didn't ask that the facts be corrected in future printings of the book; she simply wanted to express hurt with regard to her mother's death being misrepresented. (In truth, her mother's death had been more disfiguring than Laurents described it in *Original Story By*.)

She also wanted Laurents to know something else that

was inaccurate in his book. It had to do not with her mother but with the movie *The Way We Were*. Laurents complained vigorously about the "ugly" hairnet Streisand wore in the Union Station scene. No woman would have worn such a thing, Laurents opined. Kingsland disagreed, and she had the proof of her mother's old snood, which she kept in a drawer, "with my scarves." In her letter, Kingsland enclosed a photo of Jigee Viertel wearing that elegant hairnet in a passport photo dated 1946.

Epilogue

The Reporter and His Subjects

In my work as an entertainment journalist, I met and interviewed Sydney Pollack, Arthur Laurents, and Tom Hatcher.

In 1995 I wrote weekly columns on the movies for the Reuters news agency and the *Miami Herald*. Those two gigs forced me to clock in several interviews a week. Pollack, at the time, was doing press duties for his new film, *Sabrina*, and it was clear from his press conference that he didn't think much of the movie remake, based on the Billy Wilder classic starring Audrey Hepburn and Humphrey Bogart. I'd heard a rumor that Pollack had recently shown Wilder his *Sabrina* remake. Naturally, I brought it up during our one-on-one interview, asking, "So what did Billy Wilder think of your version?"

Pollack shook his head. "What could he say? He had to be nice. It's very difficult," he said. "Billy did tell me before the screening, 'Someday someone will do this to you. They will do a remake of *The Way We Were*.'"

It was a segue dropped straight from heaven! That day, Pollack much preferred talking about *The Way We Were* to talking about his *Sabrina*, and I jumped at the opportunity to ask about all the Hollywood blacklist scenes that had been cut. That was when he told me, "There will not be an extended director's cut of *The Way We Were*. The blacklist scenes don't work."

When I asked about a recently published Streisand biography that contended she would have won the Oscar if the UCLA scene had not been cut, he responded with the utmost firmness, "That's bullshit!"

I left that interview knowing that Pollack preferred *The Way We Were* to remain as he had last edited it in 1973, and that he wanted no changes made. He wanted no "cut" scenes reinserted. I found the man to be as honest and forthright as any person I've ever met in the film business.

I often interviewed Arthur Laurents when I was the theater reporter for *Variety*, from 1999 to 2005. At the time, I was also working on a biography of the agent Henry Willson, to be titled *The Man Who Invented Rock Hudson*. Since Laurents had lived and worked in Hollywood in the late 1940s and early 1950s, I hoped that his path there might have crossed with Willson's.

Laurents was quick to reply. "No, I didn't know him. But I know someone who did. Call Tom Hatcher," he said, and he gave me the phone number. At times like this, Laurents could be a reporter's dream. He also never failed to give great quotes. It was not until I had prepared for the interview, quickly skimming *Original Story By*, that I learned the identity of Laurents's longtime partner at 9 St. Luke's Place. Years before, I'd worked for an editor in chief who lived next door to "Arthur Laurents, the guy who wrote *West Side Story*, and his boyfriend." This magazine editor spoke disparagingly of his two next-door neighbors, because he believed they had poisoned one of his cats that often wandered into their garden.

The day of the Henry Willson interview, Laurents answered the door of the historic brownstone and immediately introduced me to Hatcher, who stood behind him. Both men were nearly identical in height, about five feet six or seven. Hatcher then invited me to his sparsely decorated ground-floor office, which led to a lush garden, the possible crime scene regarding my editor in chief's pet cat.

Having just read *Original Story By*, I recognized an old photograph from the book on one of the shelves in Hatcher's office. Taken in the mid-1950s, it shows Laurents and his boyfriend posed on a diving board as they are about to fall or jump into a swimming pool. Despite the twelve-year age difference, Laurents is every bit as buff as his younger partner; in fact, in their tight matching swim trunks, the two men's small yet compact bodies are nearly interchangeable. They were both amazing male specimens in an age when there weren't gyms on every other block of Los Angeles and New York City.

Before I could turn on my tape recorder, Hatcher informed me, "I renovate houses. That's what I do." He then turned himself into a veritable quote machine. After a couple of warm-up questions, he immediately launched into an anecdote regarding how Willson had fired him as a client and, on the same night, made an offer that the teenage John Saxon, a recent Brooklyn émigré, could not refuse.

It was a short but productive interview. Hatcher didn't have much contact with Willson beyond his signing him and then his firing him. In between those two events, the young actor did find himself questioned and harassed by the police for having attended a Willson pool party one Saturday afternoon.

Laurents and Hatcher's housekeeper soon made an appearance to invite me to lunch, and sitting down across from the couple in an elegant dining room on the parlor floor, as overloaded with paintings and memorabilia as the office downstairs was devoid of them, I had to wonder if this was the first time a reporter had come to this house to interview Hatcher and not Laurents. From there, it was clear who held court at 9 St. Luke's Place. Laurents wasted no time dropping the name Paul Newman, whom, he informed us, had just turned down the offer to perform in one of his plays. I assume it was *Two Lives*. "Paul told me he had tried to learn the first page of the play, and had spent all day trying and couldn't even remember a paragraph, much less a page," said Laurents. Newman would soon end his career in the theater in a Broadway production of Thornton Wilder's classic *Our Town*, in which he essayed the role of the Stage Manager, a character that carries, and sometimes reads from, the script.

I had my own stories regarding Newman. Years before, I'd been the entertainment editor at *Life* magazine, and I'd met the actor for articles on his Oscar-winning performance in *The Color of Money* and his summer retreat for children with terminal illnesses, the Hole in the Wall Gang Camp, supported by the Newman's Own charity. Laurents didn't want to hear those stories. The man I met that day for our impromptu lunch of Campbell's tomato soup and toast was the man Mary Corliss would describe to me two decades later for this book. "Arthur was very loquacious," she said. "He had a history and he had the stories. He didn't care about you. He didn't ask questions about you. But it didn't matter. You never wanted him to stop talking."

Indeed, his Paul Newman stories were much better than my Paul Newman stories.

Hatcher and I were there to listen, to be the audience. The two men were deeply in love and committed to each other. It was also clear the two men knew their place. While they continued to share the West Village brownstone, they had long lived in separate houses on Quogue, where Hatcher spent most of his time.

In his eighties then, Laurents more resembled himself in that photograph downstairs than Hatcher resembled his younger self. Age had thickened and quieted him. He was what his partner would call "a former beauty," and I don't recall him ever smiling that day. Over lunch, Laurents never stopped smiling. When he spoke, he exposed every tooth in his mouth, and he never stopped talking. His thin body was as wiry, tight, and bound with energy as it had been years ago on a diving board in Los Angeles.

I eventually had my falling-out with Laurents, as most people in the New York theater world did. He was that rare theater legend who, post-death, did not receive a memorial in one of the Broadway theaters. My contretemps came when I was researching my biography on the producer Allan Carr, to be titled *Party Animals*. Carr had brought the musical *La Cage aux Folles* to the Broadway stage, and Laurents had directed it. In one of his memoirs, he accused Carr of having prematurely closed the musical rather than transferring it from the Palace Theatre to the Mark Hellinger Theatre. Barry Brown, another producer on the show, and the musical's lawyer, John Breglio, insisted otherwise. Rock Hudson had recently died of AIDS, and tourists no longer wanted to see a light gay-themed comedy. It made financial sense to close *La Cage* at the Palace in 1987 rather than spend a quarter of a million dollars to move it to the Hellinger.

Laurents gave another version of what happened to the show. "We were set to move to the Mark Hellinger," he wrote in *Mainly on Directing*. "The Moonies, however, wanted the Hellinger for their tabernacle. They offered Allan Carr a lot of money." According to Laurents, Carr grabbed the money and closed *La Cage*.

Anyone who took the time to walk by the venue once known as the Mark Hellinger Theatre knew that it became in 1987 the Times Square Church, which has nothing to do with Sun Myung Moon, his wacky Unification Church, or illegal payoffs. Laurents always knew how to make a false story even better, not to mention more flagrantly wrong. When I challenged him on his account, he put all future telephone calls with me in his proverbial "cigar box."

Fortunately, in our previous phone interviews, he had much enjoyed being quoted in *Variety*, and I often managed to ask about *The Way We Were*, even though it was never the subject of anything I was writing about at the time. I played the curious fan, and Laurents loved having fans.

"With *The Way We Were*, were you writing about you and Tom?" I asked. Even though I asked the question in a slightly different form on various occasions, Laurents never altered his response, and he always kept it simple before changing the subject.

"I was writing about myself and my time in college and Hollywood," he replied.

Barbra Streisand visited Laurents shortly before his death, at age ninety-three, on May 5, 2011. They had had a minor dustup a decade earlier when, in his first memoir, he gave full credit to Herbert Ross for the office chair on wheels in *I Can Get It for You Wholesale*. Streisand had phoned him to complain. In their last meeting, she also brought up the subject of *Wholesale* and how he had criticized her for being "undisciplined" and always changing her performance in the show. The dying man told her, finally, that she had been right never to stop experimenting. They had long talked about working together again, specifically on *Gypsy*. That new movie version never materialized, but in her analysis of the tyrannical stage mother Rose, Streisand could have been talking about her own stage mentor, Arthur Laurents.

"I think she's tough as nails, but a person who's vulnerable inside . . . [W]hat makes for anger is also hurt," she said.

Bibliography, Discography, and Filmography

Andersen, Christopher. *Barbra: The Way She Is*. New York: William Morrow, 2007.

Arick, Michael, dir. *The Way We Were: Looking Back*. Documentary film accompanying the DVD release of *The Way We Were*. Culver City, CA: Columbia TriStar Home Video, 1999.

Callan, Michael Feeney. *Robert Redford: The Biography*. New York: Alfred A. Knopf, 2011.

Ceplair, Larry, and Steven Englund. *The Inquisition in Hollywood: Politics in the Film Community, 1930–1960*. Berkeley: University of California Press, 1979.

Crist, Judith. *Take 22: Moviemakers on Moviemaking*. New York: Viking, 1984.

Dean, John W. *The Nixon Defense: What He Knew and When He Knew It*. New York: Viking, 2014.

Dillman, Bradford. *Are You Anybody? An Actor's Life*. New York: Fithian Press, 1997.

Edwards, Anne. *Streisand: A Biography*. Lanham, MD: Taylor Trade Publishing, 2016.

Finstad, Suzanne. *Warren Beatty: A Private Man*. New York: Three Rivers Press, 2005.

Gabler, Neal. *Barbra Streisand: Redefining Beauty, Femininity, and Power*. New Haven, CT: Yale University Press, 2016.

Goldman, Eric A. *The American Jewish Story through Cinema*. Austin: University of Texas Press, 2013.

Granger, Farley. *Include Me Out: My Life from Goldwyn to Broadway*. With Robert Calhoun. New York: St. Martin's Press, 2007.

Hayden, Sterling. *Wanderer: An Autobiography*. New York: Alfred A. Knopf, 1963.

Hofler, Robert. *The Man Who Invented Rock Hudson*. New York: Carroll & Graf, 2005.

Hofler, Robert. *Money, Murder, and Dominick Dunne: A Life in Several Acts*. Madison: University of Wisconsin Press, 2017.

Kengor, Paul. *Dupes: How America's Adversaries Have Manipulated Progressives for a Century*. Wilmington, DE: Intercollegiate Studies Institute, 2018.

Kaiser, Charles. *The Gay Metropolis, 1940–1996*. New York: Houghton Mifflin, 1997.

Koch, Hawk. *Magic Time: My Life in Hollywood*. With Molly Jordan. New York: Post Hill Press, 2019.

Laurents, Arthur. *Mainly on Directing: Gypsy, West Side Story, and Other Musicals*. New York: Alfred A. Knopf, 2009; Lanham, MD: Applause Theatre & Cinema Books, 2014.

Laurents, Arthur. *Original Story By: A Memoir of Broadway and Hollywood*. New York: Alfred A. Knopf, 2000.

Laurents, Arthur. *The Rest of the Story: A Life Completed*. New York: Applause Theatre & Cinema Books, 2012.

Laurents, Arthur. *Selected Plays of Arthur Laurents*. New York: Back Stage Books, 2005.

Laurents, Arthur. *The Way We Were*. Novel. New York: Harper & Row, 1972.

McGilligan, Patrick. *Backstory 2: Interviews with Screenwriters of the 1940s and 1950s*. Berkeley: University of California Press, 1991.

McGilligan, Patrick, and Paul Buhle. *Tender Comrades: A Backstory of the Hollywood Blacklist*. New York: St. Martin's Griffin Edition, 1999.

Mann, William J. *Hello, Gorgeous: Becoming Barbra Streisand*. Boston: Houghton Mifflin Harcourt, 2012.

Navasky, Victor S. *Naming Names*. New York: Hill and Wang, 1991.

Riese, Randall. *Her Name Is Barbra: An Intimate Portrait of the Real Barbra Streisand*. New York: Birch Lane Press, 1993.

Rodgers, Mary, and Jesse Green. *Shy: The Alarmingly Outspoken Memoirs of Mary Rodgers*. New York: Farrar, Straus and Giroux, 2022.

Russo, Vito. *The Celluloid Closet: Homosexuality in the Movies*. New York: Harper & Row, 1981.

Spada, James. *Streisand: Her Life*. New York: Crown Publishers, 1995.

Streisand, Barbra: *Just for the Record . . .* Recorded 1955–88. Columbia Records, 1991, 4 compact discs.

Taylor, Theodore. *Jule: The Story of Composer Jule Styne*. New York: Random House, 1979.

Zec, Donald, and Anthony Fowles. *Barbra: A Biography of Barbra Streisand*. London: New English Library, 1981; Paperback edition. New York: New English Library, 1982.

Ziesmer, Jerry. *Ready When You Are, Mr. Coppola, Mr. Spielberg, Mr. Crowe*. Lanham, MD: Scarecrow Press, 1999.

Acknowledgments

The performances of Barbra Streisand, Robert Redford, and James Woods in *The Way We Were* continue to entertain and inspire, and I am indebted to them for the interviews they granted me for this book. Fortunately, they were not the only generous storytellers who spoke to me, whether those interviews were face-to-face or conducted by phone or email. I am also indebted to Don Bachardy, Alan Bergman, André Bishop, Michael Britton, Barry Brown, John F. Burnett, Mary Corliss, Grover Dale, Marty Erlichman, Ashley Feinstein, Dave Fiske, Jesse Green, Hawk Koch, Hal Luftig, Patti LuPone, Kevin McCollum, Patrick McGilligan, William Mann, Rachel Pollack, Rebecca Pollack, Judith Rascoe, Lynne S. Rayfiel, Michael Riedel, Zvi Howard Rosenman, Richard N. Roth, Scott Rudin, Harry Seibert, Art Smith Jr., David Stone, David Strick, Matt Tyrnauer, John Weidman, Victoria Wilson, and a couple of anonymous sources. Not everyone listed here is quoted in the book, but even if their names do not appear in the text, they provided invaluable information.

Dave Fiske and Becky Ford were especially helpful in reconstructing the *Way We Were* shoot in Ballston Spa, New York. Matt Howe, who edits the Barbra Archives website, never failed to provide speedy and accurate answers to my many queries. And a very special thank-you goes out to Lynne S. Rayfiel, who gave me not only photographs but also copies of David Rayfiel's rewrites of *The Way We Were*.

My friends Gay Haubner and Laurence Sutter read an early draft of this book and offered wonderful suggestions. Nick Buchholz, Justin Ross Cohen, Howard Mandelbaum, Christine Pittel, and Philip Rinaldi made introductions to interviewees, who were essential to the writing of this book.

I'm proud to pay the taxes that support libraries throughout the country. Nonfiction books don't get written without the enormous help of librarians. With this book especially, I relied mightily on those librarians at the Cornell University Library, the Library of Congress, the New York Public Library for the Performing Arts at Lincoln Center, the Margaret Herrick Library, and the New York Public Library's Stephen A. Schwarzman Building.

Last and foremost, I thank my photographer friend Jill Krementz; my agent, Lee Sobel; and all the talented people at Kensington Publishing, including designers Andrew Elias and Kristine Nobel, copy editor Rosemary Silva, and, of course, my editor, John Scognamiglio.

Notes

The Sydney Pollack Archives and the Arthur Laurents Archives are housed at, respectively, the Margaret Herrick Library in Beverly Hills, California, and the Library of Congress, in Washington, D.C. The dates of interviews conducted by the author are listed after the interviewees' names at the beginning of the notes for each chapter. Some interviews involved more than one session. Only the date of the first session is listed here.

Chapter 1

Quotes from Ashley Feinstein (October 7, 2021), Judith Rascoe (November 12, 2021), and Barbra Streisand (July 22, 2022) are from interviews with the author, except where noted.

1 "**Arthur remembers**": *The Way We Were: Looking Back*, directed by Michael Arick (Culver City, CA: Columbia Tri-Star Home Video, 1999). Documentary film accompanying the DVD release of *The Way We Were*.

1 "**I want this**": Randall Riese, *Her Name Is Barbra: An Intimate Portrait of the Real Barbra Streisand* (New York: Birch Lane Press, 1993), 331.

2 "**fantasy WASP**": *The Way We Were: Looking Back* documentary film; and Arthur Laurents, *Selected Plays of Arthur Laurents* (New York: Back Stage Books, 2005), 241.

4 Rock-hard buttocks/female guests: Sharon Waxman, "A Producer Who Loved Both Art and Ribaldry," *New York Times*, May 11, 2005.

4 "It's wonderful": Anne Edwards, *Streisand: A Biography* (Lanham, MD: Taylor Trade Publishing, 2016), 334.

4 property of Rastar: Pollack Archives.

4 "This will be the first-ever": Michael Feeney Callan, *Robert Redford: The Biography* (New York: Alfred A. Knopf, 2011), 232.

5 "It started there": "Eye View," *Women's Wear Daily*, April 3, 1972, 14.

6 David Lean reference: *The Way We Were: Looking Back* documentary film.

6 "That's me": Edwards, *Streisand*, 331.

7 Mary Martin reference: William J. Mann, *Hello, Gorgeous: Becoming Barbra Streisand* (Boston: Houghton Mifflin Harcourt, 2012), 225.

7 "looked awful": Theodore Taylor, *Jule: The Story of Composer Jule Styne* (New York: Random House, 1979), 226.

7 "She's terrible": "Hello, Gorgeous," in *Barbra Streisand: Her Life and Unrivaled Career*, ed. *People* editors, special issue, *People*, April 15, 2022, 30.

8 "Fanny was beautiful": Mann, *Hello, Gorgeous*, 237.

8 "corrective schnoz bob": "Barbra Streisand," *Variety*, November 22, 1961.

8 "amiable ant-eater": John McClain, "Reviews," *New York Journal-American*, March 23, 1962.

8 "cut off her nose": Eric A. Goldman, *The American Jewish Story through Cinema* (Austin: University of Texas Press, 2013), 126.

9 "Since the action": Barbra Streisand, *Just for the Record* liner notes.

9 "She actually has": "His Words Are Music to Our Ears," *New York Newsday*, December 14, 1987.

9 "David Merrick was": "Eye View," *Women's Wear Daily*, April 3, 1972, 14.

10 "She was incredibly": Mann, *Hello, Gorgeous* interview transcript.

11 "She gives him sex": *The Way We Were: Looking Back* documentary film.

11 "You've gotta have": "Hello, Gorgeous," in *Barbra Streisand: Her Life and Unrivaled Career*, 30.

11 "There is a joke": "An Interview with Barbra Streisand: Who Am I, Anyway?" *Life*, January 9, 1970, 91.

11 "is not a member": "Bios," *I Can Get It for You Wholesale*, *Playbill*, 1962.

12 Streisand letter to Laurents: Laurents Archives.

13 "People will no longer": Joanne Stang, "She Couldn't Be Medium," *New York Times*, April 5, 1964.

13 "You're never gonna make it": Ben Brantley, "Barbra Streisand Sets the Record Straight," *New York Times*, August 3, 2016.

14 "Katie Morosky, the campus political": Arthur Laurents, *The Rest of the Story: A Life Completed* (New York: Applause Theatre & Cinema Books, 2012), 10–11.

15 "three of the most successful": Stanley Kauffmann, "Homosexual Drama and Its Disguises," *New York Times*, January 23, 1966.

15 "[T]he central character": Arthur Laurents, *Original Story By: A Memoir of Broadway and Hollywood* (New York: Alfred A. Knopf, 2000), 190.

15 **"my closest friend"**: Laurents, *The Rest of the Story*, 69.

15 **"I know where Rose"**: Ibid., xiii.

16 **"starring Barbra Streisand and Robert Redford"**: Pollack Archives.

Chapter 2

Quotes from Streisand are from an interview with the author, except where noted.

17 **"We've got Streisand"**: Pollack Archives.

18 **"unheroic"**: Laurents Archives.

18 **"Barbra had never worked"**: Riese, *Her Name Is Barbra*, 332.

18 **"In acting, you have to sense"**: David Ansen, "Robert Redford: An American Superstar," *Newsweek*, May 28, 1984, 76.

19 **"Stark had no affection"**: Callan, *Robert Redford*, 232–33.

19 **twenty different Porsches**: Ibid., 102.

19 **"Everything was as phony"**: Ibid., 231.

20 **"It sounds to me"**: Ibid., 323.

20 **"Nick just died"**: Ibid., 128.

20 **"It'll be better this time"**: Arthur Laurents, *The Way We Were* (New York: Harper & Row, 1972), 71.

21 **"Almost all of Redford's"**: Robert Hofler, "Sydney Pollack Interview," *Miami Herald*, December 10, 1995.

22 **"If you didn't look"**: Larry Dubois, "Robert Redford Interview," *Playboy*, December 1974, 98.

22 **"Well, I've got news"**: Ibid.

23 **"felt like a fish"**: David Enser, "Dialogue with Sydney Pollack," *Premiere*, n.d.

23 **"He identified"**: David Ehrenstein, "*Robert Redford: The Biography* Reviewed," *Film Comment* 47, no. 4 (July–August 2011), 78.

23 **"envy"**: Laurents Archives.

24 **"narcissistic"**: Callan, *Robert Redford*, 149.

24 **"I spent literally"**: James Spada, *Streisand: Her Life* (New York: Crown Publishers, 1995), 300.

24 **"It was payback"**: Callan, *Robert Redford*, 232.

24 **Pollack letter dated December 4, 1971**: Pollack Archives.

25 **"Her reputation"**: Ibid., 234.

25 **"She's not going to sing"**: "Robert Redford Surprises Barbra Streisand" segment, *The Oprah Winfrey Show*, aired November 16, 2010.

25 **"That really got me"**: *The Way We Were: Looking Back* documentary film.

25 **"In those days"**: Barbra Streisand, interview by Raina Douris, *World Café*, NPR, September 3, 2021.

26 **"Barbra was smart"**: *The Way We Were: Looking Back* documentary film.

26 **"Because no one ever"**: Callan, *Robert Redford*, 233.

26 **"Barbra wanted to 'go straight'"**: Richard Natale, "Director Pollack Tells of 'The Way We Were,' " *Women's Wear Daily*, October 22, 1973.

27 **"camp"**: Pollack Archives.

28 **"This has nothing to do with"**: Karina Longworth, "Bogie and the Blacklist," *Slate*, March 4, 2016.

29 **Committee for the First Amendment**: Larry Ceplair and Steven Englund, *The Inquisition in Hollywood: Politics in*

the Film Community, 1930–1960 (Berkeley: University of California Press, 1979), 275.

29 **Bogart's 1939 HUAC appearance:** Ibid., 150.

29 **"It was a sorry performance":** Longworth, "Bogie and the Blacklist."

30 **"Garbo's lover":** Pollack Archives.

32 **"Hubbell knows":** Donald Zec and Anthony Fowles, *Barbra: A Biography of Barbra Streisand* (London: New English Library, 1981; Paperback edition. New York: New English Library, 1982), 283.

32 **"more existential view":** Judith Crist, *Take 22: Moviemakers on Moviemaking* (New York: Viking, 1984), 222.

33 **"I don't think you have":** Sterling Hayden, *Wanderer: An Autobiography* (New York: Alfred A. Knopf, 1963), 65–66.

34 **"I'm No Communist":** Ceplair and Englund, *The Inquisition in Hollywood*, 291.

34 **"the public is beginning":** Ibid., 289.

34 **"We didn't realize":** Paul, Kengor, *Dupes: How America's Adversaries Have Manipulated Progressives for a Century* (Wilmington, DE: Intercollegiate Studies Institute, 2018), 101.

34 **"a good guy":** Callan, *Robert Redford*, 235.

34 **"I think the blacklist":** Ibid.

35 **"I don't want to go":** Zec and Fowles, *Barbra*, 283.

35 **"If blue eyes":** Jane Wilson, "What if My Eyes Turn Brown?" *Saturday Evening Post*, February 24, 1968.

35 **"a guy who":** Hofler, "Sydney Pollack Interview."

35 **"There was resistance":** Zec and Fowles, *Barbra*, 295.

36 **"uninformed":** Laurents Archives.

Chapter 3

Quotes from Scott Rudin (October 29, 2021) are from an interview with the author.

37 **"rewrite" and "cliché"**: Laurents Archives.

38 **"Very talented, David"**: Laurents, *Original Story By*, 270.

39 **"master rewrite man"**: Alex Ward, "David Rayfiel's Script Magic," *New York Times*, April 6, 1986.

39 **"ice rink"**: Pollack Archives.

39 **"We practically live"**: *The Way We Were: Looking Back* documentary film.

40 **wearing a matching sling**: Laurents, *Original Story By*, 269.

40 **"Don't patronize me"**: Ibid., 403.

41 **chicken anecdote**: Anonymous source to author.

41 **"What an asshole"**: Ibid., 270.

42 **"He could be the wisest"**: Anonymous source to author.

42 **"[E]verything Sydney wore"**: Laurents, *Original Story By*, 270.

43 **"[I]t was a little bit"**: Zec and Fowles, *Barbra*, 295.

43 **"yenta-ism carried to the extreme"**: Crist, *Take 22*, 220.

44 **March 10 memo from Pollack to Laurents**: Laurents Archives.

45 **"Jewish!" and "Gentile!"**: Laurents Archives.

Chapter 4

47 **"You've never seen bad tennis"**: Spada, *Streisand*, 299.

47 **"No sexual tension"**: Ibid.

48 **"One of her convictions"**: Christopher Andersen, *Barbra: The Way She Is* (New York: William Morrow, 2007), 209.

48 **"The Phantom of the Beverly Wilshire"**: Suzanne Finstad, *Warren Beatty: A Private Man* (New York: Three Rivers Press, 2005), 407.

48 **"One of my flings"**: Elizabeth Kaye, "Barbra: The Superstar Who Wants to Be a Woman," *McCall's*, April 1975.

49 **"Why don't I play"**: Finstad, *Warren Beatty*, 403.

49 **"apathetic"**: Ellis Amburn, *Warren Beatty: The Sexiest Man Alive* (New York: HarperEntertainment, 2002), 162.

49 $320,000: Ibid., 165.

50 **"Malice in Wonderland"**: Laurents, *The Way We Were* (novel), 256.

51 **"This is playwright"**: Jack Conroy, "Review: 'The Way We Were,'" *Chicago Sun-Times*, March 19, 1972.

51 **"The author never grapples"**: Raymond A. Sokolov, (book) review of *The Way We Were*, by Arthur Laurents, *New York Times*, April 16, 1972.

Chapter 5

Quotes from Robert Redford (November 22, 2021) are from an interview with the author, except where noted.

52 **"All of her pictures"**: Zec and Fowles, *Barbra*, 284–85.

52 **"Redford walks on the screen"**: Brad Darrach, "Meryl," *Life*, December 1987, 13.

53 **"at all costs"**: Zec and Fowles, *Barbra*, 284–85.

53 **"I wanted him in that part"**: "Robert Redford Surprises Barbra Streisand" segment, *The Oprah Winfrey Show*, aired November 16, 2010.

53 **"Bob and Paul"**: Vito Russo, *The Celluloid Closet: Homosexuality in the Movies.* (New York: Harper & Row, 1981), 81–82.

54 **"He was shallow"**: Spada, *Streisand*, 300–01.

54 **"Ken doll"**: "Robert Redford Surprises Barbra Streisand" segment, *The Oprah Winfrey Show*, aired November 16, 2010.

54 **"Pollack, you're crazy"**: "Pollack," *Premiere*, July 1980.

54 **"I went for a vacation"**: Callan, *Robert Redford*, 232.

54 **"Aw, that piece of junk"**: Spada, *Streisand*, 300.

54 **"No, it doesn't work"**: Ibid., 300.

54 **"overly sentimental"**: Andersen, *Barbra*, 208.

55 **"Look, I'm not going"**: Zec and Fowles, *Barbra*, 284.

55 **"You've got an hour"**: Spada, *Streisand*, 300.

56 **"Barbra Redford"**: "Robert Redford Surprises Barbra Streisand" segment, *The Oprah Winfrey Show*, aired November 16, 2010.

56 **"Robert Redford, whose last two films"**: Radie Harris, "Robert Redford Set in 'Way We Were,'" *Hollywood Reporter*, June 6, 1972.

57 **"Redford Will Not"**: "Sidney [sic] Pollack to Direct 'Way,'" *Hollywood Reporter*, June 7, 1972.

58 **"Ray Stark phoned"**: "Retraction of a Retraction," *Hollywood Reporter*, June 12, 1972.

Chapter 6

Quotes from Rudin and Streisand are from an interview with the author, except where noted.

59 **June 27, 1972 letter**: Laurents Archives.

60 **"No, indeed not"**: Jeanne Miller, "It Might Suit Barbra but He Didn't Write It for Her," *San Francisco Examiner*, April 25, 1972.

62 **Pollack letter to Laurents**: Pollack Archives.

64 **"Ray and Sydney started to muck"**: Edwards, *Streisand*, 335.

64 **"bonuses" and "chintzy"**: Laurents Archives.

64 **"collapsed"**: Pollack Archives.

65 **"survivor"**: Laurents Archives.

66 **"Many people have remarked"**: Callan, *Robert Redford*, 210.

66 **"One day Sydney called"**: "His Words Are Music to Our Ears," *New York Newsday*, December 14, 1987.

66 **"I know how you feel"**: Edwards, *Streisand*, 335.

66 **"he's the blond goy"**: Ibid.

Chapter 7

Quotes from Don Bachardy (August 12, 2021), Grover Dale (November 7, 2021), Feinstein, and Zvi Howard Rosenman (October 23, 2021) are from interviews with the author.

68 ***The Way We Were* musical treatment**: Laurents Archives.

68 **"Novel" chapter and Tyrone Power anecdote**: Laurents Archives.

70 **"Arthur had been very meaningful"**: Farley Granger, *Include Me Out: My Life from Goldwyn to Broadway*. With Robert Calhoun (New York: St. Martin's Press, 2007), 89.

70 **"striking and improbable"**: Laurents, *Original Story By*, 100.

72 **"the best sex"**: Ibid., 47.

72 **"[g]uiltless, gorgeous and gentile"**: Ibid., 154.

73 **"foster parents"**: Ibid., 344.

74 **"I left on my truck-driver outfit"**: Robert Hofler, *The Man Who Invented Rock Hudson* (New York: Carroll & Graf, 2005), 225.

74 **John Saxon anecdote**: Ibid., 295.

77 **Letter dated July 15, 1962**: Laurents Archives.

77 **"did you ever see"**: Jesse Green (September 22, 2021) to author.

78 **"I don't intend to have"**: Laurents, *Selected Plays of Arthur Laurents*, 155.

78 **"I don't want to be put up"**: Ibid., 165.

79 **"kept" and "rebound"**: Laurents Archives.

80 **"Chernobyl" and "For years, people were cruel"**: Jesse Green, "When You're a Shark You're a Shark All the Way," *New York*, March 23, 2009, 41.

80 **"How does Arthur get"**: Laurents, *The Rest of the Story*, 59.

Chapter 8

Quotes from John F. Burnett (October 11, 2021), Hawk Koch (July 14, 2021), Rebecca Pollack (January 7, 2022), Rascoe, Lynne S. Rayfiel (January 11, 2022), and Richard N. Roth (October 28, 2021) are from interviews with the author.

82 **"One day Sydney Pollack"**: "His Words Are Music to Our Ears," *New York Newsday*, December 14, 1987.

82 **Laurents's last letter to Pollack:** Laurents Archives.

82 **"It was about a relationship":** Callen, *Robert Redford*, 234.

84 **"I threw up again":** Laurents, *The Way We Were* (novel), 210.

86 **Chayefsky, Gardner, and Grodin references:** Pollack Archives; and *"The Way We Were,"* IMDb (website), https://www.imdb.com/title/tt0070903/.

87 **"We believed in the Constitution":** Rascoe to author.

87 **"I was hung up":** Callan, *Robert Redford*, 237.

88 **"What emerged out of the rewrites":** Ibid., 300–01.

89 **"Why can't I sit":** Spada, *Streisand*, 301.

89 **"Finally it started to get":** Ibid.

89 **"He believes very strongly":** Ibid.

90 **"Barbra was delighted":** Callan, *Robert Redford*, 236.

90 **"She was simply mesmerized":** Andersen, *Barbra*, 213.

90 **"She was infatuated":** George Rush, "Laurents Goes Stargazing and Hazin'," *Daily News*, April 4, 2000.

90 **"The only problem with working":** Jami Ganz, "Jane Fonda Fell in Love with Robert Redford," *Entertainment Weekly*, March 20, 2017.

90 **"fell head over heels":** Callan, *Robert Redford*, 137.

90 **"I had a big crush":** Darrach, "Meryl."

90 **"Barbra, if we're going":** Spada, *Streisand*, 301.

92 **"cute" outfits:** Pollack Archives.

92 **"I haven't been this excited":** Dorothy Manners, "Dorothy Manners Hollywood," *The Tribune*, July 25, 1972.

93 **Streisand, B. Pollack, S. Pollack, and Redford quotes re-**

garding the navy-uniform costume: Ziesmer, *Ready When You Are*, 52–55.

94 "When we started on": Callan, *Robert Redford*, 238.

95 Studio bled over two hundred million: John F. Berry and Jack Egan, "Filmdom Agonizes over High-Level Juggling of Company Funds," *Washington Post*, January 15, 1978.

95 "Everyone knows the Hollywood 10": Donna Perlmutter, "The Birth of the Hollywood Blacklist," *Los Angeles Times*, October 28, 1993.

95 "The pressure I was getting": Zec and Fowles, *Barbra*, 280.

96 "We have done a pretty good": Perlmutter, "The Birth of the Hollywood Blacklist."

97 "Meta was a great person": Patrick McGilligan and Paul Buhle, *Tender Comrades: A Backstory of the Hollywood Blacklist* (New York: St. Martin's Griffin Edition, 1999), 641.

Chapter 9

Quotes from Michael Britton (October 29, 2021), Dale, Koch, Rascoe, L. S. Rayfiel, Roth, and James Woods (December 2, 2021) are from interviews with the author.

100 "I am now crew": Ziesmer, *Ready When You Are*, 62.

100 ROTC uniforms: Pollack Archives.

101 Jason Streisand: Andersen, *Barbra*, 215.

101 Stark's on-set injury: Koch to author.

101 "short-haired, clean shaven": "Streisand-Redford Movie Filming in Area Spots," *Times Record*, September 16, 1972, 12.

102 **"You can go only"**: Crist, *Take 22*, 223.

103 **"Bobby needs your help"**: Ziesmer, *Ready When You Are*, 65.

104 **"Will you just relax"**: Riese, *Her Name Is Barbra*, 337.

104 **"talked everything to death"**: Andersen, *Barbra*, 214.

105 **"Streisand is hard"**: Craig Wilson, "Streisand Films Movie at College," *Post-Star and Times*, September 22, 1972.

105 **Pollack, Redford and Streisand quotes regarding the peace strike**: Ziesmer, *Ready When You Are*, 69–70.

106 **"I could relate"**: *The Way We Were: Looking Back* documentary film.

107 **"Sydney, the kid's"** and **"I'll kill you"**: Woods to author.

108–109 **"Okay, I'll do it"** and **"We survived Barbra"**: Dale to author.

110 **"C'mon, man, she's uncomfortable"**: Callan, *Robert Redford*, 239.

110 **"Let's do it on the set"**: "Robert Redford Surprises Barbra Streisand" segment, *The Oprah Winfrey Show*, aired November 16, 2010.

111 **"I was in my place"**: Callan, *Robert Redford*, 239.

111 **"Always automatically, even when"**: Wayne Warga, "A Camera Innovator with Cinematic Vision," *Los Angeles Times*, May 20, 1973.

112 **"sort of pop out on camera"**: Andersen, *Barbra*, 213.

112 **"She was fun"**: Lisa Russell, "Evergreen," in *Barbra Streisand: Her Life and Unrivaled Career*, ed. *People* editors, special issue, *People*, April 15, 2022, 49.

Chapter 10

Quotes from Koch, Rascoe, Harry Seibert (May 11, 2022), Streisand, and Woods are from interviews with the author, except where noted.

114 *You All Want Something* and *The Young Go First*: Cornell University Library.

114 "incompetent" and "respond": Pollack Archives.

116 "green and verdant": Pollack Archives.

116 "Your father never did it": Warga, "A Camera Innovator with Cinematic Vision."

117 "I think Barbra's a little": Andersen, *Barbra*, 211.

117 "Anyone who can sing": *The Way We Were: Looking Back* documentary film.

118 "A lot of directors": *The Way We Were: Looking Back* documentary film.

118 "[T]rying to make actors": Janet Maslin, "The Pollack Touch," *New York Times*, December 15, 1985.

119 Hopper painting and "Are you sure this place": Koch, *Magic Time*, 99.

119 About fifty Polaroids: Dillman, *An Actor's Life*, 154.

120 "The water looks beautiful": "Williams Crew Stages Race for Columbia Film," *The Transcript*, September 27, 1972, 4.

120 "just beautiful town": "Hollywood Comes to Ballston Spa," *Democrat and Chronicle*, October 7, 1972, 1.

121 "They used my barber shop": Wayne Bailey, "Moviemakers Shoot Scenes in Area," *Times Record*, September 30, 1972, 14.

122 "She called me around eleven": Zec and Fowles, *Barbra*, 287.

123 "No, you're not": Ziesmer, *Ready When You Are*, 72.

123 "Good evening, ladies and gentlemen": Dillman, *An Actor's Life*, 153.

124 "Their extraordinary color": *The Way We Were: Looking Back* documentary film.

124 Tony Blue Eyes supplied marijuana: Feinstein to author.

126 "Like his character in our film": Ziesmer, *Ready When You Are*, 68.

127 "He's a man of depth": Callan, *Robert Redford*, 239.

127 "Barbra wanted precision": Edwards, *Streisand*, 340.

127 penchant for looking at himself: Lois Smith to author.

128 "Paul [Newman] was a Method actor": Callan, *Robert Redford*, 245.

128 "You surprise them": Janet Maslin, "The Pollack Touch."

129 Selznick letter: Pollack Archives.

129 "two editors": Pollack Archives.

130 "Bob didn't get along": Spada, *Streisand*, 302.

131 "clearly defined," every antique car, and "contrast dramatically": Pollack Archives.

132 "J.J.'s apartment had to be": Ziesmer, *Ready When You Are*, 84.

133 "Whenever there was an outdoor": Spada, *Barbra*, 303.

Chapter 11

Quotes from Britton, Rascoe, and Streisand are from interviews with the author, except where noted.

136 **"I'll help you guys"**: Ziesmer, *Ready When You Are*, 89.

136 **"Why don't you call Robert"**: Ibid., 93.

136 **"The heart of his agent"**: Roth to author.

137 **"So that neither star"**: Ziesmer, *Ready When You Are*, 93.

137 **"Many times Redford"**: Ibid.

137 **138-page script and $25,000**: Pollack Archives.

138 **"It works so well"**: *The Way We Were: Looking Back* documentary film.

139 **"That [phone] scene was about"**: Ibid.

140 **"heavily shadowed nude scene" and "fuck"**: Pollack Archives.

140 **"[T]hen he threw back the coverlet"**: Laurents, *The Way We Were* (novel), 42.

141 **"If Streisand has been in makeup"**: James Powers, "Dialogue on Film, Sydney Pollack," *American Film*, April 1978.

141 **"She's bound to blow up"**: Natale, "Director Pollack Tells of 'The Way We Were,'" 24.

141 **"Aramis"**: Charles Michener, "The Great Redford," *Newsweek*, February 4, 1974, 50.

143 **"loses his integrity"**: Callan, *Robert Redford*, 229.

144 **"anything"**: Pollack Archives.

144 **"She heard a sound"**: Laurents, *The Way We Were* (novel), 71.

145 **"chivalrous"**: Pollack Archives.

145 **"stubborn" and "superfluous"**: Pollack Archives.

146 **"big-boobed dames"**: Pollack Archives.

146 **original member of the Committee**: Victor S. Navasky, *Naming Names* (New York: Hill and Wang, 1991), 80.

147–148 **"Friends of the sensationally talented"**: Dorothy Kilgallen, *New York Journal-American*, August 29, 1962.

148 **"I don't like Groucho"**: Rascoe to author.

149 **"They were named after friends"**: Robert Hofler, *Money, Murder, and Dominick Dunne: A Life in Several Acts* (Madison: University of Wisconsin Press, 2017), 83.

152 **100 extras and air terminal references**: Pollack Archives.

153 **"one of the most successful operations"**: Kengor, *Dupes*, 101.

153 **"He's a very theatrical"**: Dick Kleiner, "A 'Chile' [*sic*] Star Is Born," *El Dorado Times*, December 21, 1972.

154 **"Hubbell isn't a victim"**: Callan, *Robert Redford*, 237–38.

Chapter 12

Quotes from Alan Bergman (December 29, 2021), Marty Erlichman (February 2, 2022), Koch, Roth, and Streisand are from interviews with the author, except where noted.

155 **Laurents delivered a rewrite**: Laurents Archives.

156 **"Columbia was going under"**: Spada, *Streisand*, 302.

156 **Stark memos to Stanley Schneider:** Pollack Archives.

156–159 **"bullshit practice" and "cockeyed":** Pollack Archives.

157 **"While we were rewriting":** Spada, *Streisand*, 302.

158 **Rayfiel, the writer's two-thousand-dollars:** Pollack Archives.

159 **"I knew Ray Stark":** *The Way We Were: Looking Back* documentary film.

160 **Hamlisch meeting with Pollack:** Koch to author; and Koch, *Magic Time*, 98.

160 **"If I'd left it in the minor":** Edwards, *Streisand*, 341.

161 **"It's a wonderful title":** *The Way We Were: Looking Back* documentary film.

161 **"How many singing prostitutes":** Lisa Russell, "Evergreen," in *Barbra Streisand: Her Life and Unrivaled Career*, 50.

162 **"It just didn't feel":** *The Way We Were: Looking Back* documentary film.

163 **"So is 'My Funny Valentine'":** Andersen, *Barbra*, 218.

163 **"I needed a road map":** *The Way We Were: Looking Back* documentary film.

164 **"And when it's wrong":** Ibid.

165–166 **United Nations Building and Korean War anecdotes:** Pollack Archives.

166 **Koch would pick up Redford:** Pollack Archives.

166 **"Mr. Koch! Mr. Koch!":** Koch to author.

166 **"I wanted to find":** *The Way We Were: Looking Back* documentary film.

167 **Laurents insisted it was Ross's:** Laurents, *Original Story By*, 236.

167 **"In the sunlight":** Laurents, *The Way We Were* (novel), 276.

167 **female strangers would attempt:** *The Way We Were: Looking Back* documentary film.

Chapter 13

Quotes from Barry Brown (August 17, 2021), Feinstein, and Streisand are from interviews with the author, except where noted.

168 **"For all those 11 o'clock":** Edwards, *Streisand*, 338.

168 **"Producer Robert Evans failed":** Ehrenstein, *"Robert Redford: The Biography* Reviewed."

169 **"You win, pal":** Laurents, *Original Story By*, 273.

169 **"They started shooting":** Edwards, *Streisand*, 335.

169 **"my concept":** Pollack Archives.

170–172 **"cold" and "too classy" and "disaster":** Laurents Archives.

171 **"Kate" and "Katie" controversy:** Laurents Archives.

172 **"Oh, but look what I've got!":** Rebecca Pollack to author.

172 **"Barbra had been told":** Edwards, *Streisand*, 331.

172 **"I liked *Up the Sandbox*":** Kaye, "Barbra: The Superstar Who Wants to Be a Woman."

174 **"It's only what he thinks":** Green, "When You're a Shark You're a Shark All the Way," 40.

175 **"I think you're a shit"**: Greg Lawrence, "Ballets over Broadway," *Vanity Fair*, May 2001.

176 **"loathed" and Lindfors anecdote**: Laurents Archives.

Chapter 14

Quotes from Burnett, Rebecca Pollack (January 7, 2022), and Roth are from interviews with the author.

177 **"difficult to get through"**: Pollack Archives.

177 **"Redford's the best leading man"**: Riese, *Her Name Is Barbra*, 338.

178 **Hubbell as "a shit"**: Pollack Archives.

178 **"Considering that they are both"**: James Spada, "Streisand: The Way She Is," *New York Sunday News Magazine*, October 25, 1981, 29.

179 **"Sydney cried"**: Patrick McGilligan, *Backstory 2: Interviews with Screenwriters of the 1940s and 1950s* (Berkeley: University of California Press, 1991), 152.

181 **"a Trotskyite mother"**: Laurents, *The Way We Were* (novel), 209.

181 **"wedding montage"**: Pollack Archives.

182 **Pollack memo to Stark**: Pollack Archives.

182 **"wonderful" and "crawl"**: Pollack Archives.

182 **"Steps" scene**: Pollack Archives.

183 **"favorite moments"**: Pollack Archives.

183 **"We must support the faculty"**: *The Way We Were: Looking Back* documentary film.

183 **"corny"**: Pollack Archives.

184 **"scab" and screenplay credits anecdote:** Laurents Archives.

186 **"lifeless" and "damned bore":** Pollack Archives.

186 **"And there's this film on the docket":** Berry and Egan, "Filmdom Agonizes over High-Level Juggling of Company Funds."

187 **"the opening scene of the worst political":** John W. Dean, *The Nixon Defense: What He Knew and When He Knew It* (New York: Viking, 2014), xvii.

Chapter 15

Quotes from Brown, Mary Corliss (March 1, 2022), Feinstein, Rosenman, and Streisand are from interviews with the author, except where noted.

189 **"Malice in Wonderland":** Laurents, *The Way We Were* (novel), 256.

189 **"That Barbra Streisand is so obnoxious":** Andersen, *Barbra,* 216.

189 **"I was on Nixon's enemies list":** Daniel S. Levy, "Raising Her Voice," in *Barbra Streisand: Her Life and Unrivaled Career*, ed. *People* editors, special issue, *People*, April 15, 2022, 80.

190 **"I think it came as a complete":** Ibid., 217.

191 **"fag bill" and "My lover":** Laurents Archives.

192 **"He was my reason":** Laurents, *The Rest of the Story*, xi.

Chapter 16

Quotes from A. Bergman, Burnett, Redford, and Streisand are from interviews with the author, except where noted.

196–200 **Preview screening anecdote and quotes:** Burnett to author.

198 **"'works' because of their chemistry":** *The Way We Were: Looking Back* documentary film.

201 **"I don't know anymore":** *The Way We Were: Looking Back* documentary film.

201 **"But it's too long":** Burnett to author.

201 **"tear-jerking":** Pollack Archives.

202 **"You have to go back":** Burnett to author.

202 **"I can't! I'm stuck!"** *The Way We Were: Looking Back* documentary film.

203 **"I didn't even have the negative":** Edwards, *Streisand*, 339.

203 **"In college, I stood under a maple" and other quotes from *The Way We Were*:** *The Way We Were: Looking Back* documentary film.

205 **"She's a strong woman":** Andersen, *Barbra*, 217.

205 **"[T]he scene where the love story":** Laurents, *Original Story By*, 282.

206 **"I fought and fought":** Michael Schnayerson, "The Way She Is," *Vanity Fair*, November 1994.

206 **"It was fantastically right":** *The Way We Were: Looking Back* documentary film.

206 **"The danger was":** James Powers, "Dialogue on Film, Sydney Pollack," *American Film*, April 1978.

206 **"The audiences were just plain bored"**: Crist, *Take 22*, 219.

207 **"I was signed by Ray Stark"**: Callan, *Robert Redford*, 236.

207 **"I've hit it too many times"**: *The Way We Were: Looking Back* documentary film.

208 **Charles Champlin at preview**: Pollack Archives.

208 **"It's a star vehicle"**: Natale, "Director Pollack Tells of 'The Way We Were,'" 24.

208 **"I heard he went to the World Series"**: Earl Wilson, "It Happened Last Night," *New York Post*, October 17, 1973.

209 **"essentially just a love story"**: Roger Ebert, review of *The Way We Were*, by Arthur Laurents, directed by Sydney Pollack, *Chicago Sun-Times*, October 17, 1973.

209 **"[W]ith Streisand as the film's intellectual"**: Gene Siskel, review of *The Way We Were*, by Arthur Laurents, directed by Sydney Pollack, *Chicago Tribune*, October 17, 1973.

209 **"not at all bad"**: Vincent Canby, "Screen: 'Way We Were,'" review of *The Way We Were*, by Arthur Laurents, directed by Sydney Pollack, *New York Times*, October 17, 1973.

209 **"miraculous audience empathy"**: Pauline Kael, "The Current Cinema," review of *The Way We Were*, by Arthur Laurents, directed by Sydney Pollack, *New Yorker*, October 15, 1973.

210 **"a thoroughly enjoyable movie"**: Judith Crist, review of *The Way We Were*, by Arthur Laurents, directed by Sydney Pollack, *New York*, October 22, 1973.

211 **"It's my wife's favorite movie"**: Burnett to author.

211 **"We got sixty-five"**: Enser, "Dialogue with Sydney Pollack."

212 **"That boggles the mind"**: Riese, *Her Name Is Barbra*, 340.

212 **"I felt it was the best"**: Kaye, "Barbra: The Superstar Who Wants to Be a Woman."

213 **"Watching it on television"**: Charles Marowitz, "The Honesty of a Suburban Superstar," *New York Times*, January 19, 1975.

Chapter 17

Quotes from Feinstein, Jesse Green (September 22, 2021), R. Pollack, Patti LuPone (June 22, 2022), Redford, Rudin, David Stone (November 9, 2021), Streisand, and Victoria Wilson (June 8, 2022) are from interviews with the author, except where noted.

214 **eight million dollars each:** Jack Martin, "Bob and Babs," *New York Post*, June 3, 1980.

214 **"when she phones for help"**: Marilyn Beck, "Streisand and Redford to Carry On," *Daily News*, February 20, 1980, 8.

214 **"You could literally see them"**: Stephen M. Silverman, "Pickin' Up the Pieces," *New York Post*, March 20, 1986.

215 **"Gloria Steinem kind of lady"**: Crist, *Take 22*, 219.

215 **"The sequel can begin with a funeral"**: Rascoe to author.

215–216 ***The Way They Changed*** screenplay: Laurents Archives.

217 **"Barbra Streisand and I have had"**: *The Way We Were: Looking Back* documentary film.

217 **"When do we get to *The Owl and the Pussycat*"**: Maureen Dowd, "Baby, It's Sue," *Vanity Fair*, April 2013.

217 **"There will not be a director's cut"**: Hofler, "Sydney Pollack Interview."

219 **protesting the war in Vietnam**: Laurents, *Original Story By*, 281.

222 **"In a way, he was like the country"**: Laurents, *The Way We Were* (novel), 47.

223 **"Imagine getting jobs"**: Touré, "New Musical 'Black No More' Asks: If You Had the Chance to Be White, Would You Take It?" Yahoo (website), February 15, 2022, https://www.yahoo.com/video/musical-black-no-more-asks-194520243.html.

223 **"Jewish!" and "Gentile!"**: Laurents Archives.

224 **"It's wonderful because it addresses"**: Christina Newland, "*Longing for The Way We Were*," *Vulture* (a *New York* magazine website), August 18, 2021.

225 **Hatcher complained to Prince**: Laurents Archives.

225 ***Two Lives* production at Lincoln Center**: André Bishop (July 7, 2022) to author. Also, Laurents Archives.

225 **"He's written me dead"**: Laurents, *The Rest of the Story*, viii.

226 **"I don't count on Howard"**: Laurents, *Selected Plays of Arthur Laurents*, 413.

227 **"flaw"**: Laurents, *Original Story By*, 258.

228 **some of the show's producers**: Michael Riedel, "Laurents' Beast-side Story," *New York Post*, May 11, 2011, 36.

228 **"He's an extremely truthful person"**: Tim Murphy, "*West Side Story*'s Karen Olivo on Her Tony Nomination

and Surviving Her Choreography," *Vulture* (a *New York* magazine website), May 26, 2009.

229 **"Matt Cavenaugh is absolutely straight"**: Charles Kaiser interview/transcript, *The Gay Metropolis.*

229 **"too preppy"**: Laurents, *The Rest of the Story*, 108.

229 **"best Tony ever" and "that was the worst performance"**: Pat Cerasaro, "Jeremy Jordan: InDepth Inter-View," BroadwayWorld (website), April 6, 2013.

229 **"Yes, but we don't talk"**: Green, "When You're a Shark You're a Shark All the Way," 41.

230 **"I am a Jewish boy"**: McGilligan, *Backstory 2*, 155–56.

230 **"I couldn't even get an interview"**: Laurents, *Selected Plays of Arthur Laurents*, 291.

230 **"The whole thing about Arthur's being blacklisted"**: Rodgers and Green, *Shy*, 435.

232 **"idiosyncratic"**: McGilligan, *Backstory 2*, 146.

232 **dated January 6, 1952, not 1948:** Laurents Archives.

233 **"While Arthur was absolutely"**: Anonymous source to author.

236 **"I never went near Los Angeles"**: McGilligan, *Backstory 2*, 150.

236 **"Katie and Hubbell facing what"**: Laurents, *Original Story By*, 161.

236 **her mother's described in the book:** Ibid., 199.

237 **Kingsland letter to Laurents:** Laurents Archives.

Epilogue

242 **"We were set to move"**: Arthur Laurents, *Mainly on Directing: Gypsy, West Side Story, and Other Musicals* (New York: Alfred A. Knopf, 2009), 142.

244 **"I think she's tough"**: Brantley, "Barbra Streisand Sets the Record Straight."

Index

Academy Awards, 1974: 212–13
Actors Studio: 12, 26, 122
Adler, Stella: 25
Akerman, Malin: 221
Albee, Edward: 15, 75, 78, 191
Alcoholics Anonymous: 226
Alfred A. Knopf, Inc.: 69
All About Eve: 27
Allen, Charles: 186
Allen & Company: 186
Allen, Woody: 220
All the President's Men: 128, 207
Altman, Robert: 218
American Academy of Dramatic Arts: 121
American Ballet Theatre: 71
American Film Institute: 6
Anastasia (film): 233
Anastasia (stage play): 63
Arnstein, Nicky: 2, 40
Arrangement, The: 63

Arthur Laurents Archives: 69
Arthur Laurents Enterprises: 78
Astaire, Fred: 11
Austin, Chuck: 120
Avco Theatre: 207

Bacall, Lauren: 28, 33–34, 151, 171, photo
Bachardy, Don: 72–73
Ballard, Kaye: 7
Ballet Theatre: 71
Bancroft, Anne: 143, 148, 213
Barbra Streisand Album, The: 12–13
Barefoot in the Park: 20, 21
Bartley, Anthony: 236
Beatty, Warren: 46–49, 53, 90, 96, 189, photo
Beck, Marilyn: 214
Beekman Place: 22, 131–33, 139, 169, 178, 181

Beekman Tower: 133, 150
Begelman, David: 16
Benjamin, Richard: 219
Benny, Jack: 219
Berenson, Berry: 84
Bergman, Alan: 120, 161,
    162–64, 177, 183,
    197, 213, photo
Bergman, Marilyn: 120,
    161, 164, 177, 183,
    197, 213, photo
Bernstein, Leonard: 72, 74,
    photo
Beverly Hills Hotel: 28,
    37–39, 62, 135,
    150, 158, 175, 182
Beverly Wilshire Hotel: 48
Beymer, Richard: 219
Billy: 108
Bishop, André: 225
Black No More: 222–23
Black Theatre United: 223
Blue Angel: 12
Bogart, Humphrey: 28–29,
    33–35, 151, 153,
    171, 210, 238,
    photo
Bonjour Tristesse (film):
    233
Bonjour Tristesse (novel):
    63
Bon Soir: 8, 10, 12, 93
Booth, Margaret: 115–16,
    129, 159, 169, 179,
    196, 205

Booth, Shirley: 71, photo
Brando, Marlon: 19, 32
Branning, Eugene R.: 77
Breglio, John: 242
Brice, Fanny: 1, 7–8, 11,
    14, 147, 148, 198
Britton, Michael: 102, 112,
    127, 137, 140, 141,
    148, 160, 166
Broadcast Music Inc.
    (BMI): 174
Brown, Barry: 173–74,
    194, 242
Browne, Coral: 57
Burnett, Carol: 147, 148
Burnett, John F.: 97, 98,
    129, 141, 159, 169,
    178, 181, 196, 200,
    202, 211
Burns, George: 219
Burton, Richard: 20
*Butch Cassidy and the Sun-
    dance Kid*: 53, 135,
    photo

Campbell, Bruce: 136
Canby, Vincent: 209
Candidate, The: 24, 31, 53,
    56, 112, 143, 154,
    207
Cannes Film Festival: 54–
    55, 185
Capote: 23
Carr, Allan: 242
Carson, Johnny: 146

Caught: 63, 232
Cavenaugh, Matt: 229, photo
Champlin, Charles: 208
Chaplin, Charlie: 5, 71, 209
Chaplin, Sydney: 140, photo
Chase, The: 19
Chayefsky, Paddy: 86
Chicago Sun-Times: 51, 209
Chicago Tribune: 209
Chiles, Lois: 106, 132
Christie, Julie: 49, photo
Cinderella Liberty: 212
Clearing in the Woods, A: 75
Cohn, Harry: 36, 95
Cole, Dennis: 47
Color of Money, The: 241
Columbia Broadcast System Radio (CBS Radio): 231
Columbia Pictures: 4, 16, 35, 39, 56, 94, 95, 109, 119, 137–38, 156–57, 175, 186–87, 189, 208, 210, 218
Columbia Records: 197
Come Back, Little Sheba: 15
Committee for the First Amendment: 28–29, 33, 34, 146, 153
Committee for the Re-Election of the President (CREEP): 188
Communist Party: 5, 23, 25, 80, 117–18, 180–81, 183
Conroy, Jack: 50–51
Cooper, Gary: 28, 52
Coppola, Francis Ford: 86, 196, 197, 201
Corliss, Mary: 192–93, 241
Corliss, Richard: 192
Cornell Daily Sun: 231
Cornell University: 114, 123, 231
Corsaro, Frank: 107–08
Cosmopolitan: 79
"Coward, The": 65
Crist, Judith: 210, 215, 224
Curb Your Enthusiasm: 221

Daily Worker: 5, 232
Dale, Grover: 74–75, 107–109
Dall, John: 70
David, Larry: 221
"David Rayfiel's Script Magic": 38–39
Dean, James: 92
Dean, John: 118
Della-Porte, Ted: 121

Democrat and Chronicle:
     91, 120
Democratic National Com-
     mittee: 50, 188
Dillman, Bradford: 106
Dirty Dancing: 221
"Don't Rain on My
     Parade": 8
Dorchester Hotel: 55, 63
Dorothy Chandler
     Pavilion: 213
Dougherty, Marion: 115
Douglas, Helen Gahagan:
     31
Douglas, Melvyn: 31
Downhill Racer: 53
Dumont, Margaret: 146
Dune Road: 77–78
Dunham, Lena: 221

Easy Rider: 173
Ebert, Roger 209
Ehrenstein, David: 168
Ellsberg, Daniel: 189
El Morocco: 91–93, 156,
     167, 171
Empire of Their Own, An:
     14
Enclave, The: 78, 192, 224
Erasmus Hall: 14
Erlichman, Marty: 93, 163,
     211
Essman, Susie: 221
Evans, Robert: 168

Exodus: 95
Fat City: 97, 115, 159
Faye, Alice: 170
Feinstein, Ashley: 9, 71–72,
     75–81, 173, 193–
     95, 230
Firehouse: 90–91, 225
Fitzgerald, F. Scott: 33
Five Easy Pieces: 173
Fonda, Jane: 19, 26, 76,
     90, 96, 188, photo
For Pete's Sake: 178
Forum: 49
Franco, Francisco: 104,
     106, 180, 199
Front Street: 121–22, 125
Funny Girl (film): 1–2, 4,
     94, 111, 116, 129,
     130, 156, 197
Funny Girl (stage musical):
     1–2, 7, 11, 12, 129,
     140, 147–48, 159,
     photo
Funny Lady: 209, photo

Gabler, Neal: 14
Garbo, Greta, 30, 115
Gardner, Herb: 86
Gay Activists Alliance
     (GAA): 191, 225
Getty Museum: 19
Girls: 221
Godfather, The: 33, 196

Goldwyn, Samuel: 95
Good Whip: 121, 125–26
Goodbye, Columbus (film): 219, 220
Goodbye, Columbus (novel): 219
Goodwin, Cornelius: 126
Gould, Elliott: 61, 140, photo
Gould, Jason: 64, 101, 190, photo
Granger, Farley: 70–73, 76, 173, 235, photo
Graziani, Bettina: 235
Great Gatsby, The: 168
Green, Jesse: 77, 227–31
Green, Morris: 77
Grey, Jennifer: 221
Grimes, Stephen: 37, 130–32
Grodin, Charles: 66, 170
Guess Who's Coming to Dinner: 212
Guettel, Hank: 40, 78–79
Guettel, Mary Rodgers: 40, 41, 78–79, 230, 232
Gypsy (original Broadway production): 4, 8, 12, 15, 38, 244, photo
Gypsy (1973 London production and 1974 Broadway revival): 173–74, 191, 194

Gypsy (1989 Broadway revival): 227
Gypsy (2009 Broadway revival): 226, 228

Haley, Jack: 212
Hall, Conrad: 115
Hamilton, Patrick: 63, 70
Hamlisch, Marvin: 159–63, 164, 183, 197, 207, 213, photo
Hanks, Tom: 23
Harper & Row: 37
Harris, Radie: 56–58
Harrison, George: 190
Hart, Gary: 49
Harvard University: 22
Haskell, Molly: 192
Hatcher, David: 191
Hatcher, Tom: 32, 39, 67, 72–80, 173–74, 190–95, 215, 222, 224–28, 230, 233, 235, 238–42, photos
Hatcher Road: 78
Hayden, Sterling: 33–34, 153, photo
Heartbreak Kid, The (1972): 86, 219–20
Heartbreak Kid, The (2007): 221
Heart Is a Lonely Hunter, The: 179
Heckart, Eileen: 76

Hepburn, Katharine: 11, 210, 212
Hill, George Roy: 53
Hines, Cheryl: 221
Hirschfield, Alan: 186, 198
Hitchcock, Alfred: 4, 70, 234, 235
Hodsoll, Pat: 121
Hoene, Chris: 120
Hoffman, Philip Seymour: 23
Holden, William: 198
Hole in the Wall Gang Camp: 241
Hollywood Nineteen: 28, 30
Hollywood Reporter: 56–58, 197, 210
Hollywood Ten: 28, 32, 86, 135, 152, 203, 232, 235
Holm, Celeste: 76
Holt, Fritz: 173, 194
Home of the Brave: 5, 66, 232
"Homosexual Drama and Its Disguises": 15
Horne, Lena: 12–13
House Un-American Activities Committee (HUAC): 4, 5, 6, 28–32, 43, 44, 50, 55, 57, 61–63, 83, 85, 88, 95–96, 150–52, 155, 158, 175, 187, 189–90, 193, 200, 204, 218, 231, 233, 236, photos
Howard, Ken: 46–47, 59
Hud: 212
Hudson, Rock: 73, 242
Hughes, Howard: 28
Hunter, Tab: 73
Hurt, William: 23
Huston, John: 28–29, 34, 97, 115, 152, 153, 159, 171, 200, photo

I Can Get It for You Wholesale: 9, 11–13, 26, 46, 61, 77, 128, 140, 147, 167, 243, photo
Inge, William: 15, 80
Inside Daisy Clover (film): 23–24, 27, 90, photo
Inside Daisy Clover (novel): 24
Intro 475: 191
Invitation to a March: 75–76, 194–95, photo
Isherwood, Christopher: 30, 72–73
Ivy League: 22, 93

Jack Paar Show, The: 8
Jackson, Glenda: 212, 213

Jeakins, Dorothy: 91–92, 100, 213, 219
Jeffrey, Howard: 90
Jeremiah Johnson: 18, 24–25, 53–54, 56
Jesus Christ Superstar: 107
"Jet Song": 230
Jolson Sings Again: 226
Jordan, Jeremy: 229

Kaiser, Charles, 229
Karger, Dave: 14
Kauffmann, Stanley S.: 14–15
Kaye, Danny: 28, photo
Kaye, Nora: 46–47
Kazan, Elia: 32, 42, 63, 103
Kelly, Gene: 28, 71, 108, 219
Kerr, Deborah: 235
Kershner, Irving: 142
Kingsland, Vicki: 236–37
Kiss of the Spider Woman: 23
Koch, Emily Anne: 166
Koch, Hawk: 85, 87, 117–18, 119, 139, 152, 158, 160, 164, 166
Koch, Rita: 166
Kramer, Larry: 174
Kristallnacht: 3
Lambert, Gavin: 24

Lang, Harold: 10, 71–72, 173
Larner, Jeremy: 143
Last Picture Show, The: 94
Laurents, Arthur: 1–2, 6, 11, 15–16, 18–20, 23, 25, 27–29, 33, 35–36, 37–43, 46–47, 49–51, 53, 55, 103, 111, 123–25, 140, 143, 150, 154, 155, 159, 164–65, 167, 173–74, 177–80, 184–85, 190, 200–01, 203–06, 215–17, 222–23, photos
   Altercations with Pollack: 38–39, 41, 44–45, 59–67, 82–83
   Altercations with Stark: 60–66, 82–83
   Criticism of *TWWW*: 169–72, 175–76, 181, 205, 209, 198
   Early life and career: 4–5, 8–10, 12–14, 32, 68–81, 113–114, 128, photos
   Life and career post-*TWWW*: 224–37, 238–44, photo

Laurents, Arthur: (*Cont.*)
  Name change: 195, 229–31
  Relationship with
    Hatcher: 32, 39, 67, 72–81, 191–95, 224–28, 235, 239–243
Laurents Way: 78
Lean, David: 6, 201
Lee, Gypsy Rose: 174
Lee, Peggy: 212–13
Legend of Lylah Clare, The: 27, 57
Lemmon, Jack: 213
Lennon, John: 190
Levine, Irving: 231
Liberace: 12
Library of Congress: 69, 226
Liddy, G. Gordon: 188
Life: 11, 241
Lincoln Center Theater: 225
Lindfors, Viveca: 155, 176, 199
Lindsay, John: 208
Lion in Winter, The: 212
Loew's State Theatre: 208
Loren, Sophia: 212
Los Angeles Times: 208
Luftig, Hal: 229
Lumet, Sidney: 57

Mabry, Moss: 91–92, 213
McCarthy, Joseph: 35

McCollum, Kevin: 229
McGovern, George: 48–50, 188
MacGraw, Ali: 219
MacLaine, Shirley: 49
Mainly on Directing: 242
Man for All Seasons, A: 212
Man Who Invented Rock Hudson, The: 239
Marjorie Morningstar: 219
Mark Hellinger Theatre: 242
Martin, Mary: 7
Marx Brothers: 145, 200
Marx, Groucho: 135, 146–49, 200, photo
Marx, Harpo: 146, 200
Mason, Marsha: 212
Mean Streets: 211
Medbery Hotel: 121, 123, 125, 170, 182
Meisner, Stanford: 25–26
Memo from David O. Selznick: 129
Menjou, Adolphe: 28
Merman, Ethel: photo
Merriam, Eve: 65
Merrick, David: 9–10
Merrill, Bob: 11, 148, photo
Miracle Worker, The (film): 40, 62, 159, 212
Miracle Worker, The (stage play): 40, 62, 159

Miranda, Lin-Manuel: 228
*Mirror Has Two Faces,
    The:* 221, 234
"Miss Marmelstein": 10
Mitchell, Joni: 190
Monroe, Marilyn: 92. 141
Moon, Sun Myung: 243
Morris, Anita: 107–09
Motion Picture Alliance for
    the Preservation of
    American Ideals: 96
"My Funny Valentine":
    163
My Good Name: 2–3, 231
"My Man": 7

Neal, Patricia: 212
Neighborhood Playhouse:
    25
Newland, Christina: 224
Newman, Paul: 35, 53, 96,
    128, 135, 178, 198,
    241, photo
Newman's Own: 241
Newsweek: 141
New York: 210, 224, 227–
    30
*New York Journal-Ameri-
    can:* 8
New York Times: 13, 15,
    38, 51, 209, 227
New Yorker: 209
New York/Vulture: 224
Niagara: 92
Nichols, Mike: 20

Nixon, Richard M.: 31,
    49–50, 61, 96, 185,
    187
    Enemies list: 5,
    188–90
Northpoint Theatre: 197,
    199, 200, 204
Now Playing Tomorrow:
    231
Nureyev, Rudolf: 174

O'Horgan, Tom: 107
Olivo, Karen: 228
*On a Clear Day You Can
    See Forever:* 116,
    173
O'Neal, Patrick: 153, 199,
    photo
O'Neal, Ryan: 17–18, 45,
    46, 52, 54–55, 60,
    140, 211, photo
Ono, Yoko: 190
Original Story By: 38, 65–
    66, 69–70, 76, 216,
    226, 231–32, 236,
    239, 240
Out of Africa: 52, 90
Owl and the Pussycat, The:
    4, 46, 94, 97, 116,
    130, 161, 179, 197,
    202, 217

Paar, Jack: 146
Palace Theatre: 242
Palm Court: 3

Paramount Pictures: 168
Parker, Dorothy: 8
Parsons, Louella: 185
Party Animals: 242
"People": 8, 49
Perkins, Anthony: 109
Perkins, Millie: 210
Philadelphia: 23
Picnic: 80, 198
Playbill: 11, 25
Playboy: 141
Plaza Hotel: 3, 164–66, 201, 207, 208, 223
PM East: 8
Pollack, Bernie: 93–94, 160
Pollack, Rebecca: 95, 179–80
Pollack, Sydney: 4, 6–7, 17, 21, 27–29, 30–36, 37, 52–57, 88–89, 93–95, 97, 99–100, 103, 109–10, 116, 121–23, 133, 137, 140, 149, 151–53, 160–61, 163–65, 168–69, 176, 178–80, 181–84, 186, 196–97, 199, 201–11, 214–15, 217–219, 234, 238–49, photos
   Altercations with Laurents: 38–39, 41, 44–45, 59–67, 82–83
   Altercations with Stark: 16, 55, 114–15, 128–32, 143–45, 156–59
   Directing Redford and Streisand: 26, 104–06, 111, 117–18, 127, 130, 136, 139, 141, 158, photo
   Early life and career: 18, 22–23, 25
   Life and career post-*TWWW:* 218
   TWWW pitches to Redford: 20, 24–35, 53–55
Polo, Teri: 221
Polonsky, Abraham: 31
Portnoy's Complaint: 219
Post-Star and Times: 80
Preminger, Otto: 95, 234
Price, Fannie: 14
Prince, Hal: 224–25
Prince of Tides, The: 221, 234
Production Code: 24
Pulitzer Fountain: 164, 208, photo

Rabinowitz, Ada: 190
Random House: 129
Rascoe, Judith: 7, 83–84, 86–87, 91, 101, 115, 133, 149, 150

Rastar Productions: 4, 83, 91

Rayfiel, David: 38–39, 43–44, 82, 84–85, 87–88, 101–03, 138–39, 143, 145, 149, 157–59, 165, 167, 172, 175, 181, 184–85, 200, 202, 224

Rayfiel, Lynne S.: 101, 185

Ready When You Are: 91

Rebel Without a Cause: 92

Red Channels: 5, 232

Redford, Lola: 53, 54, 89, 90

Redford, Robert: 16, 17, 28, 29, 32–33, 42, 46, 50, 57–58, 59–62, 66, 84, 88–94, 97–99, 102–07, 109–111, 120–23, 125–27, 130–31, 133–34, 139–41, 148–49, 151, 154, 164, 166–67, 170, 173, 182–83, 197–200, 203, 206–10, 214–17, 224, photos

Early life and career: 18–20, 22–24, 30–31, photo

Initial rejection of *TWWW:* 6, 19, 20–25, 27, 34–35, 38, 53–56, 81

Lateness and pranks: 112, 135–37, 142–43, 166, 208

Life and career post-*TWWW:* 52–53, 90, 128, 168, 211, 212

Refusal to speak a certain line: 20–21, 143–46, 171–72, 177–78, 202

Sex appeal: 90

Remick, Lee: 78

Rest of the Story, The: 14, 226, 230

Reuters: 238

Rice, Donna: 49

Riviera: 12

Robbins, Jerome: 32, 42, 46, 74–75, 108, 175, photo

Rockefeller, Nelson: 208

Rockford Files, The: 97

Rogers, Ginger: 11, 30

Rogers, Lela: 30

Rope (film): 4, 70

Rope (stage play): 63

Rosenberg, Meta: 29, 31, 97

Rosenman, Zvi Howard: 79–80, 195

Rossen, Carol: 30–31, 66

Rossen, Robert: 30–31

Roth, Lillian: 10
Roth Philip: 219
Roth, Richard R.: 85, 88,
     99, 115, 161, 186
Rubin, Richard: 146
Rutgers University: 3

Saint, David: 15, 225
St. Luke's Place: 39, 77, 79,
     192, 195, 239, 241
Samburu National Reserve:
     56
San Francisco Examiner:
     60
Sargent, Alvin: 82, 84–85,
     87–88, 103, 125,
     143, 145, 149, 151–
     54, 158–59, 165,
     167, 170, 181–82,
     184–85, 200, 202,
     224
Sarris, Andrew: 192
Save the Tiger: 213
Saxon, John: 74, 240
Schary, Dore: 29–30
Schary, Jill: 30
Schneider, Stanley: 95,
     156–57
Scofield, Paul: 212
Screen Actors Guild: 96,
     153
Seesaw: 107
Segaloff, Nat: 95
Seibert, Harry: 121

Seinfeld, Jerry: 221
Senate Watergate Commit-
     tee: 189
Shapiro, Barbara: 193
Shapiro, Monty: 193
Sharif, Omar: 2, 140
Sherman, Ellen: 183, 218
Shore, Dinah: 219
Short, Raymond E.: 114
Silverman, Stephen M.:
     214
Simon, Neil: 20, 86, 219
Shy: 230
Snake Pit, The: 63
Sokolov, Raymond A.: 51
Solomon, Jack: 122–23
Sondheim, Stephen: 11, 74,
     75, 78–79, 191,
     225, 231, photos
Sound of Music, The: 159
Spartacus: 99
Stanislavski, Konstantin:
     25
Star Is Born, A: 221
Stark, Fran: 7, 11, 40
Stark, Ray: 1, 4, 6, 17–18,
     19, 37–39, 46, 51,
     52–58, 59–61, 63,
     86, 91, 92, 96–98,
     100–01, 133, 140,
     146, 149–51, 155,
     161, 163, 165–66,
     169, 172, 175, 177–
     78, 180–82, 184–86,

196–97, 199, 201–
02, 206–208, 210–
211, 215–17, photo
Altercations with
  Laurents: 43, 64,
  82–83
Altercations with
  Pollack: 16, 55,
  114–16, 128–32,
  143–45, 156–59
Early life and career: 3,
  7, 11, 12
Stark, Wendy: 149
Starr, Ringo: 90
Sting, The: 53, 128, 168,
  178, 211, 212
Stone, David: 227
Strasberg, Lee: 25
Streep, Meryl: 52, 90
Streetcar Named Desire, A:
  15
Streisand, Barbra: 2, 6, 15–
  18, 25, 33, 37, 46–
  48, 53–57, 59–62,
  65, 84, 92–94, 99–
  112, 125–31, 133–
  34, 136, 142, 144,
  149, 155–56, 159–
  64, 166–64, 168,
  172, 175, 177, 178,
  182, 186–87, 197–
  200, 204, 207–10,
  212–16, 237, 239,
  photos

Anxieties: 89, 104, 110–
  11, 116–18, 122,
  137, 141
Criticism regarding
  deleted scenes: 169,
  206, 217–18, 233
Crying scenes: 117–18,
  139, 170, 183, 205–
  06
Early life and career: 1,
  3–4, 7–14, 21, 26,
  52, 146–48, photos
Infatuation with
  Redford: 90, 127,
  139
Life and career post-
  TWWW: 221, 234,
  243–44
Politics: 5, 49, 188–90
Sex appeal: 10–11, 81,
  91, 139–40
Styne, Jule: 7–8, 147, photo
Summertime: 233
Sunday in New York: 21
Sunset Boulevard: 27
Sun Valley Lodge: 38–39
Swayze, Patrick: 221

Taffel, Bess: 97
Taylor, Elizabeth: 20, 124,
  212, photo
Tell Them Willie Boy Is
  Here: 31
Tender Comrade: 30

They Shoot Horses, Don't They?: 26, 38, 43, 87, 97

This Property Is Condemned: 18, 19

Thomas, J. Parnell: 50, photo

Thomas Crown Affair, The: 161

Thought Control Conference: 28, 62, 150–51, 158, 171, 172, 184

Time of the Cuckoo, The: 15, 71, 233, photo

Times Record: 92

Times Square Church: 243

Tonight Show, The: 8, 146–48

Touch of Class, A: 212

Touré: 222–23

Treasure of the Sierra Madre, The: 34

Turner Classic Movies: 14

Turning Point, The: 47, 63

Two Women: 212

Ullman, Tracey: 221

Unification Church: 243

Union College: 99–100, 104, 120

Up the Sandbox: 56, 117, 142, 172

Variety: 197, 210–11, 239

Viertel, Peter: 235–36

Viertel, Salka: 30–31, 155, 235

Viertel, Virginia "Jigee": 235–37

Vietnam War: 102, 103, 215, 219

Wallace, Mike: 8

War Hunt: 18

Ward David: 128

Warner, Jack: 34, 36, 96

Warner Bros: 19, 25, 34, 56, 92, 132, 142, 148

Watergate scandal: 50, 187, 188–89

Way We Changed, The: 216

Way We Were, The (film): 22, 23, 27, 35, 47, 51, 57–58, 173, 189, 191

Cut scenes: 92, 121, 125, 137–38, 149–50, 156, 175–76, 180, 183–84, 190, 201–07, 217–19, 233–35, photo

Early screenings: 169–72, 177, 179–80, 182–83

Editing: 97, 129, 159, 169, 178–80, 196, 201–07

Legacy: 219–224
Love scenes: 20–21, 139–45, 143–46, 171–72, 177–78, 202, photo
Marx Brothers party: 145–46, 148–49, 171, 184, 200, photo
Premieres: 208–09, photo
Preproduction: 91–94, 99–101
Previews: 183, 190, 196–201, 204–05, 207–08
Production in Ballston Spa: 120–27
Production in Bel-Air and Beverly Hills: 135–36, 158, 167, 185
Production in Malibu: 136–38, 168, 199, photo
Production in New York City: 128–134, 164–67, 159, photo
Production at Union College: 99–112, 114–120, 159, photo
Production at Warner Bros.: 132, 139–45, 145–46, 148–49, 178, photo

Reshoots: 132–33, 178, 185–86
Reviews: 163–64
Rewrites: 18, 26, 37, 38–40, 43–45, 53–54, 59–65, 82–91, 97–98, 125, 129, 137, 143, 145, 151, 155, 158–59, 165, 167, 169, 172, 176, 178, 181, 184, 202
Sequel: 214–17
Treatment and original screenplay: 1–4, 14–16, 19–20, 23, 27, 28–33, 37, 44–45, 49, 54–55, 96, 103, 111, 113, 123, 124, 143, 164–65, 171, 179, 180, 184, 201
Union Station scene: 88–89, 151–53, 171, 237, photo
UCLA scene: 138, 183, 203, 205–06, 218–20, 239
Way We Were, The (novel): 3, 29, 37, 50–51, 52, 57, 59, 68, 80, 84–85, 96, 103, 111, 113, 127, 140–41, 143–44, 150–51, 165, 167, 171, 172, 180–81, 191, 201, 215

Way We Were, The (stage musical treatment): 68

"Way We Were, The" (song): 120, 159–164, 212

Webber, Andrew Lloyd: 107

Weidman, Jerome: 10

Weiss, Lou: 95

West Side Story: 4, 8, 74–75, 230, 239, photo

West Side Story (2009 Broadway revival): 228–29, photo

What's Up, Doc?: 140, photo

"When You're a Shark": 230

Who's Afraid of Virginia Woolf? (film): 20, 24, 212, photo

Who's Afraid of Virginia Woolf? (stage play): 15, 78

Wild Calendar: 63

Wilder, Billy: 27, 238

William B. Riley: 72

William Morris Agency: 95

Williams College: 99, 101, 120, 156

Williams, Tennessee: 15

Wilson, Patrick: 221

"Windmills of Your Mind, The": 161

Women in Love: 213

Wood, Natalie: 22, 27, 90, 219, photo

Woods, James: 103–04, 107–110, 116, 127, photo

Woodward, Joanne: 53, 212

Yentl: 234

Ziesmer, Jerry: 91, 100, 102–03, 105, 122–26, 132, 135–37

Zoetrope Studios: 196

Visit our website at
KensingtonBooks.com
to sign up for our newsletters, read
more from your favorite authors, see
books by series, view reading group
guides, and more!

Become a Part of Our
Between the Chapters Book Club
Community and Join the Conversation

Betweenthechapters.net

Submit your book review for a chance to win exclusive
Between the Chapters swag you can't get anywhere else!
https://www.kensingtonbooks.com/pages/review/